LEAVING THE 20TH CENTURY

THE LAST RITES OF ROCK 'N' ROLL

by

Dave Henderson & Howard Johnson

FIRST PUBLISHED 2000 BY THE BLACK BOOK COMPANY
PO BOX 2030, PEWSEY, SN9 5QZ, UNITED KINGDOM

ISBN 1-902799-02-X

The Black Book Company 1999

DESIGNED BY KEITH DRUMMOND
REPROGRAPHICS BY RIVAL COLOUR
COVER BY DAVID BLACK

Black Book Company Ltd
"We die only once, and for such a long time!"
Moliere

WE WROTE THIS...

DAVE HENDERSON AND HOWARD JOHNSON
have known each other for a pretty long time. In the '80s
they played against each other at football and wrote for
rival rock magazines. They wouldn't meet during the
former as they both played in their respective defences
and 100 yards is a long way, but they had been known
to share a glass of warm Budweiser at the pre-release
airing of tracks for the new Iron Maiden album.
Eventually they buried their respective hatchets and
drowned in the Britpop tidal wave with the excellent
Johnson-created Raw. It was highly underrated. Etc.
With its departure from this mortal coil, Howard moved
on to the fields of sport, Henderson mixed Mojo's
relaxed ambience with Select's' hyper-ventilating enthusiasm and they both carried on reviewing new releases
for Q magazine. In a quiet moment, the plan for this book
was concocted in Efe's restaurant in Great Portland
Street, London. Discussions took place over their Special
Meze starter - with strange cream samosa and quick-
fried liver on the side. Paramedics were always on hand.
From that bloated badinage, they formed the Black Book
Company. Dave wrote Touched By The Hand Of Bob -
about people's lives, dreams and nightmares concerning Bob Dylan, and Howard penned Get Your Jumbo
Jet Out Of My Airport ñ a collection of random notes for
AC/DC obsessives. The publication of those tomes led
to a hearty celebration and, so the story goes, in the
morning they felt like death, and this book - a history of
rock 'n' roll expiration - seemed like a recipe for recovery.
Since immersing themselves in the dearly departed of
rock's fabled few, both Howard and Dave have developed an unhealthy medical knowledge, various related
complaints and an expanded record collection. That
grown men can still enthuse about discovering Mance
Lipscomb, Duke Ellington, Curt Boetcher and Jackson
C Frank, and rediscovering Sandy Denny, Robert
Johnson, Moondog, Gram Parsons, Alex Harvey,
Badfinger and Major Lance is, I think, highly com-
mendable.
These are strange times in music and perspective is like
gold dust. Death makes it so much easier I'm sure you'll
agree. Whatever. Enjoy!

DAVE JOHNSON (no relation)

LEAVING THE 20TH CENTURY

THE LAST RITES OF ROCK'N'ROLL

EVERY MORNING when I pick up the paper I go straight to the obituary page. There's a morbid fascination about the recently deceased and obituaries have an almost Feng Shui like quality; they catalogue a person's life in less than a dozen paragraphs and tell tales tall and proud of their halcyon days. Whether it be a circus entertainer, war hero, politician, artist, society clown or simple everyday eccentric, they all get the same treatment and their lives are all evaluated against the same set of rules.

The entertainment business has created a proliferation of superstars and these dearly-departeds have fast and exhilarating life stories to tell. But even these would-be immovable icons have been edited down in time-honoured fashion in an attempt to explain their untimely expiration.

As I perused, I realised I'd developed more than a fascination and I began to collect every one of the obituaries that related to music and music culture. I had the full SP on Jean Marais; the star of Orphee immortalised on a Smiths' sleeve. The soup to nuts on various beat poets and pop artists. No fact escaped me. I had the lowdown on the guy who invented the Gameboy, on the second trumpeter with some jazz band I'd never heard of, on Shari Lewis who brought us Lamb Chop, on Phil Harris the voice of Baloo The Bear, on Giles the cartoonist.

But the really intriguing thing for me was the way that the Telegraph, Times, Independent and Guardian dealt with the demise of the likes of Jerry Garcia, Lal Waterson, Laura Nyro, Epic Soundtracks and Jeff Buckley and how the music press followed it up. The results are a magnificently flowery thumbnail of their lives. Way before rock 'n' roll, stories about musicians created some great images. As I read more, I became intrigued by the jazz, blues and folk legends that were elevated to the level of heroic icon in death. Every inch the James Dean or Jack Kerouac, the likes of Charlie Parker and Eddie Cochran made for life stories as fascinating as those of any modern rock star. They also introduced me to a whole new raft of music.

And, as a lover of bleak, morbid and mesmerising music, the dual attractions of incredibly miserable songs coupled with the tragic stories of their purveyors haunted me further. There's the ludicrous anecdote of Johnny Ace's losing Russian roulette hand, Randy Rhoads' poor attempts at flying and even Jeff Buckley's impromptu swim that saw him dragged under a boat in the Mississippi. All of them underline the offbeat irony that permeates the music scene. I quickly became fascinated with the tragic Joe Meek and his obsession that Phil Spector was recording his every conversation. Then there's the roughhouse madness of Spade Cooley, who died in prison on the verge of parole after his wife-beating exploits.

Add to all of that volatile levels of drug abuse and the stories became at once tragic and by turns ridiculous. Take, for example, the demise of Ricky Nelson's Stone Canyon Band. They were blown up in midair after their plane caught fire as someone freebased cocaine. And then there's the tragic death of Nico; a renowned drug imbiber who continually looked on the verge of the big sleep. Her fate was surprisingly subdued. She was knocked off her bicycle.

There's the none-more-black experience of Spinal Tap's ever-expiring drummers, but who would have thought that Jeff Porcaro from Toto would have followed suit and died from a bizarre gardening accident, as was first reported? Unfortunately subsequent reports revealed that a body full of cocaine might also have contributed to his death.

Rock 'n' roll is a precarious business. Just look at the premature ends of John Lennon, Buddy Holly, Sam Cooke, Otis Redding and Tupac Shakur. But, while you're about it, spare a thought for top Latino superstar Selena who was shot dead by the president of her own fan club.

This book delves deep into those murky waters, following a trail of departed icons. It asks the fans, their friends and the famous how their death affected them. It also tries to make some sense out of the heaven-bound procession. Pretty soon, as you'll see from our unique diary, every day will be a rock star commemoration day. And those thinking about living the life would do well to take heed of Howard Johnson's examination of rock tragedy by cause. It's a risky business and no mistake.

Dave Henderson

LEAVING THE 20TH CENTURY
THE LAST RITES OF ROCK 'N' ROLL
A day-by-day guide to the valley of death...

January 1
Hank Williams, 1953. Alexis Korner, 1984. Ted Hawkins, 1995. Townes Van Zandt, 1997.

January 2
Randy California (Spirit) 1997

January 4
Phil Lynott 1986.

January 5
Sonny Bono, 1998. Ken Forssi (Love), 1998

January 6

January 7
Larry Williams, 1980.

January 8
Steve Clark (Def Leppard), 1991.

January 9

January 10
Howlin' Wolf, 1976.

January 11

January 12

January 13
Donny Hathaway, 1979.

January 14
Jerry Nolan (The New York Dolls), 1992.

January 15
Harry Nilsson, 1994. Junior Wells, 1998.

January 16

January 17
Junior Kimbrough, 1998.

January 18
Roger Ruskin Spear (The Bonzo Dog Band), 1990.

January 19

January 20
Jackie Wilson, 1984.

January 21
Champion Jack Dupree, 1992.

January 22

January 23
Big Maybelle, 1972. Terry Kath (Chicago), 1978. Billy MacKenzie (The Associates), 1997.

January 24
George McCrae, 1986.

January 25
Johnny Funches (The Dells), 1998.

January 26
Donnie Elbert, 1989.

January 27
Mahalia Jackson, 1972.

January 28
Billy Fury, 1983. Puma Sandra Jones (Black Uhuru), 1990

January 29
Willie Dixon, 1992.

January 30
Mance Lipscomb, 1976. Professor Longhair, 1980. Lightnin' Hopkins, 1982.

January 31
Slim Harpo, 1970.

February 1
Vincent Crane (Atomic Rooster), 1989.

February 2
Sid Vicious, 1979. David McComb (Triffids), 1999.

February 3
Buddy Holly, 1959. Ritchie Valens, 1959. Big Bopper, 1959. Joe Meek, 1967. Gwen Guthrie, 1999.

February 4
Alex Harvey, 1982. Karen Carpenter, 1983.

February 5

February 6

February 7

February 8
Del Shannon, 1990.

February 9
Bill Haley, 1981. Brian Connolly (The Sweet), 1997.

February 10
Dave Alexander (The Stooges), 1975.

February 11

February 12

February 13

February 14

February 15
Mike Bloomfield, 1981.

February 16
Brownie McGhee, 1996.

February 17

February 18
Bob Stinson (Replacements), 1995.

February 19
Bon Scott (AC/DC), 1980.

February 20

February 21

February 22
Florence Ballard, 1976.

February 23
Melvin Franklin (Temptations), 1995.

February 24
Memphis Slim, 1988. Johnnie Ray, 1990.

February 25

February 26
Bukka White, 1977.

February 27
February 28 Frankie Lymon, 1969. Bobby Bloom, 1974. David Byron (Uriah Heep), 1985.

February 28/9

March 1
Frank Eisler-Smith (Air Supply), 1991.

March 2
Serge Gainsbourg, 1991. Dusty Springfield, 1999. David Ackles, 1999.

March 3

March 4
Trevor Lucas (Fairport Convention), 1989.

March 5
Patsy Cline, 1963. Vivian Stanshall, 1995.

March 6
Ron "Pigpen" McKennan (Grateful Dead), 1973. Richard Manuel (The Band), 1986. Delroy Wilson, 1995.

March 7

March 8

March 9
Andy Gibb, 1988. Notorious BIG, 1997.

March 10
Stuart Sutcliffe, 1962.

March 11
Sonny Terry, 1986. Stacy Guess (The Squirrel Nut Zippers), 1998.

March 12
Charlie Parker, 1955. Judge Dread, 1998.

March 13
March 14 Linda Jones (Linda Lane), 1972.

March 14

March 15
Joseph Pope (The Tams), 1996.

March 16
T-Bone Walker, 1975.

March 17
Rick Grech, 1990.

March 18

March 19
Paul Kossoff (Free), 1976. Tampa Red, 1981. Randy Rhoads (Blizzard Of Ozz), 1982. Andrew Wood (Mother Love Bone), 1990.

March 20

March 21

March 22
Dan Hartman, 1994.

March 23

March 24
Harold Melvin, 1997.

March 25
Tom Jans, 1984.

March 26
Little Willie John, 1968. Duster Bennett, 1976. Ananda Shankar, 1999.

March 27
Eazy E (NWA), 1995.

March 28
Arthur "Big Boy" Crudup, 1974.

March 29

March 30

March 31
The Singing Nun, 1985. O'Kelly Isley, 1986. Jeffrey Lee Pierce (Gun Club), 1996.

April 1
Marvin Gaye, 1984. Rozz Williams (Christian Death), 1998.

April 2

April 3
Richard Farina, 1966.

April 4

April 5
Cozy Powell, 1998.

April 6
Wendy O Williams, 1998. Tammy Wynette, 1998.

April 7
Lee Brilleaux (Dr Feelgood), 1995.

April 8
Kurt Cobain, 1994. Laura Nyro, 1997.

April 9
Phil Ochs, 1976. Dave Prater (Sam And Dave), 1988.

April 10
LaVern Baker, 1997.

April 11

April 12

April 13

April 14
Pete Farndon (The Pretenders), 1983.

April 15
Bob "The Bear" Hite (Canned Heat), 1981.

April 16
Tammi Terrell, 1970. Skip Spence, 1999.

April 17
Eddie Cochran, 1960. Felix Pappalardi 1983.

April 18
Bernard Edwards (Chic), 1996.

April 19
El Duce (The Mentors), 1997.

April 20
Steve Marriott, 1991.

April 21
Sandy Denny, 1978.

April 22

April 23
Johnny Thunders, 1991.

April 24

April 25
Otis Spann, 1970.

April 26
April 27 ZZ Hill, 1984.

April 27

April 28

April 29
Cisco Houston, 1961. Mick Ronson, 1993.

April 30
Muddy Waters, 1983.

May 1

May 2

May 3

May 4
Paul Butterfield, 1987.

May 5
The Reverend Gary Davis, 1972.

May 6

May 7

May 8
Graham Bond, 1974.

May 9
Neil Bogart, 1982.

May 10
Shel Silverstein, 1999.

May 11
Lester Flatt, 1979. Bob Marley, 1981.

May 12

May 13
Bob Wills, 1975. Chet Baker, 1988.

May 14
Keith Relf, 1976. William Tucker (Ministry), 1999.

May 15
Rob Gretton (New Order's manager), 1999.

May 16
Marv Johnson, 1993.

May 17
Johnny Guitar Watson, 1995.

May 18
Augusto Pablo, 1999.

May 19

May 20
West Arkeen (Gn'R composer), 1997.

May 21

May 22

May 23
Pete Ham (Badfinger), 1975. Will Sin (The Shamen), 1991.

May 24
Elmore James, 1963. Gene Clark, 1991.

May 25
Sonny Boy Williamson II, 1965. Brad Nowell (Sublime), 1996.

May 26
Jimmie Rodgers, 1933.

May 27

May 28

May 29
John Cipollina (Quicksilver Messenger Service), 1989.
Jeff Buckley, 1997.

May 30
John Kahn (Old And In The Way), 1996.

May 31

June 1
David Ruffin (Temptations), 1991.

June 2
Junior Braithwaite (The Wailers), 1999.

June 3

June 4
Stiv Bators (The Dead Boys), 1990. Ronnie Lane, 1997.

June 5
Sleepy John Estes, 1977. Richard Sohl (Patti Smith Group),
1990.

June 6

June 7
Eddie Kurdziel (Red Kross), 1999.

June 8

June 9
Arthur Alexander, 1993.

June 10

June 11

June 12

June 13

June 14
Clarence White, 1973. Pete De Freitas (Echo And The Bunnymen man), 1989. Rory Gallagher, 1995.

June 15
Jimmy Hodder (Steely Dan), 1990.

June 16
James Honeyman Scott (Pretenders) 1982. Kristen Pfaff (Hole), 1994.

June 17

June 18
Ian Curtis (Joy Division), 1980.

June 19

June 20
Lawrence Payton (Four Tops), 1997.

June 21

June 22
Jesse 'Ed' Davis, 1988.

June 23
Curt Boettcher (Sagittarius, Millennium), 1987.

June 24
Screaming Lord Sutch, 1999.

June 25

June 26

June 27
Hillel Slovak (Red Hot Chili Peppers), 1988. Stefanie

Sargent (7 Year Bitch), 1992. Brian O'Hara (The Fourmost), 1999.

June 28
G.G. Allin, 1993.

June 29
Shorty Long, 1969. Tim Buckley, 1975. Lowell George, 1979.

June 30
Carl Radle, 1980.

July 1
Snakefinger, 1987. Brent Mydland, 1990. Guy Mitchell, 1999.

July 2

July 3
Brian Jones, 1969. Jim Morrison, 1971. ## July 4

July 5

July 6
Van McCoy, 1979.

July 7

July 8

July 9

July 10
Jelly Roll Morton, 1941. John Hammond Sr, 1987.

July 11
Howard Pickup (The Adverts), 1997.

July 12
Minnie Ripperton, 1979. Chris Wood, 1983.

July 13

July 14
Malcolm Owen, 1980.

July 15
Trouble T-Roy (Heavy D And The Boyz), 1990.

July 16
Harry Chapin, 1981. John Panozzo (Styx), 1996.

July 17
Billie Holiday, 1959. Chas Chandler, 1996.

July 18
Nico, 1988.

July 19

July 20
Jim Ellison (Material Issue), 1996.

July 21

July 22

July 23
Keith Godchaux, 1980.

July 24

July 25
'Big Mama' Thornton, 1984.

July 26
Mary Wells, 1992.

July 27
Daniel Beard (Fifth Dimension), 1982.

July 28
Eddie Hinton, 1995. Jason Thirsk 1996.

July 29
Cass Elliot, 1974.

July 30
Don Myrick (Earth, Wind And Fire), 1993. Rob Jones (Wonderstuff), 1993.

July 31

August 1
Johnny Burnette, 1964.

August 2
Fela Kuti, 1997.

August 3

August 4

August 5
Jeff Porcaro (Toto), 1992.

August 6
Klaus Nomi, 1985.

August 7
Esther Phillips, 1984.

August 8

August 9
Jerry Garcia (Grateful Dead), 1995.

August 10
Euronymous (Mayhem), 1993.

August 11

August 12
Luther Allison, 1997.

August 13
King Curtis, 1971. Joe Tex, 1982.

August 14
Robert Calvert (Hawkwind), 1988.

August 15
Big Bill Broonzy, 1958. Jackie Edwards, 1992.

August 16
Robert Johnson, 1938. Elvis Presley, 1977.
Nusrat Fateh Ali Khan, 1997

August 17
Lorraine Ellison, 1985.

August 18
August 19 Blind Willie McTell, 1959.

August 19

August 20

August 21

August 22

August 23
Dwayne Goettel (Skinny Puppy), 1995.

August 24
Jesse Bloian (The Artistics), 1994.

August 25

August 26

August 27
Brian Epstein, 1967. Stevie Ray Vaughan, 1990.

August 28

August 29
Jimmy Reed, 1976.

August 30
Sterling Morrison (Velvet Underground), 1995.

September 1

September 2

September 3
Al Wilson (Canned Heat), 1970.

September 4
Lal Waterson, 1998.

September 5

September 6
Tom Fogerty (Creedence Clearwater Revival), 1990.

September 7
Keith Moon, 1978.

September 8

Cowboy (Grandmaster Flash), 1989.

September 9
Bill Monroe, 1996.

September 10

September 11
Peter Tosh, 1987.

September 12

September 13
Tupac Shakur, 1996.

September 14
Furry Lewis, 1981.

September 15

September 16
Marc Bolan, 1977.

September 17
Rob Tyner (MC5), 1991.

September 18
Jimi Hendrix, 1970. Jimmy Witherspoon, 1997. Charlie Foxx
(Inez And Charlie Fox), 1998.

September 19
Gram Parsons, 1973.

September 20
Jim Croce, 1973. Steve Goodman, 1984.

September 21

September 22

September 23

September 24

September 25
John Bonham (Led Zeppelin), 1980.

September 26

Bessie Smith, 1937.

September 27
Rory Storm, 1972. Jimmy McCullough (Wings), 1979. Cliff Burton (Metallica), 1986.

September 28
Miles Davis, 1991.

September 29
Betty Carter, 1998.

September 30

October 1
Al Jackson Jr (Booker T And The MGs), 1975.

October 2
Gene Autry, 1998.

October 3
Woody Guthrie, 1967. Victoria Spivey, 1976.

October 4
Janis Joplin, 1970.

October 5
Eddie Kendricks (Temptations), 1992.

October 6

October 7
Johnny Kidd, 1966.

October 8

October 9
Sister Rosetta Tharpe, 1973.

October 10

October 11

October 12
Gene Vincent, 1971. John Denver, 1997.

October 13

October 14

October 15

October 16

October 17

October 18

October 19
Son House, 1988. Glen Buxton (Alice Cooper Band), 1997.

October 20
Lynyrd Skynyrd members Ronnie Van Zant, Steven Gaines and his wife Cassie, 1977.

October 21

October 22
Ewan MacColl, 1989.

October 23
Leonard Lee (Shirley And Lee), 1976.

October 24

October 25
Nick Drake, 1974.

October 26
Wilbert Harrison, 1994.

October 27
Steve Peregrin Took (T Rex), 1980. Xavier Cugat, 1990.

October 28

October 29
Duane Allman, 1971.

October 30
Jo Ann Kelly, 1990

October 31
Festival of Hallowe'en.

November 1
Mexico's Day Of The Dead Festival begins.

November 2
Mississippi John Hurt, 1966.

November 3

November 4
Eugene Powell, 1998.

November 5
Fred 'Sonic' Smith (MC5), 1994.

November 6
Billy Murcia (New York Dolls), 1972.

November 7
Tom Clancy, 1990.

November 8

November 9

November 10

November 11
Jo Baker (Elvin Bishop Group), 1996.

November 12
Rainer Ptacek, 1997.

November 13
Ricky Wilson (B52s), 1985. Bill Doggett, 1995.

November 14
Keith Hudson, 1984.

November 15

November 16
OV Wright, 1980. Dino Valenti (Quicksilver Messenger Service), 1994.

November 17

November 18
Danny Whitten (Crazy Horse), 1972.

November 19
Alan Hull (Lindisfarne), 1995.

November 20
Roland Alphonso (The Skatalites), 1998.

November 21
Berry Oakley (Allman Brothers Band), 1972.
Shannon Hoon (Blind Melon), 1995.

November 22
Epic Soundtracks (Swell Maps), 1997.
Michael Hutchence (INXS), 1997.

November 23
Tom Evans (Badfinger), 1983.

November 24
Big Joe Turner, 1985. Freddie Mercury, 1991. Eric Carr (Kiss), 1991. Albert Collins, 1993.

November 25
Gary Holton (Heavy Metal Kids), 1985.

November 26
David Briggs, 1996.

November 27
Barbara Acklin, 1971.

November 28
Jerry Edmonton (Steppenwolf), 1994.

November 29

November 30
Tiny Tim, 1996.

December 1
Michael Hedges, 1997.

December 2
David Blue, 1982. Lee Dorsey, 1986.

December 3
Ray Gillen (Black Sabbath), 1993.

December 4
Tommy Bolin (Deep Purple), 1976. Frank Zappa, 1993.

December 5

December 6
Leadbelly, 1949. Roy Orbison, 1988. Patty Donahue (The Waitresses), 1996.

December 7
Darby Crash (The Germs), 1980.

December 8
John Lennon, 1980. Nicholas "Razzle" Dingley (Hanoi Rocks), 1984.

December 9
Will Shatter (Flipper), 1987.

December 10
Otis Redding, 1967.

December 11
Sam Cooke, 1964.

December 12
Tim Hardin, 1980. Ian Stewart, 1985.

December 13

December 14
Pattie Santos (It's A Beautiful Day), 1989.

December 15
Fats Waller, 1943.

December 16
Sylvester, 1988.

December 17
Big Joe Williams, 1982.

December 18
Nicolette Larson, 1997.

December 19
Les Kummel (New Colony Six), 1978.

December 20
Bobby Darin, 1973.

December 21
Albert King, 1992.

December 22
D Boon (Minutemen), 1985.

December 23
Eddie Hazel (Parliament), 1992.

December 24

December 25
Johnny Ace, 1954. Bryan MacLean (Love), 1998. Karl Denver, 1998.

December 26

December 27
Chris Bell (Big Star), 1978.

December 28
Freddie King, 1976. Dennis Wilson (The Beach Boys), 1983.

December 29

December 30
Clarence G Satchell (Ohio Players), 1995.

December 31
Ricky Nelson, 1985. Floyd Cramer, 1997.

CHAPTER ONE

To die, to sleep;
To sleep: perchance to dream: Ay, there's the rub:
For in that sleep of death what dreams may come,
When we have shuffled off this mortal coil,
Must give us pause: there's the respect
That makes calamity of so long life... William Shakespeare, Hamlet

THERE'S NO DENYING, DEATH changes everything. Tragedy touches us all. But at least it's not as prevalent today as it used to be. In the post-war, rock 'n' roll-fuelled, medicine-friendly, live-longer-and-get-a-good-pension-world, death sticks out like a sore thumb. So its arrival, through anything other than old age, sends out shock waves. People live much longer these days, so any life cut tragically short is thrust into the public domain.

In the genres of rock and pop music death elevates mere celebrity to mythological status. Death is simply a new phase in a rock star's career; it's a new aspect in their marketing strategy. Sure, not everyone ends up shrink-wrapped as an icon but our music stars, superstars and megastars acquire a larger-than-life kudos in death. Death shifts units.

And what of those who are left behind? Whether they're fans, friends or lovers, they're left lonelier and confused, often unable to come to terms with events.

Take Maureen Marsh, a lady who had a purely platonic passion for country star Jim Reeves. At the time of his death in an air crash in 1964,

Reeves had so much material in the can that his estate managed to plunder the vaults for years. His musical career simply carried on from the grave. Judy and Fred Vermorel's book Fandemonium turned up superfan Maureen, whose most treasured possession was a cowboy shirt worn by Jim Reeves. The story goes that, whenever she flew across the Atlantic to lay a wreath at the singer's grave, she always put the shirt on. If the plane crashed she wanted to die wearing something of Jim's. Touching stuff.

People, it seems, are obsessed by the passing of a legend, as the Vermorels' book goes on to report. They also turned up Greg Smith from Kansas, who served his apprenticeship as an undertaker in Hollywood and quickly became popular with visiting friends wanting to see where the stars had died. Quick to grasp the possibilities, Greg amassed information on the most gruesome of celebrity deaths and started up Grave Line Tours. This tour included various death-inducing trees, places of ill repute and the hotel room where Janis Joplin OD'd. Sick? Perhaps.

Then there's the Internet, it's become a place

where folks like to talk of star deaths and share their stories. Original Big Brother And The Holding Company guitarist, vocalist and songwriter, Sam Andrew has revealed his most intimate thoughts on the web, remembering his time with Janis Joplin. His eloquent letters to Janis were written in the '90s, some 20 years after her heroin overdose. Andrew's epistles are filled with a very personal insight into her world:

Dear Janis,

Remember the day when Otis Redding died? You called me and your voice was trembling. I had never heard you like that before and you seemed so forlorn. We met at your place and played all of Otis' records. It was a good night because we honoured the man, but now and then you would get a troubled expression on your face and I knew that you wanted him to still be there and that you knew he could do so much more if he had only lived.
Extract from 'A Letter To Janis' from Sam Andrew, 22 October 1996

Rock stars, more than any other species known to the devoted trend follower, create incredible emotional ties with their fellow rock stars and their fans. In many cases these ties are almost inexplicable to the impartial onlooker. But being a fan of anyone from The Osmonds through to Cradle Of Filth has its own rules and regulations and, should tragedy strike, the repercussions are inevitable.

As for the stars themselves, well, they're immortal until, well, they're not any more. Then the process of mass adulation really starts to take hold. And the tag-line "Live Fast, Die Young, Leave A Good Looking Corpse", simply adds zeroes to the value of the fan in the street's collection of rock memorabilia; spurring them on to a yet firmer and more besotted bond.

If a measure of the eccentricities of fan worship for the dearly departed were needed, we need look no further than the September 1999 issue of Record Collector magazine and its ad from Fraser's (a double page spread with pix). Fraser's specialise in autographed photographs, letters and documents. One presumes they make a virtual killing from their £19.99 a throw selection of wills and autopsy reports.

Their archives include the last testimonials of the likes of Karen Carpenter, Patsy Cline, Sam Cooke, Miles Davis, Mama Cass, Jerry Garcia, Marvin Gaye, Jimi Hendrix, Billie Holliday, Buddy Holly, Janis Joplin, John Lennon, Keith Moon, Jim Morrison, Roy Orbison, Elvis Presley, Frank Sinatra and Ritchie Valens. As for autopsies, the gruesome facts are available on Marilyn Monroe, River Phoenix and Sharon Tate along with a clutch of other sorry souls.

The Elvis will is a big seller. Put together by the great man in the March prior to his death it doesn't read like the work of a bloke who was about to allegedly fake his own death. But, to many, that option is certainly still a possibility. Since that fateful day in 1977, Presley has done the rounds and been spotted in chip shops the world over. Not to mention Mars. Surprisingly for a man who rarely left the States when he was alive, the stories and subsequent sightings in every territory known to man prove that he must have kept his passport and visas updated.

The spiritual side of the Elvis World Tour began the moment he passed on and hasn't let up yet. According to Elvis After Life by Dr Raymond A Moody Jr, one fan went home on the night of the great man's death to discover that her Presley collection had melted.

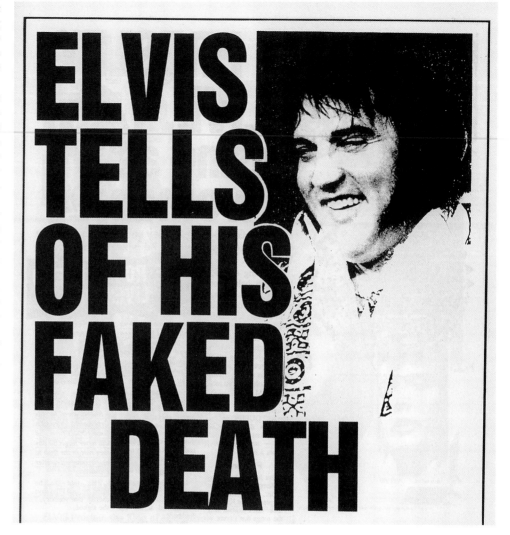

ELVIS TELLS OF HIS FAKED DEATH

Simultaneously, a couple were left in shock when their Elvis statue broke in half. There was no stopping the King; he turned up in visions helping police officers and his face was embedded in an overweight woman's pantry door. It spoke volumes.

There are hundreds of apocryphal Elvis tales, and none better than that of barmaid Elizabeth Prince from Atlanta, Georgia, who claimed she lived with Elvis between 1978 and 1981. And, although their relationship is now long over, they still speak regularly on the phone. Which is nice. Then there were the Elvis Tapes, in which the be-quiffed crooner claimed to be planning a

comeback from his Hawaiian hideaway. And imagine the surprise of Presley fan Mike Joseph who, while visiting Graceland on New Year's Day 1978, saw Elvis watching him from a window in the P's mansion. As you do...

Spookily two years later in Chicago, Illinois, John Turnbull recognised a busker as the former millionaire. They had a quick chat and Elvis told him he'd faked his own death to get away from all the "pressure". Just one year on in Encino, California, a window cleaner, John Carter, bumped into the renowned burger chomper in the queue outside of, where else, Burger King. Meanwhile, in 1987 in Alzey, Germany, a farmer

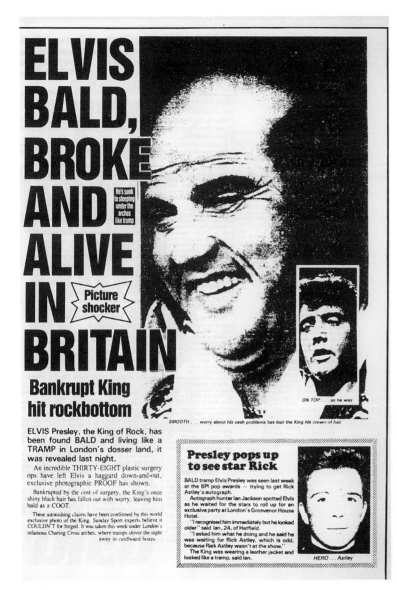

ELVIS BALD, BROKE AND ALIVE IN BRITAIN

He's sunk to sleeping under the arches like tramp

★ **Picture shocker**

Bankrupt King hit rockbottom

ELVIS Presley, the King of Rock, has been found BALD and living like a TRAMP in London's dosser land, it was revealed last night.

An incredible THIRTY-EIGHT plastic surgery ops have left Elvis a haggard down-and-out, exclusive photographic PROOF has shown.

Bankrupted by the cost of surgery, the King's once shiny black hair has fallen out with worry, leaving him bald as a COOT.

These astonishing claims have been confirmed by this world exclusive photographic PROOF has shown. COULDN'T for forged. It was taken this week under London's infamous Charing Cross arches, where tramps shiver the night away in cardboard boxes.

SMOOTH . . . worry about his cash problems has lost the King his crown of hair

Presley pops up to see star Rick

BALD tramp Elvis Presley was seen last week at the BPI pop awards — trying to get Rick Astley's autograph.

Autograph hunter Ian Jackson spotted Elvis as he waited for the stars to roll up for an exclusive party at London's Grosvenor House Hotel.

"I recognised him immediately but he looked older" said Ian, 24, of Hatfield.

"I asked him what he doing and he said he was waiting for Rick Astley, which is odd, because Rick Astley wasn't at the show."

The King was wearing a leather jacket and looked like a tramp, said Ian.

ON TOP . . . as he was

HERO . . . Astley

---

called Erich Lusk revealed that the ghost of Elvis was spooking his cows. It's all beef-related you see?

By 1988 the action had moved to Hounslow, Middlesex where The Daily Sport discovered that a local fishmonger was really Elvis trying to keep a low profile. The following year in Blount City, Alabama, The Sunday People tracked the man down to a health farm where he was hiding from a Mafia hit team, probably because the Daily Sport was about to announce that Mars was now home to the King. The paper published

a photograph obtained from "Russia" of a small statue of Elvis that had been found on the wayward planet. Concrete proof.

Universal success wasn't enough for Elvis. Rumour is he trekked to Turkey, where in 1991 the discovery of an Elvis statue on top of the Nemrut Dag mountain revealed that Elvis had lived before and probably ruled Turkey.

The stories got more and more bizarre from then on. The Sunday Sport lurched into the '90s with two more classic yarns concerning the big man. They surpassed themselves with the headlines: "Elvis Presley Alive - Posing As A Woman" and "Elvis, Bald, Broke And Alive In Britain".

The former centred on the "confession" of a 14-stone, 48-year old German housewife Jutte Jeuthe, who admitted, "I'm absolutely convinced... I am Elvis!". How on earth could you argue? Amazingly, Jeuthe claimed that Elvis was singing through her, but for some unexplained reason the songs came out in German. Natch.

The second story started with the immortal words, "Elvis Presley, the King Of Rock, has been found BALD and living like a TRAMP in London's dosser land." Further investigation unearthed the reason for his destitute state and his new abode under the arches at Charing Cross. The phenomenally rich superstar had squandered his hard-earned cash on extensive plastic surgery. Makes sense?

The further the world spiralled from Presley's death the more frivolous the tomfoolery in his name became and the bigger the Elvis merchandising industry grew. A bag of dirt from the man's yard, Presley dolls, numberplates, fetching underwear or a paperweight can all be bought in Memphis. But, why pay the airfare when you can pick up a bar of Elvis soap on your own doorstep:

PRESLEY LIVES ON IN BATTLE OF THE SOAPS

The scent of perfumed soap wafted around the courtroom of the Patents Office yesterday as an English businessman confronted the American Presley estate for the right to sell toiletries under the Elvis name in Britain.

Gasp! Just when you thought you could buy Elvis by the pound, the law steps in. This odd story rolled out a few years back, when Sid Shaw and his three million-pound Presley business fell foul of the Presley Estate. The offending soap bore the signature "Sincerely, Elvis Presley" but the Estate questioned the signature's credibility. After weeks of pontificating, the former barrow boy from Shoreditch was allowed to continue sudding up on Elvis but without the signature. The legacy of a great singer was protected. Sort of.

There's no rest for the dead. But there's definitely cash to be had. But, for me, there was still a burning yearning to know more about the Presley will. Questions needed to be answered.

Did he go around signing lots of bars of soap? Did he really work down the chip shop? Is he dead? Is he portrayed realistically by Kurt Russell in that John Carpenter film? Why on earth did his daughter marry Michael Jackson? Just what is in that will? I paid the £19.99 for you dear reader... but I'm still none the wiser. Here we present the edited highlights:

I, Elvis A. Presley, a resident and citizen of Shelby County, Tennessee, being of sound mind and disposing memory, do hereby make, publish and declare this instrument to be my last will and testament, hereby revoking any and all wills and codicils by me at any time heretofore made.

Item I Debts, Expenses and Taxes

I direct my Executor, hereinafter named, to pay all of

my matured debts and my funeral expenses, as well as the costs and expenses of the administration of my estate, as soon after my death as practicable. I further direct that all estate, inheritance, transfer and succession taxes which are payable by reason under this will, be paid out of my residuary estate; and I hereby waive on behalf of my estate any right to recover from any person any part of such taxes so paid. My Executor, in his sole discretion, may pay from my domiciliary estate all or any portion of the costs of ancillary administration and similar proceedings in other jurisdictions.

Item II Instruction Concerning Personal Property: Enjoyment in Specie

I anticipate that included as a part of my property and estate at the time of my death will be tangible personal property of various kinds, characters and values, including trophies and other items accumulated by me during my professional career. I hereby specifically instruct all concerned that my Executor, herein appointed, shall have complete freedom and discretion as to disposal of any and all such property so long as he shall act in good faith and in the best interest of my estate and my beneficiaries, and his discretion so exercised shall not be subject to question by anyone whomsoever.

I hereby expressly authorize my Executor and my Trustee, respectively and successively, to permit any beneficiary of any and all trusts created hereunder to enjoy in specie the use or benefit of any household goods, chattels, or other tangible personal property (exclusive of choses in action, cash, stocks, bonds or other securities) which either my Executor or my Trustees may receive in kind, and my Executor and my Trustees shall not be liable for any consumption, damage, injury to or loss of any tangible property so used, nor shall the beneficiaries of any trusts hereunder or their executors of administrators be liable for any consumption, damage, injury to or loss of any tangible personal property so used.

Item III Real Estate

If I am the owner of any real estate at the time of my death, I instruct and empower my Executor and my Trustee (as the case may be) to hold such real estate for investment, or to sell same, or any portion therof, as my Executor or my Trustee (as the case may be) shall in his sole judgement determine to be for the best interest of my estate and the beneficiaries thereof.

Item IV Residuary Trust

After payment of all debts, expenses and taxes as directed under Item I hereof, I give, devise, and bequeath all the rest, residue, and remainder of my estate, including all lapsed legacies and devices, and any property over which I have a power of appointment, to my Trustee, hereinafter named, in trust for the following purposes:

(a) The Trustees is directed to take, hold, manage, invest and reinvent the corpus of the trust and to collect the income there from in accordance with the rights, powers, duties, authority and discretion hereinafter set forth. The Trustee is directed to pay all the expenses, taxes and costs incurred in the management of the trust estate out of the income thereof.

(b) After payment of all expenses, taxes and costs incurred in the management of the expenses, taxes and costs incurred in the management of the trust estate, the Trustee is authorized to accumulate the net income or to pay or apply so much of the net income and such portion of the principal at any time and from time to time to time for health, education, support, comfortable maintenance and welfare of:
(1) My daughter, Lisa Marie Presley, and any other lawful issue I might have, (2) my grandmother, Minnie Mae Presley,
(3) my father, Vernon E. Presley, and
(4) such other relatives of mine living at the time of my death who in the absolute discretion of my Trustees are in need of emergency assistance for any of the above mentioned purposes and the Trustee is able to make such distribution without affecting the ability of the trust to meet the present needs of the first three numbered categories of beneficiaries herein mentioned or to meet the reasonably expected future needs of the first three classes of beneficiaries herein mentioned. Any decision of the Trustee as to whether or not distribution, to any of the persons described hereunder shall be final and conclusive and not subject to question by any legatee or beneficiary hereunder.

(c) Upon the death of my Father, Vernon E. Presley, the Trustee is instructed to make no further distributions to the fourth category of beneficiaries and such beneficiaries shall cease to have any interest whatsoever in this trust.

(d) Upon the death of both my said father and my said grandmother, the Trustee is directed to divide the Residuary Trust into separate and equal trusts, creating one such equal trust for each of my lawful children then surviving and one such equal trust for the living issue collectively, if any, of any deceased child of mine. The share, if any, for the issue of any such deceased child, shall immediately vest in such issue in equal shares but shall be subject to the provisions of Item V herein. Separate books and records shall be kept for each trust, but it shall not be necessary that a physical division of the assets be made as to each trust.

The Trustee may from time to time distribute the whole or any part of the net income or principal from each of the aforesaid trusts as the Trustee, in its uncontrolled discretion, considers necessary or desirable to provide for the comfortable support, education, maintenance, benefit and general welfare of each of my children. Such distributions may be made directly to such beneficiary or to the guardian of the person of such beneficiary and without responsibility on my Trustee to see to the application of nay such distributions and in making such distributions, the Trustee shall take into account all other sources of funds known by the Trustee to be available for each respective beneficiary for such purpose.

(e) As each of my respective children attains the age of twenty-five (25) years and provided that both my father and my grandmother are deceased, the trust created hereunder for such child care terminate, and all the remainder of the assets then contained in said trust shall be distributed to such child so attaining the age of twenty-five (25) years outright and free of further trust.

(f) If any of my children for whose benefit a trust has been created hereunder should die before attaining the age of twenty-five (25) years, then the trust created for such a child shall terminate on his death, and all remaining assets then contained in said trust shall be distributed outright and free of further trust and in equal shares to the surviving issue of such deceased child but subject to the provisions of Item V herein; but if there be no such surviving issue, then to the brothers and sisters of such deceased child in equal shares, the issue of any other deceased child being entitled collectively to their deceased parent's share. Nevertheless, if any distribution otherwise becomes payable outright and free of trust under the provisions of this paragraph (f) of the Item IV of my will to a beneficiary for whom the Trustee is then administering a trust for the benefit of such beneficiary under provisions of this last will and testament,

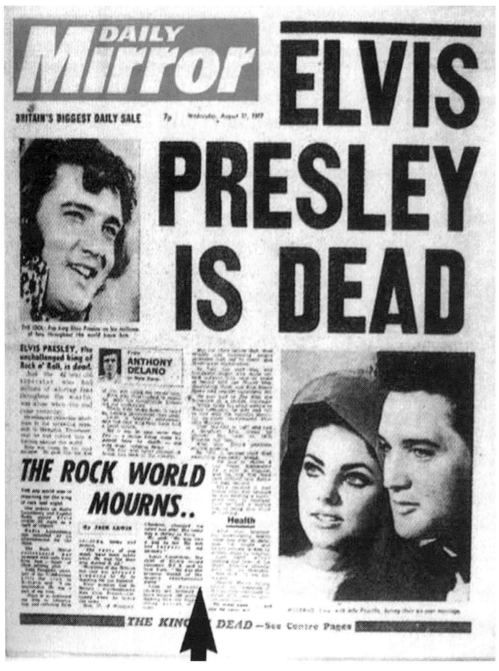

expend so much of the income and principal for the care, support, and education of such beneficiary, and any income not so expended with respect to each share so retained all the power and discretion had with respect to such trust generally.

Item VI Alternate Distributees

In the event that all of my descendants should be deceased at any time prior to the time for the termination of the trusts provided for herein, then in such event all of my estate and all the assets of every trust to be created hereunder (as the case may be) shall then distributed outright in equal shares to my heirs at law per stripes.

Item VII Unenforceable Provisions

If any provisions of this will are unenforceable, the remaining provisions shall, nevertheless, be carried into effect.

Item VIII Life Insurance

If my estate is the beneficiary of any life insurance on my life at the time of my death, I direct that the proceeds therefrom will be used by my Executor in payment of the debts, expenses and taxes listed in Item I of this will, to the extent deemed advisable by the Executor. All such proceeds not so used are to be used by my Executor for the purpose of satisfying the devises and bequests contained in Item IV herein.

Item IX Spendthrift Provision

I direct that the interest of any beneficiary in principal or income of any trust created hereunder shall not be subject to claims of creditors or others, nor to legal process, and may not be voluntarily or involuntarily alienated or encumbered except as herein provided. Any bequests contained herein for any female shall be for her sole and separate use, free from the debts, contracts and control of any husband she may ever have.

Item X Proceeds From Personal Services

All sums paid after my death (either to my estate or to any of the trusts created hereunder) and resulting from personal services rendered by me during my lifetime, including, but not limited to, royalties of all nature, concerts, motion picture contracts, and personal appearances shall be considered to be income, notwithstanding the provisions of estate and trust law to the contrary.

Item XI Executor and Trustee

I appoint as executor of this, my last will and testament, and as Trustee of every trust required to be cre-

such distribution shall not be paid outright to such beneficiary but shall be added to and become a part of the trust so being administered for such beneficiary by the Trustee.

Item V Distribution to Minor Children

If any share of corpus of any trust established under

this will become distributable outright and free of trust to any beneficiary before said beneficiary has attained the age of eighteen (18) years, then said share shall immediately vest in said beneficiary, but the Trustee shall retain possession of such share during the period in which such beneficiary is under the age of eighteen (18) years, and, in the meantime, shall use and

ated hereunder, my said father.

I hereby direct that my said father shall be entitled by his last will and testament, duly probated, to appoint a successor Executor of my estate, as well as a successor Trustee or successor Trustees of all the trusts to be created under my last will and testament. If, for any reason, my said father be unable to serve or to continue to serve as Executor and/or as Trustee, or if he be deceased and shall not have appointed a successor Executor or Trustee, by virtue of his last will and testament as stated-above, then I appoint National Bank of Commerce, Memphis, Tennessee, or its successor or the institution with which it may merge, as successor Executor and/or as successor Trustee of all trusts required to be established hereunder.

None of the appointees named hereunder, including any appointment made by virtue of the last will and testament of my said father, shall be required to furnish any bond or security for performance of the respective fiduciary duties required hereunder, notwithstanding any rule of law to the contrary.

In WITNESS WHEREOF, I, the said ELVIS A. PRESLEY, do hereunto set my hand and seal in the presence of two (2) competent witnesses, and in their presence do publish and declare this instrument to be my Last Will and Testament, this 3rd day of March, 1977.

(Signed by Elvis A. Presley)
ELVIS A. PRESLEY

The foregoing instrument, consisting of this and eleven (11) preceding typewritten pages, was signed, sealed, published and declared by ELVIS A. PRESLEY, the Testator, to be his Last Will and Testament, in our presence, and we, at his request and in his presence and in the presence of each other, have hereunto subscribed our names as witnesses, this 3 day of

March, 1977, at Memphis, Tennessee.

(Signed by Ginger Alden)
Ginger Alden residing at 4152 Royal Crest Place

(Signed by Charles F. Hodge)
Charles F. Hodge residing at 3764 Elvis Presley Blvd.

(Signed by Ann Dewey Smith)
Ann Dewey Smith residing at 2237 Court Avenue.

State of Tennessee

County of Shelby

Ginger Alden, Charles F. Hodge, and Ann Dewey Smith, after being first duly sworn, make oath or affirm that the foregoing Last Will and Testament, in the sight and presence of us, the undersigned, who at his request and in his sight and presence, and in the sight and presence of each other, have subscribed our names as attesting witnesses on the 3 day of March, 1977, and we further make oath or affirm that the Testator was of sound mind and disposing memory and not acting under fraud, menace or undue influ-

ence of any person, and was more than eighteen (18) years of age; and that each of the attesting witnesses is more than eighteen (18) years of age.
(Signed by Ginger Alden)
Ginger Alden

(Signed by Charles F. Hodge)
Charles F. Hodge

(Signed by Ann Dewey Smith)
Ann Dewey Smith

Sworn To And Subscribed before me this 3 day of March, 1977.

Drayton Beecker Smith II Notary Public
My commission expires: August 8, 1979
Admitted to probate and Ordered Recorded August 22, 1977

Joseph W. Evans, Judge
Recorded August 22, 1977

B.J. Dunavant, Clerk
By: Jan Scott, D.C.

CHAPTER TWO

Earth to earth, ashes to ashes, dust to dust;
in sure and certain hope of the Resurrection into eternal life...
From The Book of Common Prayer, 'The Burial of the Dead'

THE ROAD TO RACK AND RUIN through rock 'n' roll excess, whether it be by burger and barbiturates, or just by driving the lawnmower too fast, is a precarious one. Once the Devil's music has taken hold, then all that follow are, quite honestly, in serious trouble. The wages of sin are bad. Evil brings evil. Naughty does as naughty sees. Indeed, the trappings of superstardom are well documented and those who sip at the wineglass of mad behaviour deserve to die by the sword. Or something like that.

If proof be needed, then just click your mouse onto www.av1611.org/rockdead.html. It's here that rock stars are held up as poor examples of the way to lead a life. On this Bible-bashed site, which opens with the line: "The fear of the LORD prolongeth days: but the years of the wicked shall be shortened." Proverbs 10:27, rockism and its incumbent lifestyle just aren't the ticket.

In a no-punches-pulled tirade the site reveals that the average age at death of rock stars (who are actually dead) is 36.9 years. Obviously this doesn't take into account the ages of rock stars who are still alive, or indeed those that have yet to be born but, hey, there must be some logic to it. Did you know that on average Americans expire at the age of 75.8? Well, there you are. And, if that information weren't damning enough, the site goes on to list the many causes of "rock death", which include...

Heart Attack 41
Drug Overdose 40
Misc. Medical 37
Suicide 36
Auto/Cycle Crash 34
Cancer 23
Airplane Crash 22
Unknown 21
Murdered 18
Alcohol 9
Accident 6
Drowned 5
Brain Tumour 4
AIDS 4
Poisoned 3
Leukaemia 3
Electrocuted 3
Stroke 3
Fire 3
Choked 2
Stay away from those!

It seems death is just so final and, well, pretty hard to evaluate/swallow (delete as appropriate). How do you deal with it? How do you come to terms with its magnitude? Over to you, Jimi Hendrix, quoted in Rolling Stone magazine, just prior to his own demise.

"It's funny the way most people love the dead. Once you are dead, you are made for life."

And, how right he was. Death is quite plainly beyond rocket science and in some cases even common sense. But it counts for lots. Just look at Q magazine's person of the millennium poll, as voted by the Q readers. It's littered with those who can't quite get it together to complete that next troublesome album...

At number one (and top of the pops): John Lennon. He's closely followed by Kurt Cobain (3), Elvis Presley (5), Bob Marley (12), Freddie Mercury (13), Frank Sinatra (14), Jimi Hendrix (15), Robert Johnson (21), Marvin Gaye (25) and Marc Bolan (39).

They're the most popular ten (not forgetting Richey Edwards from the Manics who's officially missing and elevated to the late twenties between Gaye and Bolan). Bubbling under are Nick Drake (43), Charlie Parker (44), Miles Davis (52), Ian Curtis (53), Hank Williams (57), Woody

Guthrie (63), Sam Cooke (65), Jim Morrison (66), Brian Jones (71), Keith Moon (72), Buddy Holly (75), Billie Holiday (76), Fela Kuti (87), Serge Gainsbourg (88), Muddy Waters (91), Nusrat Fateh Ali Khan (93) and Frank Zappa (97).

Pretty much all dead and all still pretty famous. As they say in Corinthians, "O death, where is thy sting? O grave, where is thy victory?" Whatever that means.

Moving swiftly along, we can even gauge the top ten albums by dead icons (or bands featuring such) as taken from the Mojo 100 Greatest Albums Of All Time. They are, of course...

1 What's Going On – Marvin Gaye (6)
2 The Velvet Underground And Nico (9)
3 Are You Experienced – Jimi Hendrix Experience (12)
4 Electric Ladyland – Jimi Hendrix Experience (14)
5 The Doors – The Doors (30)
6 Otis Blue – Otis Redding (31)
7 Nevermind – Nirvana (33)
8 Grievous Angel – Gram Parsons (42)
9 New York Dolls – New York Dolls (49)
10 Closer – Joy Division (53)

For the sake of clarification, let me explain that I didn't include members of The Beatles, The Stones, Band, Sex Pistols, Byrds, Who or Moby Grape. But, I did include Nico on her only VU appearance and The Doors and Nirvana, even though not all of the members have passed on. Somehow, in those cases it just seemed right.

You see, death seems to have its own values and creates its own rules. At the end of the day, it's death. It can do whatever the hell it likes. For example, just spare a thought for the modus expiro of singer/songwriter Meir Ariel in August, 1999. Dog tick fever? You wouldn't have seen that one coming. It's a sharp contrast to the end that met rock 'n' blues innovator Robert Johnson sixty years earlier. Johnson allegedly made a deal with the devil. Maybe Ariel did too.

Anyway, Johnson and the devil? As legend has it, the Johnson escapade seems to have legs (and possibly a tail) even if the basics sound like a simple case of murder. An intellectual book of note reports: "For a subject upon which it is dangerous to generalise, it hardly strains credulity to suggest that Johnson was the fulcrum upon which post-war Chicago blues turned. His lifestyle, that of an itinerant with a ready facili-

ty to impress his female audience, was part of his demise. One such dalliance brought about his end a year after his last recording session, poisoned by a jealous husband while performing in a jook joint at Three Forks, outside Greenwood, Mississippi."

Fine. But the legend is much more interesting. Robert Johnson went down to the crossroads, where he struck a deal with the Devil in order to improve his guitar playing. His death was simply payback time.

So the story goes, as told by LeDell Johnson to David Evans and quoted from Peter Guralnick's Searching for Robert Johnson © 1982: "Fellow bluesman Tommy Johnson (no relation) said, "If you want to learn how to play anything you want to play and learn how to make songs yourself, you take your guitar and you go to where a road crosses that way, where a crossroad is. Get there, be sure to get there just a little 'fore 12:00 that night so you'll know you'll be there. You have your guitar and be playing a piece there by yourself... A big black man will walk up there and take your guitar, and he'll tune it. And then he'll play a piece and hand it back to you. That's the way I learned to play anything I want."

In October 1996, Q magazine examined the evidence behind Johnson's legendary encounter with Lucifer and discovered that another Blues legend, Son House, knew the score. House

revealed the facts of this Faustian exchange service. In 1930 House let Johnson play in the interval between his sets. According to House, it was a "terrible racket". A mere year later, the two met up again and House was astounded to hear how good Johnson had become. House immediately exclaimed that Johnson "sold his soul to the Devil to play like that."

The idea of Robert Johnson selling his soul to the devil is far sexier than the law-abiding sensible trousers of real life. Quite plainly the deal also spawned the Johnson cut 'Hellhound On My Trail' just for good measure.

This psycho-drama style of song was quickly played out on numerous bloody ballads and murder stories. And a succession of tunes basking in the glow of death have topped charts and broken hearts. Bobby Goldsboro's torch ballad 'Honey', Terry Jacks' squishily sentimental 'Seasons In The Sun', Twinkle's proto-motorbike sadness 'Terry' and its inspiration, The Shangri-la's 'Leader Of The Pack', all sound hauntingly intense.

Everybody likes a happy song but loads of people also like the maudlin sound of Tindersticks' harrowing 'My Sister' or Joy Division's Ian Curtis intoning 'The Eternal'. Just a hint of disaster and trauma can work wonders, as Elton John's Di-friendly 'Candle In The Wind' can only testify. Ah, yes, the music of death is big business.

CHAPTER THREE

THERE'S AN ORDER TO DEATH. A time of lying in state, a time to mourn, a time to deal with your grief. There's also the focal point of a funeral where people can pay their respects and try to come to terms with their loss. But that's not always the case in the world of music.

In the world of rock the death rulebook is thrown out of the window. Values are inverted. Reality remains several streets away. And privacy? There is none. And, once there's a screenplay, well, nobody comes up smelling of roses. Hollywood Babylon goes into overdrive.

We're still waiting for the inevitable batch of dead rock star bio-pics. Oh, yes, the world of the recently canonised rock hierarchy is rich for the picking. Existing attempts to unravel the story of rock's tragically demised have been patchy at best, inevitably striking a balance between reality and entertainment, with tragedy given a reasonably wide berth where possible.

The Buddy Holly Story, which starred Gary Busey as our bespectacled hero, glossed up his rags to riches story till it resembled an episode of Happy Days. Although to his credit, Busey learned to play the guitar and he puts in a believable, sickly sweet portrayal when needed.

THE CEREMONY IS ABOUT TO BEGIN - APRIL 1991

AN OLIVER STONE FILM
the **doors**

In a different stratosphere of consciousness, Val Kilmer as Jim Morrison in The Doors was just wild. Kilmer became Morrison for the movie.

And, whether Oliver Stone's direction or the screenplay are true to life or not, Kilmer proceeded to swan around Hollywood as if he really were the reincarnation of our Jim - or at least a reasonably cleaned-up version.

Now, I have no idea what it was like to live in Elvis Presley's house but John Carpenter's Elvis - The Movie, starring Kurt Russell as The King, is delivered almost like a fly-on-the-wall docusoap and as such retains a certain air of authenticity. Portraying the real-life rhinestone world of Elvis - or at least as much as director John Carpenter was brave enough to show circa 1979 (just after Presley's death) - the footage steers clear of food or drug binges and instead portrays Elvis as an amiable, almost knockabout guy who can sing into the bargain.

By contrast La Bamba, starring Lou Diamond Philips as Ritchie Valens, goes to the other extreme. At 17 Valens didn't have much of a life story to fill 90 minutes, so the film's shortfalls shouldn't come as too much of a surprise. But then, why bother making it at all? Of course, we won't mention The Rose starring Bette Midler. Of course not. Having started life as a project about Janis Joplin, the film drifted so far from

home that the character Midler portrays was later described as an amalgam of all the edgy ne'erdowells of rock. So, let's forget then. Until the next Janispic.

Can Hollywood do better next time around? In the works as 1999 closed, are film biographies of John Lennon, Joplin as mentioned (she's the subject of no less than two projects), wicked jazz stylist Miles Davis, still-warm rapper The Notorious BIG, original soul crooner Otis Redding and short lived '50s teen sensation Frankie Lymon. Sounds like it'll be a busy time for the merchandising moguls.

If Hollywood has any sense it will also be considering a batch of recent stories about the controversial and quite sticky demise of Michael Hutchence, Tammy Wynette's will-contesting daughters and the is-he-or-isn't-he-dead gangsta rap superstar Tupac Shakur. Not to mention

the inevitable Kurt Cobain project.

Each of these contemporary stories has its own bizarre twist, none more so than that of the former INXS singer Michael Hutchence. The tale revolves around his method of death; a protracted debate is still going on between his family, who claim he committed suicide, and his partner Paula Yates, who insists he died in the midst of some bizarre sexual act. The column inches and documentary footage are already being archived.

As for Tammy Wynette, her glowing obits: "No-one has ever heard a country singer more soulful than Tammy Wynette." (Rolling Stone). "With her big hair and rhinestone dresses, Tammy Wynette was everything a country singer should be." (The Times) were followed by family bickering. The Times' view that "She was one of those performers who seemed unable to

separate her stage personality from the real world." couldn't have been more apt. Within a year of being laid to rest Tammy's daughters succeeded in getting her body exhumed for a full autopsy. It's a tale that's bound to be immortalised by Nashville in song before time.

The reason for the uprooting is the daughters' claim that Tammy's husband of 20 years George Richey had her sedated to the point where she had to be hospitalised prior to her death and that he now controls her estate. Even in death the family feud goes on.

But, if family disbelief figures strongly in the post-Tammy world, it has an even bigger place in the after-trauma from the "demise" of gangsta rapper Tupac Shakur. Reports in American rap magazine Vibe confirmed his family had never received his ashes. This fuelled the theory that Shakur wasn't dead at all, merely hiding out in

order to cool the east-west gangsta rap conflict. And the evidence?

The Sunday Telegraph reported that there were too many "coincidences".

1 The letters of MAKAVELI - Shakur's pseudonym for the release 'Don Killuminati; The Seven Day Theory' which came out just weeks after his death - can be rearranged to say I'm Alive (without the K of course).

2 Makaveli is also a mis-spelt version of Niccolo Machiavelli; the 15th century scholar who discussed the concept of faking death in his work The Prince.

3 A track from his posthumously released 'Greatest Hits' album features a rap about his rival The Notorious BIG in which Shakur prays he will "rest in peace". Of course BIG died some six months after Shakur.

4 Numerology is riddled through the details of his shooting. Shakur was shot on the seventh of September. He died at 4.03 (which added together make seven). He was 25 years old (Two and five make seven). And he was travelling in a series seven BMW when he was shot.

Add to that damning evidence the none appearance of his ashes, the cancellation of three planned commemorative services and the failure to find any possible assailants and the facts are perhaps beginning to stack up to, well, something.

The rumours had begun to fly after the release of Shakur's video for 'I Ain't Mad At You', which snook out just after his death. The video featured Shakur gazing down on the world from a cloud after being shot dead in a gunfight. An obvious portent of disaster or a retro view? It's anybody's guess.

That was followed by his well-reported parting salvo? The lyrics of another posthumously released cut, 'Only Fear Of Death', which roundly claim "Remember when I die, I'll be back".

A showbiz stunt? A get out of the mob quick card? A shrewd marketing plan?

Well, it worked for The Beatles. Sort of. Way back in the late '60s we all thought Paul McCartney was dead.

The great dead Beatle scare happened BJ (Before John), when Macca was rumoured to have died around the time of 'Sgt Pepper'. An elaborate web of deceit and look-alike replacements followed.

Triggered by the lyrics of 'A Day In The Life' from 'Sgt Pepper', which were immediately "recognised" as the story of McCartney's death in a car accident, the hoax gained further wind when the sleeve of the album bore a floral tribute in the shape of the letter 'P'. It was an obvious clue. Wasn't it?

Further investigation led people to open the sleeve, where they found a picture of Paul wearing a black armband emblazoned with the letters 'OPD', which stand for 'Officially Pronounced Dead'. Don't they?

A University Of Michigan newspaper put six and two together and the story gained momentum. Had he died prior to 'Pepper' and been replaced by a workmanlike double. Michigan quickly became a hotbed of Beatles' rumours. The Detroit Free Press picked up the story, adding yet more "facts" from the 'Pepper' sleeve - like McCartney sporting a Medal Of Valour, having his back turned on the reverse of the sleeve - it all made sense.

Suddenly every bit of Beatles material became fair game. The fade out of subsequent single 'Strawberry Fields' was singled out as having a Lennon-muttered phrase 'I buried Paul'. Then the booklet for the 'Magical Mystery Tour' EP contained a message saying 'The best way to go is by M&D', the M&D in question being a well-known northern funeral parlour.

Before long, everyone started playing Beatles records backwards and you'd be amazed what they heard. 'Your Mother Should Know' breathed "Why doesn't she know me dead?". 'I'm So Tired' revealed "Paul is a dead man, miss him, miss him". And 'I Am The Walrus' chortled "Ha, ha, Paul is dead!". What further proof could you need?

When McCartney appeared barefoot on the sleeve of 'Abbey Road' the final nail was knocked in his coffin. And, as the media circus went global, Paul was confronted by his sad demise.

"Rumours of my death have been greatly exaggerated." he quipped.

And, lest we forget, similar morbidity surrounded the sojourning Dylan after his traumatic Electric tour of 1966. An alleged motorcycle accident forced him into retirement in Woodstock. The rumour mill clanked into action and included stories of his demise. His return with the album 'John Wesley Harding' sent critics into confusion. It couldn't be by the same electric youth. His voice was different and the album was hardly 'Blonde On Blonde II'.

So, McCartney not dead, then? Dylan not dead, too. Tupac Shakur? The jury is out. Richey Manic - missing! And Nikki Sixx? And Dave Mustaine? Evidently they were both dead... but they're not anymore.

Motley Crue's big-haired panstick, Sixx took his body to such excess in the '80s that his heart stopped beating and he was announced dead, before he snook back to consciousness. "It's a hazard of the profession." he guffawed.

Then the very same thing happened to Dave Mustaine of Megadeth. It *must* be a hazard of the profession.

The former Metallica guitarist had been slipping in and out of addiction for some years when, on February 17th 1992, he went a tad too far.

"My heart stopped and I was pronounced clinically dead," he told Kerrang! magazine. "The doctors phoned my wife and told her not to bother to come to the hospital because it was too late."

But Mustaine lived to tell the tale. And, so did Dave Swarbrick. The Fairport Convention fiddle player and man about folk was, quite frankly, shocked to read on the morning of April 20th, 1999, a particularly well written obituary for none other than Dave Swarbrick.

Checking his pulse, he was after all in intensive care in hospital, he read:

"Violinist with the British group Fairport Convention who in the late '60s opened the door for a fusion of folk and rock, Dave Swarbrick died aged 58. A small, dynamic, charismatic figure, 'Swarb' - cigarette perched precariously on his bottom lip, unruly hair flapping over his face, pint of beer at hand - could electrify an audience with a single frenzied sweep of his bow."

Phew! Rock 'n' roll. The Telegraph printed an apology the following day.

CHAPTER FOUR

Self-destruction is the effect of cowardice, in the highest extreme.
Daniel Defoe†

ONE PERSON WHO IS DEFINITELY dead is Kurt Cobain, but how he got into that condition is still the cause of much voice-raised conversation. Confusion reigns. According to the now-also-deceased El Duce, Courtney Love had tried to hire him to "hit her man" way back in December 1993. Truth or dare? We'll never know.

So the story goes, a week before Kurt's death, Cobain had entered The Exodus Recovery Centre in Marina Del Rey in an attempt to wean himself off drugs. And, according to people about Seattle, wife Courtney was again on the prowl looking for El Duce.

Within two days Kurt had checked out of rehab and hooked up with long-time pal Dylan J Carlson, from whom he'd secured a Remington M-11 20-guage shotgun.

On April 2nd Cobain phoned Love, who was on a promotional tour for her imminent Hole album release, and informed her, rather ominously you might think, not to worry "whatever happened".

Courtney panicked and rang around everyone in the rock world to try and track him

down, eventually hiring a private detective and informing the LA police about her concern. The police visited the Cobain residence twice but found no one.

Then, on the evening of April 5th, high on heroin and Valium Cobain, secreted in his former nanny's apartment above his garage, penned a note to Courtney and his daughter Frances Bean:

To Boddah
Speaking from the tongue of an experienced simpleton who obviously would rather be an emasculated, infantile complain-ee. This note should be pretty easy to understand.

All the warnings from the punk rock 101 courses over the years, since my first introduction to the, shall we say, ethics involved with independence and the embracement of your community has proven to be very true. I haven't felt the excitement of listening to as well as creating music along with reading and writing for too many years now. I feel guilty beyond words about these things.

For example when we're backstage and the lights go out and the manic roar of the crowd begins, it doesn't affect me the way in which it did for Freddy Mercury, who seemed to love, relish in the love and adoration from the crowd which is something I totally admire and envy. The fact is, I can't fool you, any one of you. It simply isn't fair to you or me. The worst crime I can think of would be to rip people off by faking it and pretending as if I'm having 100% fun.

Sometimes I feel as if I should have a punch-in time clock before I walk out on stage. I've tried everything within my power to appreciate it (and I do, God, believe me I do, but it's not enough). I appreciate the fact that I and we have affected and entertained a lot of people. I must be one of those narcissists who only appreciate things when they're gone. I'm too sensitive. I need to be slightly numb in order to regain the enthusiasm I once had as a child.

On our last 3 tours, I've had a much better appreciation for all the people I've known personally and as fans of our music, but I still can't get over the frustration, the guilt and empathy I have for everyone. There's good in all us and I think I simply love people too much, so much that it makes me feel too fucking sad. The sad little, sensitive, unappreciative, Pisces, Jesus man. Why don't you just enjoy it? I don't know!

I have a goddess of a wife who sweats ambition and empathy and a daughter who reminds me too much of what I used to be, full of love and joy, kissing every person she meets because everyone is good and will do her no harm. And that terrifies me to the point to where I can barely function. I can't stand the thought of Frances becoming the miserable, self-destructive, death rocker that I've become.

I have it good, very good, and I'm grateful, but since the age of seven, I've become hateful towards all humans in general. Only because it seems so easy for people to get along and have empathy. Only because I love and feel sorry for people too much I guess.

Thank you all from the pit of my burning, nauseous stomach for your letters and concern during the past years. I'm too much of an erratic, moody, baby! I don't have the passion anymore, and so remember, it's better to burn out than to fade away.

Peace, Love, Empathy.
Kurt Cobain

Frances and Courtney, I'll be at your altar.
Please keep going Courtney, for Frances.
For her life, which will be so much happier without me.

I LOVE YOU, I LOVE YOU!

Placing the note in a mound of earth from a spilt pot plant, Cobain then shot himself. The following day the phone rang incessantly but it wasn't until the next day that his body was found by electrician Gary Smith. Reporting his findings to his workplace after he'd rung the police, Smith witnessed the speed of the media in action after his boss phoned the local radio station and the whole world descended on the house. Smith couldn't get his van out for hours.

A series of accusations, counter-accusations, threats, rumours and wholesale fabrication followed. Love's friend Dr Nikolas Hartsthorne flew to the scene to take on the role of officiating coroner, this fuelled rumours of dodgy work afoot. Cobain's credit card was used in the following days, suggesting he may have been robbed. And, it was eventually revealed that Kurt had so much heroin in his system that he would have died anyway. So why did he bother shooting himself?

In the melee, divorce rumours persisted. His "suicide" note was examined and conspiracy theorists began to suggest that it never even mentioned suicide. Investigative journalists arrived on the scene and Love's father, Hank Harrison, denounced his own daughter.

Within five days, Nirvana fan Richard Lee had a Seattle Public Access TV show called Who Killed Kurt Cobain? The title quickly changed to Kurt Cobain Was Murdered.

Hot on its heels came Andrew Amirault's in-depth, multi-layered and fact-heavy web site The Murder Of Kurt Cobain. This led to a web ring covering the same subject matter. Five years on no-one was any nearer unravelling the hours of testimony, thousands of stories and painfully slow police enquiries. Amirault's site (www.tiac.net/users/tobya/) still thrives. It's the work of a cross-referencing perfectionist. It's easy to be pulled in by its analysis, backed up by reams of seemingly sensible reasoning. Amirault quotes roundly from the Bible and seems to hold everyone, from the media to Courtney to fellow Seattle musicians, to blame.

So, in the final analysis, whodunit? Way back in May 1998, Mojo rounded up the suspects:

1 Courtney did it
2 Courtney caused him to do it
3 Courtney knows who did it
4 The nanny did it
5 His drug dealer did it
6 El Duce did it
7 His accountant did it
8 Geffen (his label), Gold Mountain (his management company)/Time Warner (they had some shares) did it
9 William Burroughs' dream machine did it
10 Kurt Cobain did it

None the wiser? Then get out on the Cobain web ring where the same questions are asked. Over and over again. A typical destination (**www.angelfire.com/pe/clique/webrings.html**) reveals the talking points that troubled teens of the last guitar generation of the 1990's have to ponder. "There are so many questions about Kurt Cobain's mysterious death. These are the facts that surround his death." the site intones.

1 No fingerprints on the shotgun, the catridge, or the so-called "suicide note"
2 He had three times the lethal dose of heroin at the time of his death. According to pathology experts he couldn't have shot himself, or roll down his sleeves. He would have been unconscious within seconds.

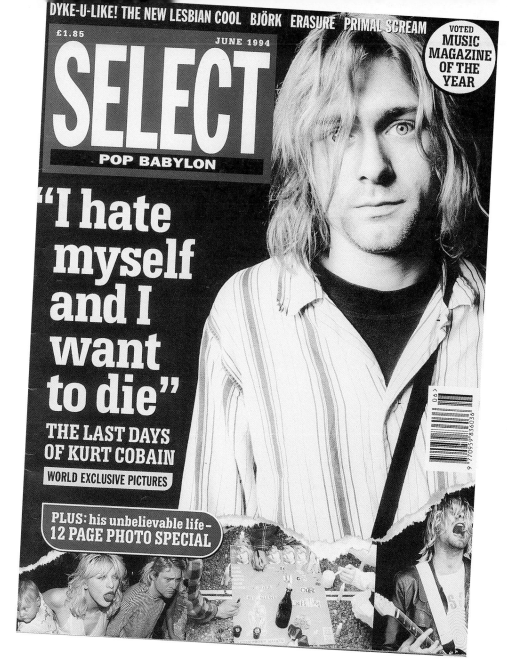

DYKE-U-LIKE! THE NEW LESBIAN COOL • BJÖRK • ERASURE • PRIMAL SCREAM

VOTED MUSIC MAGAZINE OF THE YEAR

£1.85   JUNE 1994

SELECT

POP BABYLON

"I hate myself and I want to die"

THE LAST DAYS OF KURT COBAIN

WORLD EXCLUSIVE PICTURES

PLUS: his unbelievable life – 12 PAGE PHOTO SPECIAL

3 Just weeks before he died, the police get called in from his house. Courtney had called them saying he had locked himself in with a gun and that he said was going to kill himself. While the police got there Courtney tried to knock down the door with the fire extinguisher. While Kurt screamed "Just leave me alone." When the police got there Kurt had told them that he just wanted to get away from Courtney.

4 Days before he died he told a friend he "feared for his life."

5 It was immediately declared an open-and-shut case of suicide by Seattle medical examiner Dr Nikolas Hartshorne, it was quickly accepted by the Seattle police before any investigation was conducted. Harthshorne had a potential conflict of interest as a good friend of Cobain's wife.

6 El Duce was offered $50,000 to kill Cobain. He passed a polygraph test "beyond the possibility of deception" three months later he dies mysteriously.

7 The gun was bought for protection not suicide.

8 The "suicide note" didn't say anything about wanting to kill himself. And there are two parts to it with different handwriting.

9 Why won't Courtney talk about it? Why does she become so enraged when someone tries to ask her? Why does she have to have contracts signed before every interview?

Too much to take in? Then just flit on through the web ring, there are thousands of other rambling Kurt sites...

Try **www.angelfire.com/me/ComeAsYouAre/**

"NIRVANA RULES. KURT will be back. Trust me. I should know. I am a Kurt Cobain Lover and Follower so I should know. I will bring Kurt back and we will rule the world together. Nirvana is a legacy. And Legacy's [sic] NEVER die. Will Kurt be back? Yes. Why? Cause I said so. When's he coming back? Sooner than planned. Actually Tomorrow Night when the sun goes down. Kurt's married to Courtney Love. Kurt was killed. He didn't kill himself."

As David Bowie said;
"You're too old to lose it, too young to choose it/And the clock waits so patiently on your song/You walk past the cafe but you don't eat when you've lived too long/You're a rock 'n' roll suicide."

CHAPTER FIVE

Love makes us poets and the approach of death should make us philosophers.
George Santayana

Unplugged

TOURISM *Dead rock stars don't sign autographs, but they're always at home to visitors. James McNair visits five sites where you can be just six feet away from your idol.*

VISITORS TO COBAIN'S SUICIDE scene are numerous, but the pilgrimage to Graceland for Elvis fans is like a Lourdes away day for the migraine-bothered. It holds both sadness and joy and undoubtedly brings a blessed sense of relief to most.

Similarly, Jim Morrison's grave in Paris is inhabited by sincere-looking youths deep in metaphysical debate. And the flat where Jimi Hendrix lived in London, just next door to Mozart a few years earlier, now features a blue plaque commemorating his life and times. We can all go to gawp. And many do.

At the Joshua Tree Inn in the Mojave Desert, sporadic visitors roll up to see Room 8 where Gram Parsons sipped his last Tequila on that fateful night in 1973. Twenty years on from his death in 1993, Q magazine reported that Mike and Sharon Hinshaw had booked the room a year in advance and driven 2,000 miles from Indianapolis to share this very spiritual moment with a handful of other like-minded individuals.

For many it's just too hard to let go of those memories, those songs, or that pivotal moment that changed your life. Sometimes you just have to be there. Sometimes it makes no sense at all.

At the Kurt Cobain Memorial in Seattle Center Flag Pavilion on April 9, 1994 thousands of similarly saddened fans gathered. The day after a candle-lit procession of mourners illuminated the sky of neighbouring Aberdeen, Seattle city centre became a hub of emotion as tapes from Courtney Love and Nirvana band members were played.

Steve Walken attended the event and told Q magazine: "One girl's placard said 'Kurt died for your sins', which was crap. He died because he couldn't deal with people like her."

Fan worship? It gets you down. So, do the fans take it all too seriously? Is the power of pop too demanding? Several stories during the late '90s suggest that might be the case. Richard Robinson's copycat disappearance of the Manics' Richey Edwards was tragic.

Dead Teenager Might Have Copied Pop Idol

The teenage son of a university lecturer may have

Dead teenager might have copied pop idol

THE teenage son of a university lecturer may have killed himself to mimic his pop idols, cult Welsh band the Manic Street Preachers..

Richard Robinson, 17, who disappeared 11 days ago, is believed to have been found at the bottom of 500ft cliffs at Beachy Head, a notorious suicide spot

The body will be formally identified today using dental records. But last night his father, Dr Derek Robinson, a Maths lecturer at the University of Sussex, said he was sure the body was that of his son.

Manics fan Richard, of Burgess Hill, West Sussex, disappeared shortly after seeing the band play live at the Glastonbury festival in Somerset. He was fascinated by the actions of Manics singer and guitarist Richey Edwards, 28, who disappeared in 1995 immediately before the band were due to go on a US tour.

Before the discovery of a body yesterday, his father and mother, Stephanie Robinson, hoped he may have faked his suicide in a bid to emulate Richey.

Richard disappeared after leaving his family a note saying he intended to jump from Beachy Head after seeing the Manics at Glastonbury. The note contained a line from Richard's favourite song by the group. Police feared Richard was dead when they found his bicycle, CD player and pile of CDs, including one by the Preachers, abandoned on the cliffs at Beachy Head.

Helicopter and coastguard searches failed to turn up any trace of the teenager until two anglers saw a body at low tide near Eastbourne.

James Dean Bradfi singer Manic Preac stage Glasto and R Robin who s perfor shortl before disap

killed himself to mimic his pop idols, cult Welsh band the Manic Street Preachers.

Richard Robinson, 17, who disappeared 11 days ago, is believed to have been found at the bottom of 500ft cliffs at Beachy Head, a notorious suicide spot.

Manics fan Richard, of Burgess Hill, West Sussex, disappeared shortly after seeing the band play at the Glastonbury festival in Somerset. He was fascinated by the actions of Manics guitarist Richey Edwards, 28, who disappeared in 1995 immediately before the band were due to go on a US tour.

Richard disappeared after leaving his family a note saying he intended to jump from Beachy Head after seeing the Manics at Glastonbury. The note contained a line from Richard's favourite song by the group.

Metro News

At the other end of the spectrum, 1999 saw the Trenchcoat Killings in Columbine, USA, where school authorities were quick - but in retrospect incorrect - to cite the influence of Marilyn Manson in the homicides.

This wasn't the first time that the moral majority had leapt in accusing rock stars of inspiring acts of violence. There's the legendary Judas Priest backward message case in the States, which allegedly inspired one youth to go on a gun rampage.

The case was thrown out of court when the judge heard the track in question and the backwards message "I want a biscuit" was unearthed.

And Ozzy Osbourne has received more than his fair share of allegations.

OZZY'S 'SUICIDE SOLUTION' BLAMED

The suicide of a Los Angeles youth was alleged to be a direct result of listening to an Ozzy Osbourne composition entitled 'Suicide Solution'.

This claim has been made by the parents of the boy who maintain that the 19-year-old student shot himself to death with his father's .22 revolver after hearing the track from Osbourne's 1980 solo album 'Blizzard Of Ozz'.

The suicide, which took place a year ago, came to light again recently when the boy's parents threatened to sue the artist and his record company for damages.
NME

The **levels of fan abuse** reached new heights with the tragic story of John Lennon's murder at the hands of Mark Chapman. Chapman had cajoled Lennon into signing his copy of 'Double Fantasy' before shooting him on the steps of his New York apartment later that same day. George Harrison was said to have raised the level of razor blade wire around his country estate as a direct result.

Bizarrely Chapman became a star of sorts. His copy of 'Double Fantasy' went to auction years later and is reputed to be worth a staggering 1.2 million dollars; complete with Lennon's signature, Chapman's fingerprint and a detective's signature all in "evidence".

Lennon's death was as much a shock to the system as that of any rock icon. And his cruel departure left the world stunned. Chapman remains in solitary confinement in fear of being attacked by his fellow prisoners. And the explanation for Lennon's death? A Holden Caulfield Catcher In The Rye fixation, or perhaps it was a reac-

Selena: 'killed in cold blood'

Fan convicted of murdering singing star

By John Hiscock in Los Angeles

THE founder and former president of the fan club of the Grammy-winning singer Selena has been convicted of murdering the 23-year-old Tejano music superstar.

Yolanda Saldivar, 35, who also managed the singer's boutiques, sobbed after being told she could face a maximum of life imprisonment for the shooting in a motel in Selena's home town, Corpus Christi, Texas.

Outside the court in Hous-

25¢

New York,
December 10, 1980

DAILY⊛NEWS

Tonight

LATEST
STOCKS

TUESDAY NIGHT EDITION

Killer stalked him 3 days

Page 3

Lennon signing autograph for Mark Chapman, before the shooting. **News photo by Paul Goresh** © Copyright 1980 New York News Inc.

EXCLUSIVE: Lennon & suspect

tion to Lennon's much publicised quote that "The Beatles were bigger than Jesus".

If Chapman's assassination was an indication of the frightening levels that fan adulation can reach, then the shooting of Tejano singer Selena is truly a tragic tale of fandom gone wrong.

A hugely popular star in America's Latino communities, Selena had been compared to Madonna and was about to record her first English-speaking album. Her massive success had led to the employment of Yolanda Saldivar to run her fan club, which she did, by all

accounts, not very well at all. After the singer discovered that Saldivar had been embezzling money from the club, she confronted her. The pair argued and Saldivar shot Selena in the back.

The repercussions of the murder ran riot through the Latino community where her death was compared to that of Elvis and Lennon. Since recognised with the declaration of Selena Day by Texan governor George W Bush, Selena remains a victim of fan adulation gone crazy.

Today's bereaved superfan has trouble expressing their loss. In many cases they have to method act into their grief. They take on the role of their mentor to express their sadness, penning unlikely prose or poems to rationalise their emotional ties. In these missives there are no rules; these odes to Billy Fury, Nick Drake, Sid Vicious and Jeff Buckley contain enormously personal observations:

> *Let the lights*
> *Shine bright tonight*
> *We want Billy*
> *Billy Fury*
> *Lift us up*
> *Halfway to paradise*
> *We want Billy*
> *Billy Fury*
> *All alone*
> *Down the motorway*
> *I hear your voice*
> *Singing on the radio*
> *"In Thoughts Of You"*
> *And I wish I could dream*
> *My life away*
> *But then the lights*
> *Shine bright*
> *We want Billy*
> *Billy Fury*
> © bongobeat.com/poems/bfury.html

> *May I have your autograph,*
> *Mr Vicious?*
> *Busted in NYC*
> *72 hours in the holding pens*
> *at 100 Centre Street*
> *the Old Bailey*
> *of the New World.*
> *Semi-comatose vomit and piss marinade;*
> *the blacks and Latinos,*
> *sharing the cell,*
> *don't even know who*

Jimi Hendrix honoured.

English Heritage's first rock'n'roll blue plaque is unveiled by Pete Townshend and the Experience's Noel Redding, outside Hendrix's former home at 23 Brook Street, Mayfair. He shared this rented flat at the end of 1968 with the plaque's proposer, Kathy Etchingham (also pictured). There are 650 blue plaques around London, honouring Ian Fleming, George Frederick Handel and Vivien Leigh.

Experience bassist Noel Redding (left), former girlfriend Kathy Etchingham and Pete Townshend

---

this pathetic white boy is.
It was on the TV, radio
and in the papers.
The latest bad boy
of rock & roll had...
What was it this time?
Stabbed his girlfriend?
Smuggled dope?
Possessed a firearm?
The Legal Aid
Society lawyer knows.
So when he goes back
to the bullpen to talk
to Ralphie "six fingers"
about bail, he brings a pen
and a Pistol's album.
© Virgil Hervey

Troubador
The sweetest songs you sang
I, hearing them as though you, (who'd never
seen me)
Looked in rapture
Toyed with my hair,
Touched my face.
And now you are gone
Like all the others.
But you gave me more than they,
For your voice cradles my heart through all
my years

And I still sleep as though wrapped in your
arms
Forever.
© Leslie (Cloud Tiger)

The loom of consciousness,
you, a sad moon,
pale blue, and beautiful
in a halo of thought.
On November 25th the last leaf dropped,
and you slipped away
in the morning's yellow haze
with the black eyed dog.
At last, your oasis,
an eternity of darkness,
numb and safe.
a pool of strange quiet
that nothing could wake,
not even you.
© Dana Perry 1999

When Jimi Hendrix died I remember vividly the abject sadness that overtook our classroom at school. Sure, there were only a handful of us who'd invested in Hendrix compilations by that point but when he died it elevated our clique to the point of virtual manhood (or so we thought).

To commemorate the event Track Records released a special three track EP of 'Voodoo Chile (Slight Return)', 'Hey Joe' and 'All Along The Watchtower' in a picture sleeve for 6/11d. That's pre-decimalization to you. And, in some kind of solemn show of support, we queued outside of WH Smith on the morning of its release, trouping upstairs to the suitable un-hip record department to secure our Hendrix EPs.

A month later, Christmas 1970, we were convinced that Hendrix was alive - for what reason I don't know - and we'd stencilled the legend on our schoolbags to celebrate the fact. Endless nights of playing his albums and our first experience with a bootleg followed. We were insanely wrapped up in Hendrix's world of guitar burning, wild womanising and brash behaviour. Hendrix was everything we thought we wanted to be when we grew up.

I suspect if we'd been able to do so, we'd have written lengthy epistles to his greatness but we just revelled in lyrical couplets like "Roll over Rover, And let Jimi take over." That was more than enough for us.

Perhaps we could have taken a leaf from Dion Boucicault and his line "Men talk of killing time, while time quietly kills them." in our summation of Jimi. Maybe we could have resorted to Leonardo da Vinci with a line such as "While I thought that I was learning how to live, I have been learning how to die." But we never quite got it together. But we loved Jimi nonetheless. I suppose I still do. It never goes away.

DEATH BY CAUSE

"I think it looks like death. It looks like mourning."
"Every movie in every cinema is about death. Death sells."

PREFACE

DAVID ST. HUBBINS, Spinal Tap's resident 'full time dreamer', knows a lot about the world of rock, but not as much as he thinks, especially when dismissing the band's "you can see yourself in both sides" all black album sleeve. Ian Faith, meanwhile, the band's long-suffering manager, has got it all down pat. He's worked it all out. Death - the big departure, the final chord - sells.

Death and rock 'n' roll is an undeniably seductive combination, the ultimate outlaw mix. Of course, we're not talking about musicians who rock on to a ripe old age, then die peacefully in their sleep, here. While that may be very pleasant for the individuals concerned, that would be just too, well, *conventional* for us. Not that there are too many musos who would fit the category anyway. Who was it who once said 'Musicians are like dogs that chase cars. We run around a lot, make a lot of noise, but we don't last too long!'? No, what we're talking about here are the musicians who burn twice as brightly for half as long. If you're going to fill out the job application for 'rock star', you'd best not be planning on sticking around too long.

And if you don't believe us, then we'll name some names. We've got lists as long as your arm of the musical great and good who span off their mortal coils way before their sell-by date; some the victims of their own wild ways, some because of stupidity, some just down to plumb bad luck. All of them, though, have passed on before we, the fans, felt they were done, leaving behind music with a question mark. Exciting, incredible music that will always, by definition, get you thinking about what might have been. Who doesn't wonder how Jeff Buckley's 'Sketches For My Sweetheart, The Drunk', would have ended up had he decided not to go for a dip that Mississippi night in 1997. Three decades have passed since Jim Morrison did his bath tub thing, but who doesn't listen to L'America or Hyacinth House from that last Doors album and wonder just what kind of twisted, bizarre, downright bonkers stuff the self-styled shaman would have gone on to produce?

The list of casualties is long and varied, just as are the causes of death. No one would be too surprised - though no less intrigued, of course - to hear that one of the foremost killers of rock stars is the drug overdose. Car crashes rank highly too, with plane fatalities not too far behind. But wouldn't the eyebrows be raised to discover that "an allergic reaction to weed killer" did for poor Toto drummer Jeff Porcaro? Death, it seems, can come knocking when you least expect it.

Maybe by boning up on our 'Death By Causes' section, you'll be able to avoid some of the pitfalls that sadly trapped so many of our musician friends. Maybe you'll never step on a plane ever again. Possibly you'll come to the conclusion that doing the weeding is simply too scary to contemplate. Maybe you'll come to believe that being a rock star just ain't worth the candle, no matter what the fringe benefits. Whatever you decide, though, we reckon you should listen to Jerry Springer above all when he says... 'Take care of yourselves... and each other'

> "But you see Sheriff, that's the way it is. When you've got a gun you're a sort of god. If you had the gun I'd be the chump and you'd be the god. The gun gives you the power of life and death."
>
> Frank Sinatra playing Johnny Baron in the film Suddenly.

GUNS ARE AS MUCH A PART of the mythology of the rock 'n' roll outlaw image as sex and drugs. From The Clash's 'The Guns Of Brixton' to AC/DC's 'Guns For Hire' and right the way down the stylistic highway to Frankie Laine's 'Gunslinger', guns have always been one of the most glamorous of rock star accessories.

Yet while guns and gangsters will always have an endless fascination for musicians, the combination of firearms and impressionable people has often proved lethal. Marilyn Manson's schlock horror imagery and fascination with death was blamed in some quarters for the violent deaths of 13 students in America in 1999. Two kids going under the name of 'The Trenchcoat Mafia' had randomly executed fellow schoolmates at Columbine High in Littleton, Denver. And many musicians, just like many other members of society, have fallen victim to violent, gun-related deaths.

The most shocking of all these murders, of course, was the shooting of John Lennon outside his New York home The Dakota Building on 8th December 1980. Lennon had been one of the music world's most vociferous advocates of peace with his infamous Amsterdam bed-in and his universally adopted anthem 'Give Peace A Chance'. Despite a much-publicised battle against drug addiction, a short-lived separation from his wife Yoko Ono and a fight against

LENNON'S CAGED KILLER

JOHN LENNON: So nice and since

'Hunks blew out of him—I felt nothing'

LOYAL WIFE: Gloria

MEETING: Lennon signs his autograph for Chapman hours before the killing

faced Chapman shot John Lennon.

SATURDAY MORNING, DECEMBER 6, 1980

Chapman arrived in New York from Hawaii for the second time in as many months.

But this time he was determined to carry out his plan to kill Lennon.

He dropped his bags off at the YMCA and set off for the Dakota—Lennon's home—nine blocks away.

He waited for hours before giving up and going to see a movie.

SUNDAY MORNING, DECEMBER 7, 1980

Although Chapman had booked into the YMCA to save money, he suddenly left and took a room in the smart Sheraton hotel.

There he assembled a bizarre exhibition of his posessions which he believed would provide police with the motive for the crime he was about to commit.

Among the jumble was a picture of Judy Garland wiping away the Cowardly Lion's tears in the Wizard of Oz, his passport, a picture of himself with refugee children, a photograph of his car and his favourite book, Catcher in the Rye, scrawled with the words: "The Gospel According to John Lennon."

He went back to the Dakota building clutching his autograph book as a cover.

This time he waited for 10 hours before giving up and going for a final dinner of hamburger, fish-and-chips, cottage cheese and chocolate mousse,

Steady

"Then Lennon looked at me and I heard a voice in my head say: 'Do it, do it, do it.'

"I walked a few feet. I pulled the gun out of my pocket, put it in my left hand—I don't remember aiming.

"I just pulled the trigger steadily five times."

Chapman used flat-nosed dum-dum bullets which ripped huge holes in Lennon.

Chapman says: "The guy had five bullets in him. Big hunks came out of him, they had to.

"I was using a gun big enough to blow a man off his feet."

Lennon was dead and today in a chilling step-by-step account put together from police and psychiatric tapes, The News of the World pieces together the full untold story of the crucial days before baby-

washed down with beer.

Back in his room he phoned a massage parlour and ordered a call-girl. They didn't have intercourse and after she left he called his wife Gloria to say he was missing her and would be home soon.

MONDAY MORNING, DECEMBER 8, 1980

Chapman said later that he knew today would be the day.

He got to the Dakota just before noon and started talking to two women fans he'd met there on the Saturday.

He hadn't been waiting long when a station wagon pulled out with Lennon's five-year-old son Sean and his nanny inside.

Cutest

Chapman recalls: "The girls knew Sean and introduced me to him.

"He had a cold and I said, 'You better take care of that cold.'

"He was the cutest little boy I'd ever seen. It didn't enter my mind that I was going to kill the poor young boy's father and he won't have a father for the rest of his life."

Then at mid-afternoon

Lennon emerged. Chapman recalls:

🔘 All of a sudden John came out with Yoko. I went up to him and I said: "John, would you sign my album please?"

He said: "Sure" and signed it. He looked at me very sincerely and handed back my album.

Then he said: "Is that what you wanted?" I said: "Yeah, thanks. Thanks a lot." I was overwhelmed by his sincerity.

There was a little bit of me going: "Why didn't you shoot him?" And I said: "I can't shoot him like this." I wanted to get his autograph.

Chapman then almost went home rather than kill him.

He said: "Some very serious thoughts came into my mind of leaving, abandoning the idea of murdering him, going back to the hotel, checking out, getting a cab to the airport and flying the hell out of there.

"I kept saying, 'You have his autograph you can just go home now, Gloria won't believe that that's John Lennon's autograph, but you'll tell her you met him.'"

He adds: "I remember

I was praying to God to keep me from killing Lennon and I was also praying to the Devil to give me the opportunity."

Then suddenly Lennon's limousine came into view on the windswept street.

"I said, 'This is it.' So I got up, the car rolled up and the door opened and Yoko got out.

"She was about 30 or 40 feet in front of him. It was all meant to be. If they were together, I don't know if I could have shot him or not. But he was alone.

"He looked right at me, and I didn't say anything. He walked past me. But I know he remembered me."

Chapman dropped to his knees in the classic combat position, arms outstretched, and emptied his .38 into John.

Yoko's scream rang out in the deathly silence, she ran to him and cradled her husband in her arms, weeping uncontrollably.

A shock wave went around the world. The voice of a generation was silenced for ever.

🔘 *The Man Who Shot John Lennon, First Tuesday, will be shown on the ITV network on Tuesday at 10.35pm.*

Caption in her here here Caption in her here here

deportation from America, Lennon had finally managed to settle in New York. He would often remark about how enjoyable it was to be recognised and yet still left alone to get on with his life in New York. Sadly, the city he had grown to love also proved to be the city where he was brutally murdered by Mark Chapman, a fan who shot him five times at point blank range with a .38 revolver. Lennon was rushed to hospital, but was pronounced dead on arrival. Chapman later claimed he had been incited to kill Lennon following a flippant comment Lennon had made 14 years earlier, in 1966, when he had claimed that the Beatles were bigger than Jesus. Most people believe that Chapman was simply an obsessed lunatic.

The sad fact that nothing much seems to have changed in New York City is proved by the death of Christopher Wallace 17 years later although the rapper's violent end was much less of a shock to the system than that of the peaceable Lennon. Wallace was born in Brooklyn on 21st May 1972 and had been surrounded by violence and death at every stage of his life. His 1994 debut album as The Notorious B.I.G. was prophetically titled 'Ready To Die' and went on to sell more than two million copies. He traded on the gangster image and quickly established himself as one of the figureheads of the burgeoning East Coast rap scene. As rivalry between crews from East and West grew more intense Wallace found himself going head to head with a former mate of his, Tupac Shakur, who had signed up with the notorious West Coast rap label Death Row, run by Suge Knight

While Biggie worked on his second album Shakur himself was shot and killed in Las Vegas. Much media speculation followed as to whether the East Coast rap crew had been responsible for the shooting. Both the Notorious B.I.G. and his mentor and producer Sean 'Puffy' Combs strongly denied the rumours. However, it appeared that not everyone was convinced of their innocence. On the morning of 9 March, Biggie was heading back to his LA hotel after an awards party when another car pulled up alongside and opened fire. Wallace was killed instant-

ly. The double album, 'Life After Death', was released three weeks after the shooting. It went straight to number one.

Less publicised rap deaths include Freaky Tah of the socially conscious The Lost Boyz, who was shot in the back of the head in New York in March of 1999. Then Scott LaRock was shot dead in his pick-up in 1987, while trying to mediate in another dispute. Brandon Mitchell of Wreckx-N-Effects was also shot dead in New York in 1990

in an argument over a woman.

America's free and easy attitude to gun control has surely resulted in a society that may not be inherently more violent, but which simply offers more violent solutions to its problems. Legendary singer Marvin Gaye, is another high profile victim. Gaye's name is now synonymous with some of the very greatest soul recordings ever. His creative peak began in 1971 with the release of 'What's Going On'; a beautiful, socially-aware record that reflected the singer's concerns with ecology, long before such thoughts had entered most people's heads. Yet such was the breadth of Gaye's emotional scope that his very next album, 'Let's Get It On', was a far more personal and sexual album; a record which still stands out as one of the all-time great love

albums.

Troubled by his constant battle between a love for God and a love of women, Gaye's moods became more and more erratic as the decade came to an end. Tax problems didn't help and a move to Europe in 1980 only seemed to unsettle him even more. There were stories of prodigious use of cocaine. After settling back in the States again Gaye moved into his parents' home in California, but cocaine-fuelled depression made it impossible for him to commit to any new music. His condition was so bad that Marvin talked many times about suicide and his difficult personality meant that he often argued with his Apostolic minister father.

On 1st April, the day before Marvin's forty fifth birthday, the two men argued yet again. Marvin was upset about how his father was treating his mother. In a fit of rage Marvin struck out and beat his father, who left the room but immediately returned with a gun. He shot his son twice at point blank range and one of the greatest soul singers of all time died instantly.

Another soul great who died violently and disturbingly was Sam Cooke, whose songs such as 'You Send Me' and 'Cupid' are still classics of laid-back delivery. He died in a shooting at a Los Angeles motel, The Hacienda where he had checked in with a woman. Cooke had met Linda Boyer at a party that same night, 11th December, 1964. Boyer had run out of the motel room and Cooke had gone after her, breaking into the manager's office where he believed she was hiding. The manager's wife, Bertha Franklin, shot Cooke three times with a pistol.

While her name may not be familiar to mainstream music audiences, the death of Selena in Corpus Christi, Texas on 31st March 1995, sent enormous shock waves throughout the Latino community. Born Selena Quintanilla on 16th April 1971, she began performing at the age of 10 and recording by the age of 12. With a backing band, Los Dinos, that included her brother Abraham on bass and her sister Suzette as drummer, Selena quickly rose in the business. In 1987 she was named Female Vocalist Of The Year and Performer Of The Year at the Tejano Music

Awards. Selena's fame grew quickly and by 1993 she was awarded a Grammy for Best Mexican American Performance for her album 'Selena Live'.

It seemed that there was no end to her success, she went on to set up a clothing range and even made her film debut in Don Juan De Marco. Her album, 'Amore Prohibido', also won her another Grammy in 1995. Tragically Selena was killed that same year after an argument with Yolanda Saldivar, a woman who ran one of her shops in San Antonio and was founder of the Selena fan club. Selena's father had found out that Saldivar had been stealing money from the fan club funds. After a fiery meeting in a motel room Selena was shot in the back as she left. She died in hospital later that day, having named Saldivar as her killer.

Like Selena, Jimmy Ellis' name may not be familiar to you, but the 53-year-old had forged a big reputation as America's foremost Elvis impersonator. Using a stage character called Orion, who always performed wearing a mask, many claimed that Ellis' voice was the closest to The King's they'd ever heard. But Ellis' was tragically shot behind the counter of his Alabama convenience store on 12th December 1998, when a robber burst into the shop and blasted Ellis and his ex-wife Elaine Thompson with a sawn-off shotgun. Thompson died instantly, Ellis lost his struggle for life shortly afterwards.

The most bizarre case of a gunshot death, however, simply has to be that of '50s rocker Johnny Ace. Born John Alexander, his string of hits included 'Cross My Heart' and 'The Clock'. Ace came to a sad and untimely end on Christmas Day, 1954 when he embarked on a solo game of Russian Roulette to impress a crowd of backstage hangers-on at one of his gigs. Believing the gun chamber to be empty he pulled the trigger and shot himself. Paul Simon eventually recorded a tribute to him, 'The Late Great Johnny Ace'.

The Troutman brothers, Larry and Roger, made their names in the eighties with the band Zapp, while Roger enjoyed a renaissance in the rap-dominated '90s by performing on Tupac Shakur's hit 'California Love'. The brothers died in April of 1999 when Larry shot Roger several times in an argument about the family music business. Larry then shot himself in the head.

From drummer Al Jackson of the MGs, shot

by a burglar in his own house in 1975 to Walter Scott, frontman of big band Bob Kuban And The In Men, who was killed by his wife's lover in December of 1983, the list of gun-related deaths makes for sobering reading. Even Dizzy

Gillespie's trumpet player, Lee Morgan, was shot and killed by a jealous lover at New York's Slug Club in 1972, while former Earth Wind & Fire saxophonist Donald Myrick was shot and killed by a police officer in Santa Monica in 1993. The policeman had a warrant to search the place and shot Myrick when he mistook a lighter he was holding for a gun.

Of course anywhere where the culture tolerates guns is likely to see more firearms-related deaths and Jamaica has suffered badly under the gun. The Wailers' guitarist and pianist Peter Tosh was shot to death by three burglars at his Kingston home, while the group's drummer Carlie Barrett was shot twice in the head in the same city. His wife Albertine and her lover Glenroy Carter were charged with the murder. Dub legend King Tubby was also murdered outside his home in Kingston by an armed robber.

Strangest of all is the story of Terry Kath, founding member and guitarist with the 70s American phenomenon Chicago. On 23rd January 1978 Kath, aged 31, was at the home of one of the

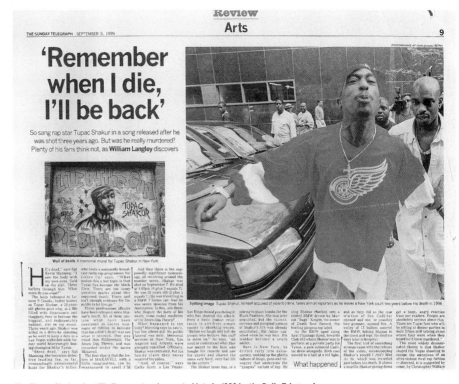

The 'Tupac Shakur is still alive mystery' reported late in 1999 by the Daily Telegraph

band's roadies, Don Johnson. Kath was a serious collector of guns and enjoyed shooting. He started messing around with an automatic pistol and when Johnson told him to stop fooling around, Kath laughed and told him not to worry because there was no clip in the gun. To prove his point Kath put the gun to his head and pulled the trigger. Unfortunately for him a bullet was in the gun chamber before the clip cartridge had been removed. Kath was killed instantly.

Of course the pattern of violence remains the same no matter what the country and no matter what the era. Such high profile music-related deaths are only the tip of the iceberg. People die from guns all over the world. But imagine how many great musicians could have contributed so much more if guns hadn't been so freely available.

MOTORBIKE CRASHES

Marlon Brando, all sulky lips underneath battered leather peaked cap, was the man who sealed the motorcycle's status as fashion icon. Riding into town as the leader of the delinquent motorcycle gang in The Wild Ones, Brando pushed a button with rebellious young people looking to express themselves after the dark and repressive days of the Second World War. And tearing about dressed in black leather with a throbbing motorbike at your command seemed just about the best, the loudest way to say that you weren't going to be a part of the machine.

Some of the film's stylised rebellion looks awfully twee with the benefit of hindsight, but while film style has changed, the impact of the motorbike on youth culture has endured. And as film stars started to give way to rock stars in the '60s, the motorbike went along for the ride. Hell's Angels, Easy Rider, Dylan wiping out at Woodstock; the bike had a real good go at knocking the hot rod off top spot as the ultimate rock 'n' roll accoutrement. It was flash, fast and fierce and, as youthful rebellion became the order of the day, the message was clear. As Dylan himself retorted when asked by a reporter exactly what he was rebelling against, "What have you got?"

Dylan, though pretty mashed up when he lost control of his two wheeler up there in Woodstock, at least made a full recovery. Other rock stars weren't so lucky. Of course the most tragic music-related motorcycle fatalities have to be the two which occurred in rapid succession. On 29 October 1971, while returning from wishing his band member Berry Oakley's wife Linda a happy birthday, Duane Allman swerved to avoid a truck while riding his bike in Macon Georgia. He lost control of the motorcycle and crashed and, after three hours of emergency surgery, died in Macon Medical Center. At the age of 24 Duane was at the very outset of his musical career and had already garnered a massive reputation as a blues rock guitarist. With his brother Gregg playing keyboards and singing, the Allman Brothers Band debut in 1970 impressed Eric Clapton so much that Duane was invited to record with the English legend at Miami's Criteria Studios as part of Derek & The Dominoes. Within 10 days a double album had been recorded, which included a song featuring a guitar duet between the two players that would enter the annals of rock history. 'Layla' is for many Duane Allman's true lasting legacy.

The death of Allman had a devastating effect on The Allman Brothers Band, but as 1972 came around the album 'Eat A Peach' was released, which featured the last three tracks ever recorded by Duane. But then tragedy struck again. Another band member was killed in a motorcycle accident, this time Berry Oakley. The 24 year-old bassist was killed when his bike collided with a bus just three blocks away from the spot where Duane had died a year before. Oakley was finally laid to rest in Macon's Rose Hill Cemetery, where Allman was also buried. Despite the double blow, The Allman Brothers continued and the following year's Brothers And Sisters, an album dedicated to Oakley, topped the American charts for five weeks.

Despite the obvious dangers of motorcycles, Allman and Oakley remain the two highest-profile musicians to have been killed in cycle accidents, though of course there have been other deaths. 28 year-old Richard Farina, a little-known but much-respected musician and novelist was killed on 30th April 1966 when he crashed his bike during a party to celebrate the launch of his novel Been Down So Long. His first album, 'Celebration For A Grey Day', is now regarded as an underground classic.

Jimmy Domengeaux was 44 when he was killed in a hit-and-run accident while riding his bike in southern Louisiana. During a long musical career Domengeaux's guitar playing had been heard in the bands Steve Riley And The Mamou Playboys, Cajun Heat and Gumbo Cajun Band.

Echo And The Bunnymen's Pete DeFreitas was killed in a motorbike crash in Rugeley, Staffordshire in 1989. Don Rich of The Buckaroos, meanwhile, died on 17 July 1974 in a motorcycle accident in California and Moody Blues touring member Jimmie Spheeris was killed ten years later in Venice Beach when a drunk driver ignored a stop sign a few blocks from Spheeris' home. Nicky Hammerhead, drummer with Julian Lennon and occasionally Bo Diddley, also died in 1992 from internal injuries following a bad bike smash.

The motorbike's place in rock history will always be assured. After all, surely it's the sense of danger that makes the two-wheeler sexy. Yes, of course there's the chance that a motorbike will kill you, but for many musicians its allure is something that's simply impossible to resist.

"I give so much pleasure to so many people. Why can I not get some pleasure for myself? Why do I have to stop?"

Comedian John Belushi

'SEX AND DRUGS AND ROCK AND ROLL/All my brain and body needs' sang Ian Dury on that legendary record back in 1978. No doubt a clever chappie like Dury was being heavily ironic at the time, not-very-gently mocking all those Class A losers who thought that sex, drugs and rock 'n' roll were a passport to greater enlightenment. The trouble with irony, though, is that too often too many people miss the point. How many people saw his single as a call to arms, a rallying clarion, a big two fingers up to a straight and sedate life? As far as most young people with a taste for discovery were concerned sex and drugs and rock 'n' roll were all that the brain and body needed.

The trouble is, like the advert says, drugs really can screw you up. And everyone's seen the clear-as-day evidence; people so fucked up on stuff that they simply can't function any more. And that's not nice. And not only is it not nice, it can be a lot worse than that. It can kill you.

Rock stars die from drugs. That's a plain, bald, statistically proven fact. Not all rock stars, of course. But plenty of rock stars do cop it. Like the appropriately named Ken 'Dimwit' Montgomery, drummer with rock band The Four Horsemen. He died in 1984 from a heroin overdose. Like John Ritchie (aka Sid Vicious), who was carried out of a Greenwich Village apartment in a body bag, full to the brim with heroin, aged 22 in 1979. It should be a lesson to us all. What we should learn above all is that

drugs are particularly dangerous in the hands of people who don't really have to do too much at all until about 9.30pm when they go on stage. These people have too many lackeys kissing their ass and making them believe that not only is their judgement impeccable, but that they're also indestructible. It's a bad combination. Ask any of this lot...

Jimi Hendrix, the greatest rock guitarist of them all, died in a bedroom at the Samarkand Hotel in London's Notting Hill aged 27 on 18th September, 1970 after taking the barbiturate quinalbarbitone. The coroner recorded an open verdict with the death being attributable to "inhalation of vomit due to barbiturate intoxication". Jimi, apparently, had a very low tolerance of drugs.

Singer songwriter Tim Buckley (father of Jeff, see 'Drowning' section) died on June 29th, 1975 from a heroin overdose, aged 28. Apparently Buckley died after snorting way too much heroin at the house of his good friend Richard Keeling in Dallas after a successful sold-out show in the city. After lurching about his pal's home he was taken back to his place and put to bed by his wife Judy, who called paramedics after Buckley turned a frightening shade of blue. Too late.

Tim Hardin, like Buckley a cult rock figure, also

tim buckley / happy sad

succumbed to heroin. Hardin described himself as a jazz singer, though most people would have opted for the folk tag. He picked up his habit while in the marines and throughout his career was blighted by addiction. He even nodded out on stage at London's Royal Albert Hall in 1968. Hardin stumbled through a series of personal catastrophes before finally succumbing in Los Angeles aged 38 on December 29th, 1980. The LA County Coroner's Office returned a verdict of death from acute heroin-morphine intoxication due to an overdose.

While Hardin's audience has always remained selective, his contemporary Janis Joplin established a massive reputation in the wake of her drug-related death. The Texan belter had redefined people's conception of female folk singers with her impassioned and almost scary performances; a million miles removed from the polite and sanitised interpretations of Joan Baez and Judy Collins. Joplin was a misfit, though, an awkward-looking girl whose early amphetamine addiction indicated some kind of emotional void. Her performing tour de force, an absolute showstopper at the Monterey Pop Festival of 1967, sent her reputation soaring. But before she had even begun to explore the possibilities of a seemingly limitless range, Janis died aged just 27 from a heroin overdose at the Hollywood hotel where she was staying while working on her 'debut' album with new act The Kozmic Blues Band. She was found with a needle sticking out of her arm.

It certainly appears that 20-something musicians appear to be at the most risk from heroin-related deaths. From 25-year old 'boy wonder' Frankie Lymon in 1968 to 22 year old Darby Crash of LA punk band The Germs in 1980 to original Red Hot Chili Peppers guitarist Hillel Slovak, who died aged 26 in 1988, the message has remained constant across the years. Messing with the brown powder is an almighty risk. Heroin seems to waft in and out of fashion and as the nihilistic feel of grunge music infiltrated America in the mid-'90s it seemed only too obvious that heroin would once more become the drug of choice for many musicians. The movement lost its iconic leader, Kurt Cobain to a suicide shot from a gun, but he was known to have struggled with heroin. There were two other high profile heroin deaths within the movement. Kristen Pfaff, bassist with Courtney Love's band Hole, died on June 16th, 1994 aged 27, the victim of a heroin overdose. She had opted to get out of Seattle, fast becoming the centre of heroin chic, and she was only in the city to pack up the last of her things. Unfortunately she took a bath, nodded out and died during the night. Her removal truck was still outside the apartment.

34 year old Jonathan Melvoin was a member

of San Francisco band Smashing Pumpkins in July 1996 when he overdosed on heroin at the Regency Hotel in New York. He was with the band's drummer Jimmy Chamberlain at the time, himself a man with a history of drug and alcohol problems. New York police reported that it was Chamberlain who made the 911 call that alerted the authorities to Melvoin's plight, but the keyboardist was pronounced dead at the scene. His jazz-playing father had, ironically, fought hard to warn musicians of the dangers of

drugs. Melvoin had presumably also chosen to ignore the warning offered by the death of Sublime singer and guitarist Bradley Nowell less than two months earlier. Nowell was found dead of an overdose in a San Francisco hotel room, precipitating the collapse of the band.

Of course the drug-related deaths of many musicians have been a result of a slow and steady decline rather than one final grand gesture. Rocker Phil Lynott of Thin Lizzy died of heart failure in 1986 after spending a week in a coma, the result of many years of drug and alcohol abuse. The Who's drummer Keith Moon also suffered the same problems throughout his career. His notorious and prodigious use of alcohol and drugs clearly fuelled some of his wildest exploits, but also caught up on him in the end and even affected his undoubted abilities as a drummer. By the time the band were recording

'Who Are You' in 1978, Moon was unable to hold the beat on one song, 'Music Must Change', and it was simply put down on tape without one. On 7th of September of that year Moon died in his rented Mayfair flat after taking an overdose of a drug called chlormethiazole, which he had been using to combat his rampant alcoholism.

The Doors singer Jim Morrison, officially died of a heart attack in the bath of his Parisian flat, but his years of hedonistic living had clearly caught up with him. Like many addicts, Morrison had been fully aware of how dangerous his excessive appetites were. Following the deaths of his '60s musical contemporaries Janis Joplin and Jimi Hendrix, Morrison would often say, "you're drinking with number three". Troubled by asthmatic problems during his time in Paris, where he had moved to escape both his own fame and the music industry, Morrison was found dead on 3rd July 1971 by his common law wife Pamela Courson, who was herself to die of a heroin overdose three years later.

Jerry Garcia, legendary leader of The Grateful Dead, finally succumbed to long-term drug abuse while trying to kick his heroin habit by checking himself into the Marin County rehab centre in 1995. Cause of death was noted as a heart attack. Blues rock guitarist Paul Kossoff also died of drug-induced heart failure in March of 1976 on a flight from LA to New York, aged just 25.

Morrison, Moon, Garcia, Lynott, Kossoff... all were sadly only a part of a long line of musicians suffering with fatal drug problems. Legendary jazz saxophonist Charlie Parker died aged 34 on 12th March 1955, after his health had deteriorated due to heroin addiction and a love of alcohol. The Temptations' David Ruffin died in 1991 aged 50 of a crack cocaine overdose. Gene Clark of The Byrds finally saw his heart wear out on him in 1991 after years of abuse. Legendary rock star Gram Parsons died in 1973 as a result of 'drug toxicity' after taking too much morphine together with alcohol. And then there's the greatest star of them all. Elvis Aaron Presley's death from a heart attack was almost certainly due to the vast quantity of prescription drugs he had been dependent on in the later years of his life.

Yet even more tragically, musicians have not always died through their own reckless, drug-related behaviour, but rather through the stupidity of others. Scottish soul act Average White Band lost their talented drummer Robbie McIntosh in September of 1974 at the age of 24. Attending a party in the fashionable Hollywood Hills, McIntosh was the unlucky victim whose drink was spiked with a lethal dose of heroin. And while heroin is by some considerable distance the most potent killer amongst musicians, it is by no means the only one, as former Blind Melon vocalist Shannon Hoon found out to his cost back in October 1995. Embraced by the biggest rock band at the time, Guns N' Roses, who were themselves no strangers to substance abuse, Blind Melon hit paydirt early doors with their debut album of 1993. The band's second album, Soup, released in the summer of '95, failed to ignite the charts. Hoon was found dead from an accidental cocaine overdose on the band's tour bus and this event signalled the end for a promising group and a life barely begun at 28.

Famed groupie Miss Christine, who had a musician's career of sorts when she was a member of the GTOs in the early '70s (one album, 'Permanent Damage', produced by Frank Zappa), also met her end through drugs. Surprisingly, though, she didn't die of illegal substances, but rather from prescription painkillers she was taking after treatment to repair curvature of the spine.

The most incredible story of a musician's drug-related death, however, simply has to be that of little-known Lester Butler, a singer and harmonica player who lived in LA. On the night of May 8, 1998 Butler was aiming to get high at a friend's house. A woman, who screwed things up badly by administering him with too much, injected him with heroin. Butler passed out at once, scaring the two conscious people, who threw him into a bath full of ice cold water in the hope of bringing him round. It didn't work, so when the woman's boyfriend arrived they decided to try and rouse him by injecting him with cocaine. To no avail. They tried more cocaine. To no avail. But instead of getting help they tried yet another cocaine injection. This extraordinary situation was bad enough, but Butler had a gig to play that night. For some inexplicable reason the two junkies drove to the show in Butler's van with Butler in the back, then went in to watch the band perform without their frontman, telling punters that he had passed out and was just sleeping the worst of his excesses off. By two in the morning they still hadn't got Butler some much-needed medical help and instead went back to their apartment to go to bed. Butler died at some stage during these insane proceedings and the hapless duo ended up dropping his dead body back at the original house the next day. Drugs? On the evidence of this, they really do fuck you up.

Caption in her here here Caption in her here here

"Lord, Lord! methought what pain
it was to drown:
What dreadful noise of water in mine ears!
What sights of ugly death within mine eyes!
Methought I saw a thousand fearful wracks;
A thousand men that fished gnawed upon."

William Shakespeare, from Richard III.

SUEDE WROTE 'THE DROWNERS', Manic Street Preachers came up with 'Ready For Drowning'. The Beat penned 'Drowning', The Adventures 'Drowning In The Sea Of Love' and The Mobiles 'Drowning in Berlin'. Despite the common use of the drowning metaphor in contemporary songs, it still comes as something of a shock that so many of rock's top artists have fallen victim to this particularly unpleasant death. Why? On the surface it doesn't seem as if there's any particularly strong connection between musicians and water. Unless you count mixing it with whiskey, that is. But Dennis Wilson , Randy California, Johnny Burnette, Jimmy Hodder and Jeff Buckley have all drowned and that's without even mentioning the most notorious case of all... that of Rolling Stone Brian Jones.

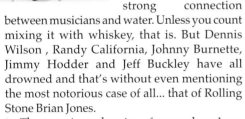

The conspiracy theories, of course, have been so much part of the Stones' folklore that it's incredibly difficult to separate fact from fiction. What is beyond dispute, however, is the fact that the prettiest and (in the early days, at least) most popular Stone had found himself in the middle of a vicious downward spiral long before leaving the group in June of 1969. As The Stones

freely experimented with drugs of all kinds, Jones was quick to embrace their full-on hedonism. The legendary '67 Morocco road trip undertaken by the unholy trinity of Jones, his girlfriend Anita Pallenberg and Keith Richards

should have been enough of a warning to Jones. Pallenberg herself observed that, "Brian began to berate me and attack me physically, beating me with a kind of sobbing frustration." Pallenberg went on to explain, "Brian was suffering badly at this point from severe fits of paranoia," and it was downhill from that point onward. Jones received a drug conviction of his own in late 1968 and Pallenberg got herself pregnant with Richards' child. When Jones left the group in mid-1969 it seemed he could sink no lower. Sadly this proved to be untrue; Jones was found dead in a swimming pool in the grounds of a Sussex house once owned by the famous writer A.A. Milne. The official verdict of 'death by misadventure' never really satisfied some of the more fanciful Stones fans, but its seemed entirely plausible that Jones could have drowned while under the influence of drink and drugs.

There was no suggestion that Jeff Buckley had been drinking or taking drugs when the California native drowned a full 28 years after Brian Jones. Nor could it be claimed that the 30-year-old had exerted anything like the influence of his fellow guitarist on the world of music at large. Yet amongst the musical cognoscenti there was genuine shock and grief when Buckley's death was announced on June 4th. The son of cult '60s songwriter Tim Buckley, Jeff had built up a solo career playing the coffee houses and clubs of LA before signing a deal with Columbia

In 1993. A year later the album 'Grace' established Buckley's credentials with the critics. Before Buckley had time to capitalise on this early buzz, though, tragedy befell him when he and a friend travelled to Mud Island Harbour on the banks of the Mississippi on the night of 29th May 1997. On the spur of the moment Buckley decided to go swimming and jumped into the water fully clothed. Within moments Buckley disappeared beneath the swell and, although the authorities were quickly alerted and a full-scale search mounted, they were unable to save him. Buckley's body was found floating near the city's famous Beale Street area on June 4th; a rock death as bizarre as it was unexpected.

The idea that Dennis Wilson would die before his time was one that had been accepted readily enough by anyone with even the most cursory knowledge of the Beach Boys. But the notion that it would be by drowning? Well, no one could have predicted the drummer's death in that obtuse manner. Dennis' behaviour had never been quite as bizarre as that of his brother Brian but his dedication to living on the very lip of sanity was no less complete. His liking of and capacity for drugs was legendary, his taste for women hardly less so. The only way to live life was in the fast lane as far as Dennis was concerned and even when his voice was reduced to little more than a hoarse whisper due to his indulgences it seemed like there would be no let-up in his pursuit of the hedonistic. Surely it would only be a matter of time before his actions caught up with him, and so it proved. During a break in recording the album 'Bamboo' in 1983 Dennis drowned diving from his yacht in California's Marina

Del Rey on December 28th. His blood-alcohol level was at a very high level. Fittingly, his family decided that he should be buried at sea. He was 39 years old.

Wilson's fellow American, guitarist Randy California, lasted another six years before suffering the same fate. California's work with Spirit had seen his guitar playing compared with the innovative style of Jimi Hendrix. There was no denying that the Seattle guitarist influenced Randy Wolfe (he was actually dubbed 'California' by Hendrix himself). Like Hendrix, California had also cut his teeth in The Blue Flames in New York's Greenwich Village in 1966 before forming Spirit in Los Angeles the following year. He never reached legendary heights, but had a hardcore following of guitar virtuoso fans. At the age of 45, however, a strong undertow took California as he swam off the coast of the Hawaiian island of Molokai. In one final act of heroism he managed to save his 12-year-old son Quinn.

The deep also claimed the life of original rockabilly hero turned teen ballad singer Johnny Burnette, who drowned in Clear lake California aged 30 in 1964 after falling out of his boat during a fishing trip. Steely Dan's Jimmy Hodder passed on in the same unfortunate manner aged 42 in June of 1990, while saxophonist Art Porter also drowned in Bangkok aged 35 in 1996.

"If we value so highly the dignity of life, how can we not also value the dignity of death? No death may be called futile." – Japanese author Yukio Mishima

SO LET'S JUST TAKE A FEW SONG titles at random...

Sex And Drugs And Rock And Roll'- Ian Dury And The Blockheads

I Want Your Sex - George Michael

You Sexy Thing - Hot Chocolate

Sex Over The Phone - The Village People

Sexy MF - Prince

(Sexual) Healing - Marvin Gaye

Sex As A Weapon - Pat Benatar

The Sex Of It - Kid Creole And The Coconuts

We could go on all night here, but that would get boring. Still, the point is clear. Making love and making music go together. It's nothing new. Music - good music - makes people feel sexy, gets their mojos working, sends a call to their subconscious that says 'Let's get it on'. Aerosmith's Steven Tyler - a man who, we can safely assume, has experienced quite a lot of bump and grind, talks about "the sex of it" when discussing a great tune. And we all know what he means. Great music makes us feel like being a little bit... naughty. Trouble is, there aren't too many musos out there who want to talk about the other side of sex, the dark side, the side that can kill. Yet that dark side is something that everybody - from musicians to politicians - have been forced to confront in the last 15 years.

There aren't many people alive today who remember the days when sexually transmitted

diseases like syphilis and gonorrhoea were killers. To most of us sex and death can mean only one thing; AIDS. David Bowie summed up the feelings of a generation well enough when he argued: "We are aware for the first time in our history that the sexual act can bring about death. But we must not let AIDS become a banner that can be waved by right wing elements to herald some new morality. AIDS is being used as a reason why nobody must experiment." Of course such a notion would naturally be anathema to one of pop music's most adventurous composers and performers, but it is also equally understandable that the liberal, 'anything goes' environs of the music industry would be hit hard by the advent of AIDS.

An industry, which more often than not relies on fantasies and the selling of dreams, was always going to find it hard to tackle such a bleak issue as AIDS head-on. An industry that had all but founded itself on the cornerstone of sexual liberation in the Sixites was never going to find it easy to stare into the abyss and see that sex and liberalism could now kill. But nevertheless, that really was the issue facing musicians in the early '80s. Sexually tolerant and sexually promiscuous artists, many with a liking for hard drugs, were always going to be a fertile breeding ground for AIDS. How much effect these AIDS-related deaths have had on the world's music-loving population is difficult to assess. The plague of deaths so hastily predicted in the early '80s, as people first got to grips with the virus, has failed to materialise. But huge stars have died from AIDS and died of it too young.

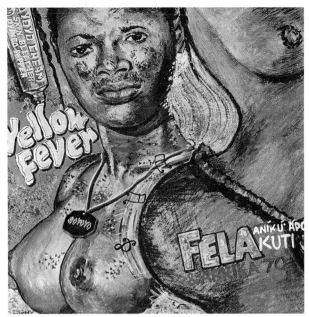

The first known musician to die of AIDS would almost certainly be Klaus Nomi. Nomi was no major star, but had garnered something of a reputation at the more avant garde end of the rock spectrum as a performer and writer of interest and intrigue. Born in Germany in 1944 as Klaus Sperber, he had dreamt of becoming a singer at the Deutsche Opera in Berlin and even worked as an usher in the building. However, he failed in his quest and moved to New York, initially to work as a pastry chef in the World Trade Centre. After founding his own baking company Nomi started working evenings in clubs and soon formed a friendship with David Bowie, who invited him to appear with him on Saturday Night Live. Nomi sang backing vocals on 'The Man Who Sold The World', 'TVC15' and 'Boys Keep Swinging'. The appearance set Nomi on his way and he continued to attract fringe interest in his work until his death on August 6, 1983.

If Nomi was the first known musician to die of AIDS, then certainly the biggest rock star to succumb to the disease has to be Freddie Mercury. The eccentric, egotistical and extraordinary lead singer of Queen flaunted the fact that he was gay without ever actually announcing it. Rumours began to circulate about the state of his health towards the end of the '80s as the once robust frontman suddenly appeared in public looking drawn and gaunt. Mercury - born Frederick Bulsara on September 5, 1946 in Zanzibar - had lived a flamboyant and careless life as Queen steadily rose to become one of the world's biggest rock bands. Talk of multiple partners and a propensity for excess in all areas of his life meant that few were surprised when Mercury finally announced he was suffering from AIDS in November of 1991. Within 48 hours the singer died of bronchial pneumonia at his home in Knightsbridge. By April of 1992 the remaining members of Queen had organised a major concert at London's Wembley Stadium to promote AIDS awareness. It attracted the world's largest ever TV audience when it was televised live.

But if anyone was tempted to claim that Mercury's death once again proved that AIDS was a disease which specifically affected the gay population, the death of Eric Wright in 1995 soon proved that notion to be far from the case. Wright, known in music circles as Eazy-E, had made his name as the unremittingly heterosexual lynchpin of rap act NWA. Niggas With Attitude prided themselves on their hard-assed approach; their songs packed full of violence and macho, chick-fucking bravado.

Eazy-E (one of whose more memorable lyrics ran as a call and response between the rapper and his female fans: 'We love you Easy / Yeah I love you too / We wanna fuck you Easy / Yeah, I wanna fuck you too') clearly had plenty of sexual encounters and was at a loss to explain exactly where he had picked up the disease when he finally realised he was suffering from AIDS. What he did know when he made the announcement about his predicament, was that "I've learned in the last week that this thing is real and it doesn't discriminate." Unfortunately for Wright the realisation came too late to save him.

Musicians of all kinds have been afflicted with the AIDS virus. From Mississippi blues guitarist Lonnie Pitchford to heavy metal singer Ray Gillen, from B52s' guitarist Ricky Wilson to Bruce Jay Paskow of The Washington Squares. But of all the musicians who have died, the one who could and should have had the greatest influence on the spread of the disease is Fela Kuti.

Fela Ransome Kuti was born in Abeokuta, Nigeria on October 15, 1938 and grew to prominence as the biggest afrobeat musician on the planet. His dedication to pan-Africanism would have made him the perfect mouthpiece for the fight against AIDS, his sheer bravery - given his constant and consistent stance against his native country's military dictatorship - should have given him the nerve to take the message to the people. Sadly, though, Kuti's private life allowed no room for manoeuvre. For this was a tremendously promiscuous man, a man capable of having multiple relationships with several women, many of whom were often members of his retinue of dancers. It's impossible to imagine Kuti preaching a message of sexual restraint and caution when he was so clearly a man with a voracious sexual appetite. The power he had over huge swathes of the African people would have been a potent weapon in the fight against AIDS on the continent most afflicted by the disease. But Kuti's nature, so steadfast in its condemnation of the killers in African military dictatorships, could never be turned to help what has proved to be just as scary an instrument of death.

> ## "I feel about airplanes the way I feel about diets. It seems to me that they are wonderful things for other people to go on."
>
> US author and playwright Jean Kerr.

EVERYONE KNOWS THE STATISTICS. You're more likely to die crossing the road than in a plane crash. Everyone knows most planes can still make it to their destination with three of their four turbo engines conked out. You try telling all of that to Patsy Cline, or Jim Reeves, or The Big Bopper, or Stevie Ray Vaughan, or Buddy Holly. Ask yourself this: - How can you *really* ever trust a form of transport that has taken away that kind of musical talent?'

The single biggest air crash to have blighted rock history remains the one that happened on February 3, 1959 between Clear Lake, Iowa and Moorhead, Minnesota. Three of the era's biggest stars - Buddy Holly, The Big Bopper and Richie Valens - had decided to hire a plane to take them between two gigs on their joint tour. Visibility was poor when the small plane took off on that night and within minutes it was in trouble. The plane came down almost immediately, killing all three musicians and the pilot, in the process obliterating three young talents, none of whom had even reached their thirtieth birthday.

Those who embraced the commercial sense that the aeroplane made in those early days of rock 'n' roll touring were taking a calculated risk. Aeroplane technology was relatively new, commercial pilots and their regulation was still something of a grey area and flight paths and safety checks were haphazard. Yet despite these enormous problems, flying still held a great appeal for musicians - particularly those working in America - who were constantly tired and frazzled from spending too long on the road.

Virginia Patterson Hensley, born in the all-too-prophetic town of Gore in Virginia in 1932, became one of country's all-time great singers under the name of Patsy Cline. Cline's greatest moments - 'Crazy', 'Walkin' After Midnight' - are still recognised as classics and you can't help but wonder what heights she might have scaled had she not been killed at the age of 31. In March of 1963 Cline agreed to do her manager Randy Hughes a favour by flying to Kansas City to play a benefit for the wife of a country DJ - and friend of Hughes' - who had died in a car crash. On the flight back home the plane ran into storms. The plane came down in a swampy wooded area in Camden, Tennessee, just 85 miles from the destination of Nashville. Cline was killed instantly alongside her manager. In a grisly finale to the tragedy, identification of the singer proved extremely difficult as only her shoulders, right arm and back of the head were in one piece.

Less than a year after the death of Patsy Cline another huge star of the American music scene was lost to an air disaster. Texan crooner Jim Reeves was flying himself down to Batesville, Arkansas in July of 1964 to discuss a prospective land deal, taking pianist Dean Manuel along for the ride. Approaching Nashville on his return Reeves' plane hit a rainstorm and was lost from the radar. Top star Marty Robbins heard the sound of a crash near to his home in the suburb of Brentwood and raised the alarm, but it still took two days to recover the bodies from the

Above: The grave of Buddy Holly in Lubbock, Texas. Right: Buddy Holly in a sad and pensive mood, gazing out to sea.

was negotiating with Bob Thiele to release the recording of 'That'll Be The Day'. Petty also made a separate contract to record Buddy Holly as a solo artist. Holly would be on the Coral label, and the Crickets on Brunswick, although the same people would be involved in making both series of records. While the Crickets' records were rock & roll, Holly's solo records were softer, what the trade used to call 'ballads with a beat'.

The first solo Holly record, 'Words Of Love', sank without trace, although it inspired a respectful and faithful version from the Beatles years later; but the second, 'Peggy Sue', was as remarkable as 'That'll Be The Day' had been. Without any irony or defence, Buddy donned a childishly simple verse over a hypnotic guitar rhythm: it worked because he sang it so adventurously, playing around with the melody and vowels until the whole thing became just sound. Anybody else who tried to sing it was obliged to follow Buddy's vocal lines, or risk losing the song's effectiveness – an important quality of Buddy's style which explains the continuing demand for his records.

The success of 'That'll Be The Day' and 'Peggy Sue' immediately created a demand for personal appearances by Buddy Holly (and the Crickets) around the world, and they made tours of the States.

Australia and Britain. On stage, Buddy confirmed and extended the impressions created on record, as one report stated:

"At the Globe, Stockton, the stage seemed huge and empty with just a drummer (Jerry Allison) behind his kit, and the bass player (Joe Mauldin) standing next to his stand-up bass. And when Buddy walked on, his face cracked by a huge grin under his glasses, it was impossible not to identify with him and feel nervous on his behalf: could this kid, who looked like he had just changed out of his school uniform, meet the audience's expectations? One blast on his guitar and those of us in the front row were ready to move to the back. How could one guitar be so loud? "I think the secret of Buddy's style," Jerry Allison ruminated later, "was

that we didn't have a rhythm guitar, so Buddy had to play a style which was lead and rhythm at the same time, he had to play a melody on chords."

Relaxed And Impressive

There were two LPs out by this time, one just called 'Buddy Holly' with an almost recognisable picture of him without his glasses, and 'The Chirping Crickets'. On stage, Buddy would run through most of the songs, which mostly sounded just like the records, but sometimes were even better because Norman Petty wasn't around to make them smooth. The audiences marvelled at how Jerry Allison could play so strongly while looking so relaxed, and remembered

46

wreckage.

Unavoidable air tragedies have accounted for many of the lives of the greatest of our singers. Otis Redding, the sublime voice behind the 'Otis Blue' album, was lost in December of 1967 aged just 26 when his light aircraft went down into Lake Monona near Madison, Wisconsin. He had recorded '(Sittin' On) The Dock Of The Bay', the song that was to become his only million-seller, just three days before the crash.

Blues legend Stevie Ray Vaughan was killed in a chopper crash aged 35 in 1990 as he headed back to Chicago following a blues guitar face-off against Eric Clapton, Robert Cray, Buddy Guy and his brother Jimmy.

Jim Croce, the Philly-born singer songwriter who scored a top 10 US single hit with 'You Don't Mess Around With Jim', also died in a plane crash in July of 1973 when the aircraft he'd chartered hit trees at the end of the airstrip at Natchitoches, Louisiana. And Paul Jeffreys, guitarist with the British group Cockney Rebel, was sadly killed in the Lockerbie air disaster when terrorists blew up a Pan Am jumbo on 21 December 1988.

53-year-old John Denver, one of the States' biggest stars of the '70s thanks to a syrupy ballad titled 'Annie's Song' and, ironically, the writer of Peter, Paul and Mary's big international hit 'Leaving On A Jet Plane', also crashed and burned in October of 1997. Denver was an enthusiastic pilot and had just taken delivery of a futuristic Long-EZ experimental aeroplane the day before he crashed in it in California's Monterey Bay and was killed instantly. Rumours circulated that Denver died after trying to switch from an empty fuel tank to what he believed was a full one, only to find that was empty too.

Empty fuel tanks were also blamed for the multiple deaths suffered by the southern rock band Lynyrd Skynyrd in 1977. Led by vocalist Ronnie Van Zant, the band had a reputation for playing raw rock and roll and leading lives that were rawer still. Yet it wasn't the partying and carousing that did for Van Zant, but the swamplands of Gillsburg, Mississippi when the twin-engined Convair 240 that was carrying the band ran out of fuel and plummeted into the water. Van Zant, Steve Gaines and his sister and backing singer Cassie Gaines were all killed alongside the band's manager Dean Kilpatrick. Band members Gary Rossington, Allen Collins, Billy Powell and Leon Wilkinson were all badly injured. The band's latest album, 'Street Survivors', was withdrawn immediately as the sleeve eerily and prophetically featured the band surrounded by flames.

As a tragic footnote to the Skynyrd saga, Allen Collins was injured in a car crash in 1986 while driving near his home in Jacksonville, Florida. His girlfriend was killed in the accident and Collins was left paralysed from the waist down. His health deteriorated and he died on January 23rd, 1990.

Tragedies like these, of course, are unavoidable. But rock fans will feel cheated by the death of Randy Rhoads, aged just 25, in 1982. The Californian guitarist had been enlisted by former Black Sabbath vocalist Ozzy Osbourne for his new band and had already proved a sensation in the hard rock world. Whilst in the middle of an American tour and heading for Florida, the band decided to make a stop at a small airfield where a friend of the driver of the band's tour bus had a small aeroplane. A couple of band members were duly taken up for a joyride; Rhoads was persuaded to get on board alongside the group's make-up artist. The pilot decided to play a prank on the people inside the tour bus and buzz the plane as low over the roof of the bus as possible - with predictable results. The plane clipped the bus, then flew hopelessly out of control before crashing, killing everyone on board. Air crashes. No matter how much they tell you planes are safe, can we ever truly believe them?

CAR CRASHES

> "Death, when it approaches, ought not to take one by surprise. It should be part of the full expectancy of life. Without an ever-present sense of death life is insipid. You might as well live on the whites of eggs."
> British novelist Muriel Spark

"HE BLEW HIS MIND OUT in a car," said John Lennon, a man who knew a thing or two about the human condition. And by setting the scene for one man's demise in the very embodiment of new-found '60s opulence, the ballsiest Beatle had identified the car not only as a symbol of freedom, but just as easily as a place of danger. Not that the car is dangerous *per se*, of course. Mix it with other particularly combustible elements, found, it has to be said, with greater frequency in the genetic make-up of your average rock star, though, and what you've got on your hands is simply a killing machine. Combine a throbbing engine with the impetuousness of youth, a primeval urge to preen and, as often as not, alcohol and the capacity for fireworks is huge. Of course the biggest teen idol to meet his end in a car was James Dean.

Having already received a ticket for speeding in his Porsche on the afternoon of September 30th 1955, Dean collided with a Ford Sedan driven by one Donald Turnupseed at 5.45pm at the intersection of routes 466 and 41. Passenger and friend Rolf Wutherich was thrown free, but Dean died within seconds. The phrase 'live fast, die young', may well have been invented right there and then; immediately bestowing on the car the mythical status of the ultimate youth status symbol.

After the post-war years of austerity in the

ELECTROCUTION

> "How you die is the most important thing you'll ever do. It's the exit, the final scene of the glorious epic of your life. It's the third act and, you know, everything builds up to the third act."
> Timothy Leary

GIVEN THE HAPHAZARD nature of live gigs, it's amazing that so few musicians have been electrocuted. There were, however, some unlucky ones and the most famous electric rock death has to be that of former Yardbirds vocalist and harmonica player Keith Relf. The man who originally found the band's name in a book by American novelist Jack Kerouac soon became the vocal foil to Jeff Beck's explosive guitar playing. Songs such as 'For Your Love' and 'Heart Full Of Soul' not only helped to define the emergence of blues-based British rock in the '60s, but also laid the foundations for the development of many vocalist/guitarist fulcrums of the superstar rock groups of the '70s. After The Yardbirds split in 1968 Relf formed Together, which soon became Renaissance, he then joined Medicine Head and finally Armageddon in 1975. Within in a year, however, Relf was dead after electrocuting himself while playing guitar in the bath at home.

Leslie Harvey, another stalwart of the British blues rock scene of the '60s, actually lost his life performing live on stage. The younger brother of the legendary Alex Harvey, Leslie first played on a 1964 Alex Harvey album titled 'The Blues' at the tender age of 16. He continued to play in his brother's groups until 1966 when he helped form Stone The Crows. While the band always did well on the live circuit their record sales never really soared and the group had already begun to fragment when Harvey was electrocuted on-stage at Swansea's Top Rank Ballroom on 3rd May, 1972. He was 27 years old. The band soldiered on and finished a fourth album with Thunderclap Newman's Jimmy McCullough handling guitar duties, but the vibe of the band had been lost and Stone The Crows folded in 1973.

In that same year another British star was also lost to electrocution. John Rostill had made his name in the '60s as bass player with The Shadows. He'd joined the band in 1963 as a replacement for the departed Brian Locking and was with the group until their break-up in December of 1968, making him the band's longest-serving bassist ever. Just under five years later, however, his wife Margaret found Rostill dead in his own recording studio on 26th November 1973. He had been electrocuted in a tragic accident at the age of 31.

States, young people were getting money in their pockets for the first time. And that meant getting their hands on these mean machines, machines that let you get away from your parents and your boring roots at ferocious speed. Dean completed the circle as far as the car was concerned, cementing its stature forever as the ultimate rebel statement. No surprise, then, that songs paying homage to the motor have been so plentiful. From 'Brand New Cadillac' to 'I'm In Love With My Car', the car's been a musical star for as long as we can remember. No surprise either, that so many musicians have met their maker either behind the wheel or as passengers in the sexiest mode of transport there ever was.

Way back in the '30s, the long and winding roads had already claimed one of its earliest musical victims. 32-year-old Milton Brown, leader of one of the most important western swing bands of the time, was involved in a head-on collision. While the accident itself didn't kill him, this precociously talented bandleader died five days later from pneumonia. He wasn't the only one whose luck ran out on the road. Chu Berry (born Leon Berry) was one of the era's most popular tenor sax players, pitching up for stints in both Benny Carter and Fletcher Henderson's bands before making the big break in 1937 by landing the gig with Cab Calloway's band. While on the road with Calloway, Berry was involved in a horrific smash and died a few days later from the terrible head injuries he received. The car has been at the sharp end of rock 'n' roll deaths ever since.

From lesser-known individuals such as Big

Girlfriend's car hits tree

MARC BOLAN KILLED IN CRASH

Star's Chris Bell (he hit a telegraph pole in his native Memphis on December 28, 1978 aged 27) to major stars such as Marc Bolan and Eddie Cochran, road kill is no respecter of reputations nor boundaries. British fans were devastated by the loss of two of their country's biggest stars.

Bolan was making a comeback as the elfin king of glam rock, having taken some time off to assimilate the onslaught of punk rock in 1977. Travelling as a passenger in a Mini driven by his common-law wife and American soul singer Gloria Jones, Bolan collided with a tree on Barnes

Common in the suburbs of London and was killed instantly.

Eddie Cochran was just 21 when he died in that most un-rock 'n' roll of places; Chippenham, Wiltshire. The taxi he was taking burst a tyre and span off the road, crashing and killing the young rocker, then riding high on the back of the smash hit 'C'mon Everybody'. Cochran's fellow passengers Gene Vincent and Sharon Sheely were badly injured in the smash, but fortunately survived. Some were just plain unlucky. Take the case of 46-year-old Jack Anglin. Anglin enjoyed success during the 1940s and 50s with his wife Louise's brother Johnnie in the vocal duo Johnnie And Jack. That run of success came to an unfortunate and ironic end on March 7, 1963, however, when Anglin became yet another car crash fatality. The singer went speeding into a curve on New Due West Avenue in Madison, lost control of his vehicle and was killed instantly in the ensuing crash. Where had Anglin been heading in such an almighty hurry? Towards a *memorial service* for his friend and fellow singer Patsy Cline, who'd recently been killed in an air crash.

There's definitely something especially disturbing about an ironic death, though Anglin's demise is surely overshadowed by songwriter Harry Chapin's auto fatality. Most famous for his 1974 US Christmas number one hit 'Cat's In The Cradle', Chapin was a multi-talented artist who also found success as a filmmaker and as the writer of the 1975 Broadway revue The Night That Made America Famous. His abilities behind the wheel, however, were less certain. He'd already amassed a pile of tickets for speeding offences and had had his licence taken away from him. He was therefore driving illegally on July 16th, 1980 when the car he was in charge of was hit by a truck in Jericho, New York. Chapin was on his way to play a benefit concert. The irony is that it, despite such a poor driving track record, the accident that finally killed him wasn't actually Chapin's fault.

Cars have claimed the lives of many more musicians across the years, of course, from the country rock act Marshall Tucker Band's Tommy Caldwell, who died in 1980 when his Toyota Landcruiser hit a stalled car, to hardcore act The Minutemen's D. Boon, killed in his band's tour

EDDIE COCHRAN HAD PREMONITION OF DEATH

Told Hotel Manager: "I Know I'm Going To Die"

THEN—FATAL CRASH

For three tormented days on his last visit to Manchester recently, rock 'n roll idol Eddie Cochran was haunted by a feeling of impending death, it was revealed to-day.

Shocked by the news of Cochran's death which he read to-day, Mr. Arnold Burlin, manager of the Milverton Lodge, Manchester, where the singer stayed while playing at the Manchester Hippodrome, said: "This is fantastic. Cochran was obsessed and in a dreadful state over a strong feeling he had that he was going to die. He told me: 'I feel so horrible —there is nothing I can do about it, but I know I'm going to die.'"

The 21-years-old star, earning £1,000 a week, died in a Bath hospital last night after a hire car taking him from Bristol to London Airport for a flight back home to Los Angeles burst a tyre and crashed into a lamp standard.

Injured in the smash was another "rock" singer, Gene Vincent. Cochran's girl-friend, 0-year-old song writer Shelley Sharon, was also seriously hurt.

IMPENDING DOOM

Mr. Burlin went on to describe scenes in his office, for three days running, towards the end of Cochran's stay at

Eddie Cochran

Friday and Saturday, although he managed to get some sleep after we called a doctor, who gave him sedatives."

PERFECTLY FIT

bus when his girlfriend nodded off at the wheel. Dave Prater of Sam & Dave fame was killed in a car crash near Sycamore, Georgia in 1988. John Mellencamp's accordion player John Cascella also died at the wheel on his way home in November of 1992, while Rob Collins, keyboardist of The Charlatans, died in his BMW driving back to a recording studio after a night in the pub in 1996 with twice the legal limit of alcohol in his bloodstream. British singer Johnny Kidd died in a car crash on the M1 motorway in October of 1966, while drummer Cozy Powell lost control of his Saab 9000 on the M4 near Bristol in April of 1998. Hard rock band Metallica's bassist Cliff Burton died on September 27th, 1986 aged 24 when the band's tour bus skidded out of control on an icy road in Sweden. Burton had been asleep in one of the bus' bunks when the bus span out of control and was crushed to death.

Weirdest of all, though, was the death of Stiv Bators, the 40-year-old American punk icon. Bators had carved himself a faintly successful career with first The Dead Boys, then The Lords Of The New Church through the '70s and '80s before pitching up in Paris to work on solo material at the turn of the new decade. He had finished six songs when he was hit by a moving car, while standing on a Parisian pavement. Incredibly, Bators actually walked away from the accident, but later died in his sleep at home. Bators hadn't even been in a vehicle at the time, but once again the car proved to be the rock star's nemesis.

Then again, just how appropriate was it? The car is after all sexy, sleek, coveted, cool, fatally attractive... and dangerous. And what rock star worth their salt wouldn't want people to think all that of them?

The two most popular ways out of a desperate situation for boys born on the wrong side of the tracks are sport and music. What other opportunities are there if you're determined to leave your tough-as-teak-world behind and 'make it'? The lack of options is what drives ambitious youngsters onwards and upwards, which is why there seem to be so many musicians out there from poor, deprived or underprivileged backgrounds. It puts fire and desperation into the music. Of course the posh kids can make it in the music business. But what you get is Genesis instead of Happy Mondays, kids from stage schools fronting manufactured pop acts rather than underground dance DJs.

The trouble for the artists themselves, though, is that they can never really leave their roots behind. No matter how far they travel, there will always be something dragging them back to those harder, tougher, nastier lives they came from. Maybe it's those kinds of backgrounds too, which influence the scene in which many musos find themselves living; a twilight world between night and day where things are never quite normal. Flitting between studio and gig, being asleep half the day and awake most of the night, the booze and the sex and of course the intensity that comes with the music. Few would argue that it's an incendiary mix, liable to erupt at any

time. So is it really any wonder that there have been so many violent deaths amongst musicians?

Jaco Pastorius is acknowledged as one of the greatest bass players of all time. His work in the

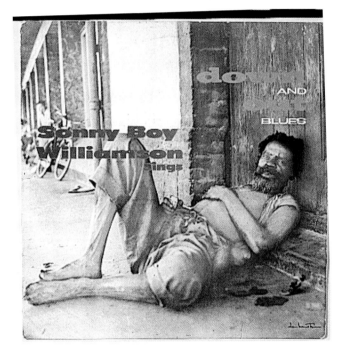

'70s, with Pat Metheny and Weather Report, marked him out as a fretless player without equal. As with so many musicians, however, Pastorius had personal problems; suffering from depression and an addiction to alcohol, his ability to perform began to wane. But it wasn't his health problems that finally killed him. Pastorius died aged 35 on 21st September 1987 after suffering fatal injuries in a brawl outside a nightclub, The Midnight Bottle Club, in his hometown

of Fort Lauderdale. The inspirational bassist, however, was far from the first musician to die in such a way.

As long ago as 1948, the greatest blues harmonica player of them all, Sonny Boy Williamson, was mugged and beaten at the age of 34 on his way out of Chicago's Plantation Club after playing a gig. He sustained a fractured skull and numerous other injuries from which he never recovered, passing away on 1st June. He was buried in his hometown of Jackson, Tennessee.

For many blues enthusiasts Little Walter picked up the mantle laid down by Sonny Boy Williamson and became the first player to shake the pop charts as a harmonica-playing frontman. First with Little Walter And The Night Caps, then with Little Walter And The Jukes, Marion Walter Jacobs put a marker down with hits like 'Blues With A Feeling', 'Last Night' and 'My Babe'. While his musical career saw him move from one success to another, Little Walter's private life was another matter altogether. Known for his boozing and his temper, Little Walter got into plenty of fights. His propensity for wild living finally caught up with him when he was killed in a street brawl in 1968, at the age of 38.

Tragically, not all musicians who have died violently have behaved so recklessly. Mia Zapata of fast-rising punk band The Gits died at 27 after being raped, strangled and left for dead on the streets near her Seattle home in 1993. What's worse is that her murderer has never been caught. Nor has the killer of Durutti Column guitarist Dave Rowbotham, stabbed to death in Manchester in 1992.

> **"Men are never convinced of your reasons, of your sincerity, of the seriousness of your sufferings, except by your death. So long as you are alive, your case is doubtful; you have a right only to your scepticism."**
> Albert Camus

KURT COBAIN WOULD DOUBTLESS have approved of Camus' overview of suicide. In the world of rock and pop; a world so often overtaken, submerged, then finally subsumed by shallowness and fakery, it still came as a fearful shock when the appointed leader of the Nothing Generation actually went and took his own life. It's not as if the warnings weren't there. All the way through the early work of his band Nirvana, Cobain had been telling the world of his despair. Yet ironically, when Nirvana became the rock phenomenon of the decade and Cobain found himself in a position where his influence on the world's young music fans was huge, he found not fulfilment, only more confusion and pain. Was it because so many of us were not convinced of the seriousness of his sufferings, wrapped up as it was in the silly machinations of pop? Was it because Cobain forever doubted he really was capable of being the spokesman for a generation? Or was it simply that he wasn't thinking straight when he shot himself in the head in March of 1994, whacked out on various drugs and confused about what the hell was going on in his private life with his wife Courtney and daughter Frances Bean?

Suicide is still the big taboo. And despite its disregard for convention, the music business still can't get its head around suicide. Suicide always means a life that ends with a question mark. There remains the question of what might have been. Lives not lived to their natural conclusion are always sad. When a life has been ended voluntarily it makes the pain all the greater. When it's a famous musician so many more millions cry. Cobain's death - and suicide note, bearing the line 'thank you all from the pit of my burning, nauseous stomach' - led to a string of copycat suicides and attempted suicides by disenfranchised, disconnected youths. The difficulties encountered by social services in trying to drag these people back from the edge were then doubled by the disappearance (presumed suicide) of Manic Street Preachers guitarist Richey James in 1995. Awkward teenagers had quickly adopted James, a beautiful and sensitive boy, as an icon. And if anything, James had spelled out his feelings in lyrics even more bleak than Cobain's:

"Scratch my leg with a rusty nail, sadly it heals. Colour my hair but the dye grows out. I can't seem to stay a fixed ideal, childhood pictures redeem, clean and so serene. See myself without ruining lines, whole days throwing sticks into streams. I have crawled so far sideways I recognise dim traces of creation. I wanna die, die in the summertime."

From 'Die In The Summertime', 1994.

Reading these words today makes it hard to believe that more people didn't see Richey's disappearance coming. Here was a man who had already slashed his wrists with a slogan, 'for real', in an attempt to convince a sceptical journalist of the purity of his art. But again as Camus said: "Men are never convinced of your reasons, of your sincerity, of the seriousness of your sufferings, except by your death." Especially when you're in the business of pop music.

While two such high profile suicides defined the dark side of pop in the nineties, this was not a new phenomenon amongst musicians. Stability - mental or otherwise - is very rarely a word associated with those of a musical bent. Take Roy Buchanan, a shy man never blessed with the worldliness that makes it that much easier to make your way in this life. A guitarist of considerable skill, his best-known work was his solo on the seminal 'Green Onions'. Buchanan was never comfortable in the limelight, though, and was deeply disturbed by the apparent contradiction between his nature and his need for performance. He made several unsuccessful attempts at suicide and finally hanged himself in a police cell after being arrested and charged with drunk driving. He was 47.

Alienation from society and an inability to cope have often been the cornerstones of the best music. The agony that the artists feel in expressing these feelings results in music of quite incredible authenticity and power. Stylistically varied and eclectic, the feeling of 'otherness' is what has bound many of our greatest musical talents. Sadly for many of these artists, it all simply becomes too much to cope with and suicide seems the logical answer. "At this moment I wish I were dead," said Joy Division singer Ian Curtis in his suicide note before he was found hanged in his hometown of Macclesfield on 18th May 1980. "I just can't cope anymore." Joy Division's music expressed this feeling of disassociation perfectly. With a deliberately downbeat musical feel linked to Curtis' monotone vocals and live interpretations bordering on the psychotic, the Manchester band's bleak musical landscape hinted all too presciently at the singer's inner struggle. As is so often the case, though, nobody sensed that Curtis' art could soon be reflected in his life and death at the age of 23.

Six years prior to Curtis' death the English music scene had lost another displaced artist in Nick Drake. Not as commercially revered as Joy

and instruments playing, knowing that the people who made the sounds have taken their own lives, brings on an incredible sense of pathos. And surely no suicides are more tragic than those of Badfinger members Tom Evans and Pete Ham. Famous for writing Nilsson's massive hit 'Without You', Ham hanged himself on 23rd April 1975 at the tender age of 27; depressed and confused by a music business which seemed to him fickle and uncaring. Eight years later his writing partner Evans also hanged himself at his home in Surrey, again brought to the point of despair by financial problems. The words to 'Without You' echoed both musicians' feelings only too clearly. 'I can't live, I can't live any more'.

The nihilistic feelings expressed in heartbreaking form by Badfinger found a far more violent outlet in the punk rock of the late '70s. Naturally the bleak worldview propagated in the songs of artists like The Clash and The Sex Pistols resulted in some punks taking reckless chances with their lives. Darby Crash, lead singer with LA punks The Germs, killed himself in 1980 with a lethal dose of heroin as part of a bizarre suicide pact with his girlfriend. It was

Badfinger, the tragedy-friendly Tom Evans (second from left) and Pete Ham (behind)

IAN CURTIS
18 – 5 – 80
LOVE WILL TEAR
US APART

Division and altogether more mellow and contemplative in approach, Drake was an unsung hero of the melancholic. His simple acoustic style sounded ethereal, other-worldy and fragile, the work of a man who was unsure of himself and his place in the world. On 25th November 1974 Drake was found dead in his bedroom, the coroner returned a verdict of suicide. In the sleeve notes to 'Way To Blue', a 1994 introduction to his work, Joe Boyd insists, however, that Drake died from "an accidental overdose of anti-depressants". Whatever the cause of death, Drake's inner isolation seems to have had a debilitating effect on him.

Such tragedies seem to have a greater resonance when musicians are involved. The eeriness of hearing voices singing

supposedly a tribute to his idol Sid Vicious of The Sex Pistols, who'd overdosed on the drug himself a year earlier. In typically chaotic punk fashion the whole event went badly wrong. The girlfriend survived and the big gesture made little impact as John Lennon was killed the following day.

Across the years, across the styles, musical suicides have occurred with depressing regularity. From clean-cut doo wop singer Del Shannon, who blew his brains out with a rifle in February of 1990, to E. William Tucker of industrial bands Ministry and Pigface, who slit his own throat in May, 1999, musicians have always been taken their own lives. Richard Manuel of The Band, John Spence of ska punk act No Doubt, Wendy O'Williams of shock punk band The Plasmatics, Chris Acland of indie band Lush, Alan Wilson of '60s stars Canned Heat, Paul Williamson of soul legends The Temptations, Screaming Lord Sutch, Paul Williams of The Temptations, Billy McKenzie of The Associates, Rozz Williams of gothic rock band Christian Death, Vincent Crane of British rock band Atomic Rooster and even Rob Pilatus from disgraced pop group Milli Vanilli. None of these talents seemed to find fulfilment in their art and all ended their lives by their own hands.

Of course the most notorious rock suicide of

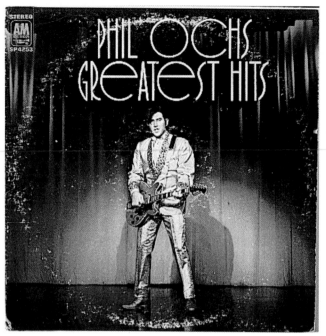

recent times has to be the death of INXS singer Michael Hutchence in 1997. Hutchence's girlfriend Paula Yates claims the Australian's death was a bizarre accident, the result of a sexual adventure gone wrong. However the evidence suggests - he was found hanged by a belt on the door of his room at Sydney's Ritz Carlton hotel - he took his own life.

A battle against addiction led to the death of Gin Blossoms songwriter and guitarist Doug Hopkins at the age of 32. Hopkins had a long-

standing history of alcoholism and had suffered from severe bouts of depression. In April 1992 he was removed from the band after his behaviour deteriorated, but after attempting to detox at a clinic in Phoenix, Arizona, Hopkins shot himself on 5th December 1993.

Somebody once gave the perfect description of a suicide victim when they explained that these people were simply too sensitive for this world, then proceeded to expand: "They just had one layer of skin too few". This seems to be the most poignant way of understanding our musical suicides. And if one tragedy were to sum up this notion in its entirety it would have to be the death of little-known '60s troubadour Phil Ochs, who was found hanged at his sister's home on 7th April 1976 aged 35. Ochs was a man who seemed to feel the pain of others even than he felt any of his own suffering. With songs like 'All The News That's Fit To Sing' and 'I Ain't Marching Anymore' bursting at the seams with political comment and an agenda which included "a comment on the spiritual decline of America", Ochs was constantly railing against the injustice he saw everywhere in the world. But his deep concern for the plight of others often obscured his own problems. His voice was permanently scarred after he was attacked and strangled during an African tour, he suffered acute attacks of writer's block and was eventually dragged down by schizophrenia. Unable to cope any more with his one layer too few of skin, he finally succumbed to suicide.

If there is anything good to be taken out of such a tragic series of deaths, though, then it has to be in the suicide of 28-year-old Texan bassist Sims Ellison. A member of little-known metal band Pariah, Ellison shot himself in his Austin apartment. His suicide, however, so shocked his former manager Wayne Nagle, that he immediately founded the SIMS Foundation, an organisation dedicated to helping suicidal musicians. Maybe there is light at the end of the tunnel.

"If anything in this life is certain, if history has taught us anything, it's that everyone can be killed."

Michael Corleone in The Godfather Part II.

IT'S A CATCH-ALL PHRASE, of course, but when people are described as dying "in mysterious circumstances" it's hard not to feel a certain sense of intrigue and, much as we might not like to admit it, excitement. And it's no surprise, of course, to discover that any number of musicians have died in mysterious circumstances, given the twilight world so many of them inhabit. Surely no death, however, could be more bizarre or mysterious than that of singer Bobby Fuller. Born in Baytown, Texas in 1943, the leader of The Bobby Fuller Four hit the American Top 10 in January of 1966 with a cover of The Crickets' 'I Fought The Law'. They followed this success with another Top 10 hit, a Buddy Holly song titled 'Love's Made A Fool Of You', but Fuller quit the group in June of 1966 after a disagreement with a record company boss over future releases. Within a month 22-year-old Fuller's body was found in his car in the garage of his Hollywood apartment. He had died from asphyxiation after being forced to inhale gasoline. No one was ever arrested for the murder, but rumours persist to this day that Fuller was dating a woman who was also involved with a Los Angeles gangster who took exception to the relationship.

Larry Williams was one of the earliest rock 'n' roll stars and his recordings for the Specialty label were a major influence on John Lennon. In fact The Beatles actually covered one of Williams' hits, 'Dizzy Miss Lizzy', as well as 'Slow Down' and 'Bad Boy'. But Williams' personal life was troubled. He was arrested for possession of drugs in 1959 and went to jail, causing Specialty to drop him from their roster. Royalties from The Beatles recordings gave him an income for the rest of his life while he tried his hand at producing, the best known of his work being two albums for Little Richard. Williams' colourful life continued all the while, with rumours flying around that he was both a burglar and a pimp. Williams died on 2nd January 1980 from a gunshot wound at his Los Angeles home. It was ruled that he had committed suicide, but many of Williams' friends and acquaintances insisted a crime syndicate had murdered him.

Robert Johnson has been hailed by many as the finest exponent of blues guitar playing ever and his wild lifestyle fitted the stereotypical image of all blues players. His liking for the ladies was notorious. On one riotous evening it seemed that Johnson was coming on to the owner's wife just a little too strongly and in a fit of jealousy the story goes that the owner poured strychnine into a bottle of whiskey Johnson was drinking. Despite fighting the poison, within three days Johnson was dead. Johnson was buried in Mississippi and Eric Clapton has since claimed "I have never found anything more deeply soulful than Robert Johnson."

Equally as influential as Johnson in his chosen musical field was Jamaican trombonist and songwriter Don Drummond. As leader of The Skatalites he pioneered the ska sound. Drummond was, however, a complex character, mentally unbalanced and with a turbulent private life. His girlfriend, Marguerite Mahfood, was an exotic dancer who deliberately gave him the wrong medicine on New Year's Eve 1964 to debilitate him so she could go out dancing. Drummond slept right through till the next morning. When Mahfood arrived home Drummond was waiting for her and stabbed her in the neck. She died from her injuries and Drummond was remanded in an asylum. On May 6th, 1969 Drummond died and while the official explanation was that he had taken his own life, there was no autopsy. The rumour mill went into overdrive and included allegations that the government had targeted him and that mobsters, who had been friendly with Mahfood, had carried out a hit.

440lb Darren Robinson of rap act The Fat Boys, meanwhile, died of a heart attack after simply falling off his chair while performing at home in New York in 1995. He was just 28. The demise of Angus MacLise, original drummer with The Velvet Underground was also truly bizarre. MacLise died in Nepal in 1979 and he's surely the only rock star to die of malnutrition.

Jud Strunk, a banjo player from New York state finally met his maker eight years after his one hit, 'Daisy A Day', when he crashed the World War II vintage plane he'd just bought in Maine. American DJ Vik Venus, meanwhile, had a minor novelty hit in 1969 with 'Moonflight', but died in 1994 whilst actually on air at WHLI on Long Island, New York.

Possibly the most bizarre death of them all, though is that of The Singing Nun. Sister Luc-Gabrielle was a Belgian nun of the Fichermont Monastery, who had had a surprise hit in the US with a single titled 'Dominique' in the early '60s. She gave all the profits of her work to help various missionary projects, but eventually left the Dominican order in 1966. Just under 20 years later, in April 1985, Jeanine Deckers as she was then known, committed suicide in a pact with her female companion Annie Pescher in Wavre, Belgium. The two women had been depressed and killed themselves with a combination of barbiturates and alcohol.

1929–1959

Boy, when you are dead, they really fix you up. I hope to hell when I do die somebody has sense enough to just dump me in the river or something. Anything except sticking me in a goddam cemetery. People coming and putting a bunch of flowers on your stomach on Sunday and all that crap. Who wants flowers when you are dead? Nobody. **J.D. Salinger**

WAY BACK since 1929, the people who made rock 'n' roll, blues, soul and pop have been exiting stage left, leaving the world to mourn and marketing execs to remake and remodel their posthumous career.

What a long strange, sad and super-real trip it's been. Let's walk down those streets of sorrow and think about who took the last train home.

1929

Blind Lemon Jefferson

The blues legend died in December 1929 from exposure following a heart attack. Legend has it that he froze to death on the streets of Chicago. A more likely story is that he died in his car of a heart attack and was abandoned by his driver. Jefferson was a highly influential rural blues singer who inspired everyone from BB King and Jerry Lee Lewis through to Bob Dylan.

Read about it in books: "If it hadn't been for his immediate and widespread success, there might never have been the rush to record men with guitars." From The Blues From Robert Johnson To Robert Cray by Tony Russell

Remember me this way: 'See That My Grave Is Kept Clean' covered by Bob Dylan on his debut album.

1933

JIMMIE RODGERS

Rogers died on May 26th from TB. He was hailed as 'The Singing Brakeman' and developed a wandering style of storytelling country blues. Rodgers recorded distinctive songs such as 'Blue Yodel' and 'Waitin' For A Train', which epitomised his bohemian, railroad-chugging lifestyle.

Read it on the internet: Jimmie Rodgers was the first figure inducted into the Country Music Hall of Fame and is fondly referred to as the "Father of Country Music". Yet his combination of Blues and hillbilly styles made him a true fore-

bear of rock 'n' roll. Born in Meridian, Mississippi, in 1897, Rodgers worked on the railroad from the age of 14, learning the blues from black workers on his crew. At 24, he contracted tuberculosis and was forced to quit his job. fromThe Rock and Roll Hall of Fame web site at **www.rockhall.com**

Read it on record sleeves: *Jimmie Rodgers is certainly the patron saint of country music. Jimmie's innovations not only gave America a new form of music, but also established the singer in the select roster of all-time international greats.*
Rodgers' short but fruitful life began in 1897, but his major musical contribution did not get under way until the summer of 1927 when he made his first recordings. In the less than six years before his death from tuberculosis, Rodgers had recorded a legacy of 113 songs, most of them original compositions. He had given the south its own musical form.
JB Walter, RCA, 1961from the sleeve of 'Jimmie The Kid'

STEVE EARLE: "Jimmie was the classic vagabond folkie and I really thank Bob Dylan for asking me to play one of his songs."

Remember me this way: The Bob Dylan-collated tribute album which snook out on Bluebird/Sony in 1997 featuring covers by Bob, Steve et al.

1937

BESSIE SMITH

Died September 26th, she bled to death after a car accident. Legend has it that she was not admitted to the local whites-only hospital. Dubbed The Queen of the Blues, she recorded 'Nobody Knows You When You're Down And Out', 'Tain't Nobody's Business If I Do' and a host of other life-buffeted ballads.

Read it on record sleeves: *In her heyday in the record business, Bessie was able to command the very respectable figure of a thousand dollars a session at which four sides were made. That was some way from her humbler days in 1933. Then, the best she could get was a flat fifty a side, and even at that their sales at that time did not justify the expense.*
From the sleeve of 'Bessie Smith. The World's Greatest Blues Singer'

Read about it in books: *No-one would call Bessie Smith a versatile singer yet she tackled a wide range of material with aplomb. Her most poignant memorial apart from her recordings is the short film drama St Louis Blues, in which she sings a magnificent extended version of that most famous song.*
From The Blues From Robert Johnson To Robert Cray by Tony Russell

Remember me this way: On the John Hammond-masterminded series of double albums featuring her '20s material.

ROBERT JOHNSON

Allegedly with a hellhound on his trail, Robert Johnson died August 16th, 1938. A well-known womaniser, he was poisoned with strychnine-laced whiskey by a jealous husband. Many favour the more exciting story that Johnson had sold his soul to the devil in exchange for his song-writing prowess (as you do.) Either way Johnson was a highly influential Bluesman whose 'Stones In My Passway' and 'Travelling Riverside Blues' impressed Led Zeppelin just a tad.

READ IT IN THE PRESS:

First hand reports on Johnson were sketchy at best but the sheer speed of his improvement on the guitar is the thing that harks back to this mystical encounter with the devil. Son House and Willie Brown encountered a rejuvenated Johnson toting an impressive guitar style a mere three months after his performance was less than not very good. The duo instantly agreed that "Little Robert done sold his soul to the devil."

The myth is, of course, further enhanced by Johnson's lyrics to 'Me And The Devil', 'Malted Milk' and 'Hellhound On My Trail', all of which has the singer possessed from the dark side.
Charles Shaar Murray in Q Magazine, 1990

ROBERT PLANT: "When we were on tour in Memphis, I rented a car and drove down to Mississippi, to Fryers Point, as in the song. It was a very strange place, very African, very other-worldly. Sleepy, woodsmoke fires, big trees all around, burnt-out hotels, deserted gas stations..."
IAN ANDERSON: "It took some serious listening before I got to the essence of Robert Johnson, the starkness is quite scary. And when you start to read things about the guy, it puts a lot of things into perspective."
KEITH RICHARDS: "Brian Jones had his first album and that's where I heard him first. I went round to Brian's crash pad - he only had a chair and a record player - and he put it on. It was just astounding stuff."
ERIC CLAPTON: "I have never heard anything more deeply soulful."
ROBERT CRAY: "For straight blues you've got to

go back to Robert Johnson. The cat put out so much emotion singing and playing guitar; he sounds like three people. He was just incredible."
ERIC CLAPTON: "When I first heard him it struck me that he wasn't playing for an audience at all. At first I found it almost too painful, but then after about six months I started listening and then I didn't listen to anything else."
KEITH RICHARDS: "You want to know how good the blues can get? Well this is it."
Those Johnson covers and disciples in full: 'Crossroads' - Cream. 'Four Till Late' - Cream. 'Steady Rollin' Man' - Eric Clapton. 'Love In Vain' - The Rolling Stones. 'Stop Breakin' Down' - The Rolling Stones. 'Come On In My Kitchen' - Mick Jagger.

'Walkin' Blues - The Butterfield Blues Band and Taj Mahal. '32-30 Blues' - Johnny Winter. 'Hellhound On My Trail' - Fleetwood Mac. 'Dust My Broom' - Elmore James. 'Kind Hearted Woman' - Muddy Waters. 'Sweet Home Chicago' - Junior Parker. 'Terraplane Blues' - John Lee Hooker and Roy Rogers.
Remember me this way: Few tracks exist but, amazingly, film footage of the legend was discovered in 1998. If in doubt revert to the Sony Legacy box set.

MA RAINEY

Died December 22nd, aged 52, of a heart attack. Ma Rainey was known as the 'Mother Of The Blues' but her vocal style and her touring tent shows covered all manner of musical styles. She recorded 'Broken Hearted Blues' and most famously 'See See Rider' and along the way she'd found plenty of time to inspire Bessie Smith. However Rainey's repertoire extended far and wide and included typical 1920's and '30s ballads like 'Tough Luck Blues', 'Leavin' This Morning', Stack O'Lee, 'Trust No Man', 'Dead Drunk Blues' and the immortal 'Shave 'Em Dry Blues'.
Remember me this way: Ma Rainey's originals or Mitch Ryder's frenetic take on 'CC Rider'.

JELLY ROLL MORTON

Died July 10th, but not before mixing his early jazz roots into primal rock 'n' roll blues and inspiring a gaggle of early hybrid musicians into the bargain. Morton recorded the brooding 'Mournful Serenade' but is renowned for his stylish and distinctive piano rolls and his customised, full-blooded and expertly-broiled New Orleans' stew, which took in elements of blues, opera, jazz, folk and brass band music.
Remember me this way: Read all about it in folklorist Alan Lomax's book Mister Jelly Roll.

1941

Fats Waller

Died December 15th of pneumonia. Fats Waller added a swing to the blues and he also took time to infuse his music with a distinctive sense of humour. Along the way he backed Bessie Smith and penned the much-covered 'Ain't Misbehavin' as well as the radio perennial 'I'm Gonna Sit Right Down And Right Myself A Letter'.

Remember me this way: That letter song covered by the Frank Sinatra is an epistle from above.

1947

BLIND WILLIE JOHNSON

Died of pneumonia after adding a touch of spiritualism and gospel soul to the blues. Johnson emoted the confessional 'Lord, I Just Can't Keep From Cryin' and was renowned for his distinctive Hawaiian-style guitar playing.

Remember me this way: Seek out The Grateful Dead's version of 'Let Your Light Shine On Me' or trek back to the originals.

1948

SONNY BOY WILLIAMSON

John Lee 'Sonny Boy' Williamson died in a mugging on June 1st. The country blues legend from Jackson, Tennessee recorded 'Good Morning Little School Girl' which became a staple of the UK blues boom of the '60s.

Remember me this way: Hanging around at the school gates.

1949

LEADBELLY

Died December 6th of lateral sclerosis. The Louisiana folk and blues player is revered for his ballad-style and quasi-spiritual lyrics. Born in 1888 (although a variety of sources offer many different dates), Leadbelly was a giant of a man, fond of women, booze and fighting. Legend has it he sang his way out of jail on more than one occasion and his legacy of tunes - whether traditional arrangements or self-penned it's unknown, he was never keen to give clues - is more than impressive. The roster includes 'Goodnight Irene', 'Cotton Fields', 'Rock Island Line' and 'Midnight Special', all of which were given a wider audience when he teamed up with field recordist John Lomax. From there Leadbelly moved through society - convict garb and all, introducing a new style of music to America.

Read it on record sleeves:

Huddie Ledbetter, or to give him the name by which the world knows and reveres him - Leadbelly - was born in Louisiana somewhere around 1885. His career never lacked drama or excitement from his early days in Texas when he was jailed for murder until the later and more tranquil years when he became established as one of the great folk singers of America. His voice has been recorded and preserved in the Library Of Congress. A great deal of the success and fame of Leadbelly is directly attributed to John and Alan Lomax. It was these two men and their efforts to find and preserve the great folk song tradition of America that established Leadbelly as one of the great originals of all time.

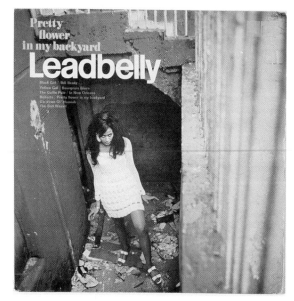

Art and Sound, London, 1965 from the sleeve of 'Pretty Flower In My Backyard.'

Remember me this way: His mid-'30s legacy, recently re-issued through Capitol, or countless covers of those old back porch serenades.

1953

HANK WILLIAMS

Died January 1st of a heart attack following endless touring, drinking and general debauchery. The legendary travelling country troubadour is justly idolised for his succinct writing style and his unique genre-straddling delivery. Copied by every rock star from Elvis on.

He was born Hiram Williams on the September 17, 1923, in Georgiana, Alabama and died in Virginia. A true musical pioneer who numerous sources and, indeed no less an expert than the Rock 'n' Roll Hall Of Fame claim, "drank too much, took drugs, played with guns, destroyed hotel rooms, threw money out of windows and permanently lived in conflict." Sound familiar? On the night of his death, Williams was in the company of a hired 18-year-old driver, Charles Carr, who was pulled over by the police for running a red light. The police officer looked in the back of the car and saw Williams looking all but

29 COUNTRY & WESTERN SINGER, 1923-1953

USA

HANK WILLIAMS

dead and asked if the singer was OK. Carr reassured the officer and then drove on, but five hours later, to Carr's surprise, the policeman was proven right. The whisky bottle-hugging Williams had died due to a "severe heart attack with haemorrhage" in which alcohol and pills had certainly played their part.

Williams' trademark songs of everyday desolation and despair were just too close to home. The man who'd taught latter day rock stars to behave badly was, according to Paul Du Noyer writing in Q Magazine, "the Expert's Expert in things debauched. In fact, rarely had somebody sung of wild times and remorse with such an obvious commitment to first hand research."

When Williams died, his then-current single release, 'I'll Never Get Out Of This World Alive' was propelled to the top of the charts. On the poster for the gig he was travelling to when he died, it said: "If the Good Lord's willing, and the creek don't rise, I'll see you at the Canton Memorial Auditorium." He never made it.

Read it on record sleeves: *Hank Williams wrote songs that everyone can feel and understand. Each and every one tells a story of basic life - of good times and bad, of love and hate, of sin and salvation. He sang them simply, soulfully, and with a sincerity that is quite uncommon. He drove himself too hard toward the end, constantly travelling and performing, trying to set down the pain and infrequent happiness of his life in song.*
Burt Korall, MGM Records from the sleeve of 'Let Me Sing A Blue Song.'

TONY BENNETT (who covered Williams' 'Cold Cold Heart'): "It was the first country song ever to be performed with strings and the first to become an international hit. Within two weeks it had sold two million copies. Hank Williams loved the royalties but he had a very strange way of thanking me for its success. He called me up and said: 'What's the idea of ruining my song?'."

T-BONE BURNETT: "More than anything, I wanted to be Hank Williams."

HANK SAID: "You got to have smelt a lot of mule manure before you can sing like a hillbilly."

The Classic Tunes: 'Your Cheatin' Heart', 'I'm So Lonesome I Could Cry', 'Kaw-Liga', 'Weary Blues From Waitin', 'Take These Chains From My Heart', 'Settin' The Woods On Fire', 'I'm Sorry For You My Friend', 'You Win Again', etc, etc.

Remember me this way: Road weary, gaunt but always soulful.

1954

JOHNNY ACE

Died December 25th aged just 25 after a drunken bout of one-upmanship resulted in an unfortunate Russian Roulette Christmas present. Ace was known for his drunken bouts of gunplay. His demise was witnessed first hand by Big Mama Thornton.

Remember me this way: With the R&B chart toppers 'My Song' and 'The Clock' and as a crazed, gun-totin' drunk.

1955

CHARLIE PARKER

Died March 12th after years of drugs and alcohol had decimated his internal organs. He took the rock 'n' roll lifestyle torch from Hank Williams. The free-form saxophonist and bandleader created beatnik cool and took body experimentation and mind-mangling to his own personal extremes.

Read it on record sleeves: *Attempts at technical analysis of the music cannot suffice to explain Parker's greatness. A vital dimension is added by the vigour and beauty of his sound, thrusting and soaring over the rhythm, expressing the extremes of emotion with a very special, personal feel.*

Michael Walters, 1966 from the sleeve of 'Ornithology'.

Remember me this way: The film 'Bird' is a good place to start, then there are the albums, the spoons and the substances.

1958

BIG BILL BROONZY

Died August 15th from cancer. Mississippi-born roots performer, who mixed folk, blues and ragtime to create a distinctive storytelling style. A prolific songwriter Broonzy had penned over

350 tunes by the time of his death.

Read about it in books: "After he died, they went on singing his songs, and Muddy Waters remembered him with an affectionate album of his best-loved numbers, 'Muddy Waters Sings Big Bill'. From The Blues From Robert Johnson To Robert Cray by Tony Russell

Remember me this way: The 'missing link' between Robert Johnson's dark delta groove and the Chicago Blues sound.

1959

LARRY PALUMBO

Died after his parachute failed to open during a routine paratrooper training exercise. Palumbo had been drafted into the services cutting short his pop career as a member of The Earls. The Earls hit the charts with their multi-part harmony on the doo-wop meets rock 'n' roll standard 'Remember Then'.

Remember me this way: Not remembering the golden

rules of parachuting but being worshiped by Sha Na Na ten years later.

BUDDY HOLLY

Died February 3rd in a plane crash. Holly had taken the flight in order to beat a long haul drive in icy conditions during a coast-to-coast US tour. The Texan singer-songwriter had introduced uptempo rhythm to a ballad-based repertoire, before going on to lushly-orchestrate his romantic storytelling.

Buddy was born Charles Hardin Holley in Lubbock, Texas on September 7, 1936. His early demos got him a deal with Decca and in 1957, he put together The Crickets with Jerry Allison, Niki Sullivan and Joe Mauldin. He left the band a year later following huge commercial success. Within five months, aged just 22, he was killed in a plane crash along with The Big Bopper and Ricthie Valens.

All three had been on a Winter Dance Party tour. Since his death his songs have been covered by Mud, Nick Berry, Peter And Gordon, The Rolling Stones, Andy Williams, The Everly Brothers, Don McLean, Santana and Elvis Presley.

Read about it in the press:

Buddy Holly and two more of America's top rock 'n' roll stars were killed in a plane crash on their way to a concert in the early hours of the morning of February 3. Earlier Holly, the Big Bopper and Ritchie Valens had entertained over 1,000 teenagers at the Surf Ballroom in Clear Lake, Iowa, then chartered a flight to take them to their next concert in Moorhead, Minnesota.

Three hours after the dance had finished, three of the top names on the show were dead, along with the pilot who was flying them. The others on the bill, The Platters and Dion, had travelled separately. The plane appeared to have come down in a heavy snowstorm, scraping along the ground before bouncing and skidding for 200 yards before coming to a halt. UPI

DAVE BRUBECK: "He knew as much about modern jazz as he did about what was happening in rock and blues and country. I was shattered by

'LADY DAY'

BILLIE HOLIDAY

They can't take that away from me
Swing brother swing
I can't get started
Do nothing till you hear from me
Billie's blues
I cover the waterfront
The man I love
Do you know what it means to miss New Orleans
Farewell to Storyville
The blues are brewing

Died July 17th. Renowned blues/jazz wailer who's ragged career was reflected in semi-auto-biographical song. From teen belter to night-club mainstay and ex-con, her life was littered with drugs and the joys of social collapse amid intense racial tension.

Read it on record sleeves: *All too often tragedy and genius seem to go hand in hand in the world of jazz. It may be the sensibility to create a certain kind of musical beauty feels too acutely the ills of the universe to come to terms with them. Whatever the reason, the lives of many of the most important figures in jazz make a sad, sorry contrast beside their musical achievements. The daughter of teenage parents who soon separated and, while her mother served a jail sentence for being a call girl, Billie became a singer and was discovered by John Hammond. Records, exacting tours and drug addiction led to brushes with the law which deprived her of a cabaret licence and limited her performances in later years. Her problems, though, probably fuelled her greatest performances.*
From the sleeve of 'Lady Day'

FRED DELLAR (journalist): "I saw her in the tiny Flamingo Club in London and she was hypnotic. Being at the end of her career her voice was quite cracked but she used that to squeeze every bit of emotion out of it."

Thge Classic Tunes: 'This Year's Kisses', 'I Must Have That Man', 'Me, Myself And I', 'Strange Fruit', 'God Bless The Child', 'Lover Man', 'Ain't Nobody's Business', 'Just One Of Those Things', 'One For My Baby' and a whole lot more.

Remember me this way: The not hugely realistic portrayal of Holliday by Diana Ross in Lady Sings The Blues or the recorded library? Probably the latter.

BLIND WILLIE MCTELL

Died August 19th of a cerebral haemorrhage. Georgian blues player whose southern roots style greatly impressed later electric rock icons. Wrote and released the awesome 'Statesboro Blues', which was later grunged and jammed by The Allman Brothers.

Remember me this way: His guitar style and the lamentable gambling ballad 'Dying Crapshooter Blues'.

the news of his death, it's just a pity that we never got the opportunity to record something together."

Jim Newcombe (fan): "Buddy Holly's voice was as raucous as the music. Make no bones about it (live), Holly was a rocker. He set out to create the same excitement as Elvis but not by using sex appeal. He used good old foot stomping rock 'n' roll. Once he was gone you were drained, left breathless."

Remember me this way: The movie, the stage play, the countless posthumous recordings and the legacy that spins back to 'Peggy Sue', 'That'll Be The Day', 'Not Fade Away' and so on and so forth.

RITCHIE VALENS

Died February 3rd in the same plane crash as Buddy Holly and The Big Bopper. He sang the rock 'n' roll love poem 'Donna' and the rousing Mexicala fling 'La Bamba'.

Remember me this way: Immortalised in the so-so film *La Bamba* or just reeling with the title track.

THE BIG BOPPER

Died February 3rd in the same plane crash as Buddy Holly and Ritchie Valens, aged 28. A master of deep-throated soul crooning, he charted with the incomparable 'Chantilly Lace', but never got the chance to capitalise on its huge international success.

Remember me this way: "Will I what? Oooh, baby, you know what I like."

BILLIE HOLIDAY

1960s

It is not that I do not want to die, I just do not want to be there when it happens. **Woody Allen**

1960

EDDIE COCHRAN

Died April 17th of severe brain injuries received in a car accident. A classic rock 'n' roll icon who brought country and blues to the genre, Cochran produced the original and definitive versions of 'Summertime Blues', 'Somethin' Else' and 'C'mon Everybody', all ironically covered much later by Sid Vicious.

Cochran was born on October 3, 1938, in Minnesota and died at the age of just 21 having topped the charts once. He's now regarded as one of the key rock 'n' roll stylists. Cochran's career went ballistic after his appearance in the teen flick The Girl Can't Help It; where he performed 'Twenty Flight Rock'. His youthful good looks ensured a strong female following and the Liberty label soon snapped him up.

Cochran was killed in Chippenham, Wiltshire, when the taxi he was travelling in crashed. Fellow passenger Gene Vincent was also badly injured, as was Cochran's girlfriend Sharon Sheeley.

Read it on record sleeves: *As plucky and good-natured as he may have been, there was also a dark, gloomy side to this Byronic young man. At what turned out to be his last session, the owner of the Freedom label bawled him out for turning up late. Cochran turned to him and said, 'Who cares?'*
From the sleeve of 'Legends of the 20th Century'

Read it on the internet: Though he died young at 21, Eddie Cochran left a lasting mark on rock 'n' roll as a pioneer who helped map out the territory with such definitive songs as 'C'mon Everybody', 'Something Else', 'Twenty Flight Rock' and 'Summertime Blues'. Cochran epitomised the sound and the stance of the Fifties-bred rebel rocker.
From the Rock and Roll Hall of Fame site: www.rockhall.com

Read it in the press:
EDDIE COCHRAN KILLED, VINCENT INJURED IN TAXI CRASH

Following a concert at the Bristol Hippodrome, Eddie Cochran, Gene Vincent, Sharon Sheeley (Cochran's fiancee) and tour manager Patrick

Thompkins set off for London in a Ford Consul taxi driven by a 19-year-old youth. Cochran was in a hurry, as he was due to fly back to America from Heathrow airport the next afternoon.

Averaging 70mph, the taxi reached Chippenham, Wiltshire at midnight. However, the driver had lost his sense of direction and control of the vehicle. As he emerged from beneath a railway viaduct, the car hit the curb, careering 150 yards before crashing into a concrete lampstand.

The impact threw Cochran upwards against the car roof and then through the door and on to the road. Gene Vincent suffered a fractured collarbone and Sheeley back injuries, while Tompkins and the driver remained unhurt. At 4pm Easter Sunday, 16 hours after the accident, Eddie Cochran died as a result of severe brain lacerations. NME
Remember me this way: Without added viciousness.

JOHNNY HORTON

Died November 5th in a car crash. The 33-year-old country singer charted with 'Battle Of New Orleans'.
Remember me this way: His wife said: "Johnny was convinced he was going to die, he always talked about it. He was terrified he was going to die in a plane crash and wouldn't fly anywhere."

1961

'CHARLIE' SHIVERS

Unfulfilled Rockabilly guitarist, who chose civil engineering over a music career. Shivers died on April 7th when a methane gas explosion destroyed his farmhouse near Scotsville, Kentucky.
Remember me this way: Scotty Moore: "If Charlie had decided to give up building bridges and concentrated on playing the guitar we'd all be looking for new jobs."

CISCO HOUSTON

Died April 29th of cancer. Houston was a Woody Guthrie sidekick who straddled the line between '50s pop music and country 'n' western songsmithery. Inspired the likes of pop folkies The Kingston Trio.
Remember me this way: With Woody singing 'Cowboy Songs'.

1962

STUART SUTCLIFFE

Died March 10th of cerebral paralysis. Sutcliffe was the original bass player in the Beatles, his life story inspired the film Backbeat. Sutcliffe was a big mate of John's, a painter and a seminal part of the Fab Four legend. His creative crisis and love tangle in Germany, while the Fabs were playing in Hamburg, led to his departure from the group.

Read it in the press:
EX-BEATLE SUTCLIFFE DIES

Following a brain haemorrhage the previous day, former Beatles bassist Stuart Sutcliffe died, aged 21, in the arms of his German fiancee, photographer Astrid Kirchherr, in the back of an ambulance carrying him to a Hamburg hospital. Since leaving The Beatles last year, Sutcliffe had been studying art in his adopted city. Sutcliffe's untimely death may have been brought about as result of being savagely kicked in the head outside a Liverpool dance

hall two years earlier. NME

Remember me this way: Hey, Backbeat was prettygood, wasn't it? Some nice paintings too.

HENRY "RUBBERLEGS" WILLIAMS
Died October 17th of a heart attack. Blues player who recorded 'Bring It On Home'.
Remember me this way: The song aside (covered by Zep and Van no less) his nickname's great.

1963

PATSY CLINE
Cline died March 5th in a plane crash that also claimed the life of her manager Randy Hughes. The renowned downbeat country singer etched a place in the public's hearts with her distinctive ballad style on songs such as 'I Fall To Pieces' and 'Crazy'.

Read it in the press:
PATSY CLINE KILLED IN PLANE CRASH
Country music stars Patsy Cline (30), Lloyd 'Cowboy' Copas (50) and Harold 'Hawkshaw' Hawkins (41) all perished when the light aircraft carrying them home after a benefit concert in Kansas City crashed at Camden, Tennessee, on March 5.
Patsy Cline was best known for a string of hits that included 'Walking After Midnight' and 'I Fall To Pieces'. Only two years ago, Patsy Cline narrowly escaped death in a road crash. She was a passenger in her brother's car when it was involved in a collision in which a man in another vehicle was killed. She overcame her injuries and fought her way back to the top again, winning Billboard magazine's DJ poll last autumn as best female country vocalist. NME

LISA STANSFIELD: "The song 'Three Cigarettes In An Ashtray' is very corny, but I love the romanticism of it. I suppose it's from listening to things like this that I write mini-soap operas into my lyrics. A lot of her songs are very sad and when I'm in a really melancholy mood I punish myself and listen to the most depressing ones."
Remember me this way: Decidedly at very lo-speed, with a cocktail in hand, in the dark, with the curtains closed and, most significantly, alone.

Patsy Cline: The queen of Melancholy

ELMORE JAMES

Died May 24th of a heart attack. A distinctive blues player who inspired many early rock acts with his melody-driven Mississippi sound. He wrote the inspirational 'Shake Your Money Maker' (adopted by Fleetwood Mac) and 'Bleeding Heart' (Jimi Hendrix).

GEORGE THOROGOOD: "Some had the guitar but not the voice, some had the voice but not the guitar. Elmore got 'em together, better than anyone except for Robert Johnson."

Remember me this way: Don't forget the seminal 'The Sky Is Crying'.

DINAH WASHINGTON

Died December 14th from an overdose of sleeping pills and alcohol. Alabama-born soulstress who spanned jazz and pop. Had hits too, with 'What A Difference A Day Makes' and 'September In The Rain'.

Read it in the press:

QUEEN DINAH FOUND DEAD

The Queen of The Blues, Dinah Washington was found dead from an overdose of sleeping pills in her Detroit home on December 14. She was 39.

Born Ruth Jones, in Tuscaloosa, Alabama, August 29, 1924, this one-time singer with the Lionel Hampton Orchestra scored 36 chart entries between 1949 and 1963. However, her private life was textbook turmoil - just five months prior to her tragic death, Dinah Washington married her seventh husband, Detroit Lions' football star Dick 'Night Train' Lane. API

Remember me this way: Sunday afternoon, MOR radio and the beautiful sadness of 'September In The Rain'.

JIM REEVES

Died July 31st in a plane crash. However, his pop and country career lived on through endless posthumous releases scheduled by his wife. Famed for the perfectly balanced tearjerker 'I Love You Because'.

Read it in the press:

JIM REEVES KILLED IN AIR CRASH

Texas-born country music star Jim Reeves became the object of instant cult hysteria when he was killed, aged 40, in an air crash on July 31.

The light aircraft, which was carrying Reeves and his manager Dean Manuel from Arkansas back to Nashville, flew into heavy rain four miles from Berry Field Airport and plunged into thick foliage. NME

Remember me this way: It ain't over until long after the (fat?) lady has signed away all your royalties.

JOHNNY BURNETTE

Died August 1st. Burnette was an upbeat Tennessee rock 'n' roller who drowned in a boating accident. He unleashed the groovy finger-picking rockathon 'Train Kept A-Rollin'.

Read it in the press:

JOHNNY BURNETTE DROWNED

Johnny Burnette has drowned in a fishing accident, aged 30. Memphis-born Burnette - whose legendary Rock 'n' Roll Trio sides for Decca/Coral rank alongside Elvis's Sun sessions as essential seminal rockabilly classics - really only found international recognition once he joined Liberty Records, smoothed out his style and appearance, and charted with such songs as 'Dreamin' and 'You're Sixteen'. NME

Remember me this way: Not by his later pop hits such as 'You're Sixteen', but by the staccato rambling of 'Train Kept A Rollin'.

SAM COOKE

Died December 11th as the result of a brawl with a hotel manageress, who shot him before clubbing him to death - Cooke had entered her office in search of an escaping floozy.

Read it in the press:

SOUL PIONEER COOKE KILLED

The manageress of a Los Angeles motel shot soul singer Sam Cooke dead on December 10. Earlier that evening, Cooke picked up an Eurasian girl named Elisa Boyer in a bar and offered to drive her home. Instead Cooke drove to a hotel on South Figeroa, where he signed the register as Mr and Mrs Cooke.

It's alleged that, once inside the hotel room, Cooke began to rip the woman's clothes off. Then, when he went to the bathroom the woman fled from the room with both her clothes and Cooke's, and hid in a near-by phone booth, from where she called the police. Emerging from the motel room in a sports coat and shoes, Cooke kicked in the door of manageress Mrs Bertha Lee Franklin. She testified that Cooke punched her twice and that, in self-defence, she fired at him three times with a .22 revolver.

One shot wounded Cooke in the chest. However, this didn't stop his attack, so Franklin bludgeoned him with a stick. Sam Cooke was already dead by the time the police arrived at the scene.

Unproven rumours within the US music industry suggest that the Mafia had taken out a contract on the singer, who refused to throw in his lot with the criminal elements that control some of the record industry. NME

The Classic Tunes: 'You Send Me', 'Only Sixteen', 'Wonderful World', 'Chain Gang', Cupid', 'Twistin' The Night Away', 'Another Saturday Night' and 'Frankie And Johnny'.

Remember me this way: You'll never forget the silkily soulful voice that delivered 'You Send Me.'

NAT 'KING' COLE

Died February 15th from lung cancer. Cole was a jazz crooner who turned his hand to pop, soul and even country, he was famed for his comforting voice and his songbirding kin. Cole released a brace of single hits and produced some landmark jazz offerings, including the 1956 album 'After Midnight'.

Those hits in full: 'Somewhere Along The Way' (1952), 'Because You're Mine' (52), 'Faith Can Move Mountains' (1953), 'Pretend' (53), 'Can't I' (53), 'Mother Nature And Father Time', 'Tenderly' (1954), 'Smile' (54), 'Make Her Mine' (54), 'A Blossom Fell (1955), 'My One Sin' (55), 'Dreams Can Tell A Lie' (1956), 'Too Young To Go Steady' (56), 'Love Me As If There Were No Tomorrow' (56), 'When I Fall In Love (1957), 'When Rock 'n' Roll Came To Trinidad' (57), 'My Personal Possession' (57), 'Stardust' (57), 'You Made Me Love You' (1959), 'Midnight Flyer' (59), 'Time And The River' (1960), 'That's You' (60), 'Just As Much As Ever' (60), 'The World In My Arms' (1961), 'Let True Love Begin' (61),

'Brazilian Love Song' (1962), 'The Right Thing To Say' (62), 'Let There Be Love' (62), 'Ramblin' Rose' (62), 'Dear Lonely Hearts' (62).

Remember me this way: Not by daughter Natalie's computer-generated duet but by the soulful muse of 'Ramblin' Rose'.

Nat 'King' Cole: Natalie! No!

SPIKE JONES

Died May 1st of emphysema. Legendary Californian band leader who pastiched all musical genres and livened up the big band era. Jones paved the way for Zappa and the Bonzo Dog Doodah Band through his twisted rewriting of the classics.

Remember me this way: Strictly mad versions of 'Mairzy Doats', 'Kookie, Lend Me Your Comb' and 'The William Tell Overture'.

SONNY BOY WILLIAMSON II

The multi-named Sonny Boy Williamson II (aka Aleck 'Rice' Miller, aka Willie Williamson) died May 25th from TB. The Mississippi blues legend hit the emerging UK scene of the '60s and played with The Yardbirds and The Animals.

Remember me this way: Telling Eric Burdon how to sing the blues.

IRA LOUVIN

Died June 20th in a drunken car crash. Ira was the crazed half of The Louvin Brothers, prone to tantrums, womanising and alcoholism. He couldn't cope when his brother left the band. Louvin's public profile of cleaner than clean God-fearing homeliness couldn't have been further from his real life excess, which was typified when he smashed his mandolins on stage in a pre-Pete Townshend frenzy.

Read it on record sleeves: *With melodies as heartfelt as a deserted girl's tears, with words as simple and eloquent as a prayer at twilight. These songs tell of lovers parted by death and unfaithfulness, of those who pine for love in vain, of hearts that loved and were left with only memories. Ira and Charlie Louvin were born and raised on a farm near Henegar, Alabama. Their father was a banjo player and singer, and music was always important in their home. At an early age the brothers just started playing and singing together. In spite of their great success, Ira and Charlie Louvin retain their sincerity and humility, their love and understanding of the sort of ordinary people they grew up with.*
From the sleeve of 'Tragic Songs of Life', Capitol Records

Remember me this way: The immortal and often re-issued album 'Tragic Songs Of Life'.

BILL BLACK

Died October 21st after surgery to remove a brain tumour. Legendary bass guitarist who worked with Elvis Presley on the 1956 sessions and later formed The Bill Black Combo.

Read it in the press:
ELVIS BASSIST DIES
Bill Black the bass player who appeared on all of Elvis Presley's pre-army recordings and live dates, as well as in the films Loving You and Jailhouse Rock, died on October 21 in Memphis, aged 39. He had been ill for some time, and had undergone surgery at the Baptist Hospital on a brain tumour, from which he did not recover. NME

Remember me this way: For his Presleyian rumble on 'Heartbreak Hotel', 'Hound Dog' et al.

RICHARD FARINA

Died April 3rd in a motorcycle accident. The New York folkie married Joan Baez's sister Mimi, after a brief hiatus with singer Carolyn Hester. Farina was active on the Greenwich Village scene alongside Dylan. He wrote the beatnik-meets-hippie tome I've Been Down So Long It Looks Like Up To Me and recorded with Dylan under Bob's pseudonym of Blind Boy Grunt in the early '60s. Along with Ric Von Schmidt, the trio played at various folk clubs and recorded an impromptu set in a record shop in Soho. Farina had been influential on Dylan through his writing and the two were to meet up again when Joan and Bob and Mimi and Farina first decamped to Woodstock.

Remember me this way: His timeless but tinny live recording with Dylan in Dobell's jazz shop.

BOBBY FULLER

Died July 18th. The leader of The Bobby Fuller Four, who charted with 'I Fought The Law', was asphyxiated when forced to inhale gasoline.
RICK STONE (The Bobby Fuller Four's manager): "Bobby was there lying in the car, all beat up real bad and gasoline all over him and these little burns on him. The cops said the gas had burned his skin in the heat. I knew he was dead. God, it was awful."
BRYAN THOMAS (Del-Fi Records): "At the time of his death, Fuller had been keeping company with a young woman named "Melody" whose ex-boyfriend was a jealous club owner who was reported to be tied to the local crime syndicate. In the days just after the discovery of Fuller's body, band member Dalton Powell had been confronted by "three real mean-looking dudes" who had come to his apartment looking for the guitarist. Then, Randy Fuller and the band's road manager were nearly run off the road. Finally, a private investigator, hired by Fuller's parents, quit the case after a few days when he was shot at.

Remember me this way: 'I Fought The Law', reworked by The Clash or in its original format.

JOE AND EDDIE

The American close harmony duo died on August 9th after the car that Joe was driving went off the road. The duo had carved a niche for themselves with their inventive selection of material, which included a host of songs from the folk archive.

Read it on record sleeves: *Joe And Eddie have become firmly established in the firmament of musical stardom. And like 'Ole Man River', they just keep rollin' along. In every way they have what it takes ñ great voices, a completely unique and exciting style and irresistible personalities, vocally and visually.*
From the sleeve of 'Walkin' Down The Line'

Remember me this way: Crooning Dylan's 'All I Really Want To Do'.

JOHNNY KIDD

Died October 7th in a car accident. London's answer to the rock 'n' roll explosion, Kidd and his stripe-shirted Pirates, produced the standard 'Shakin' All Over'. Sporting swashbuckling gear and leather slacks Kidd specialised in haunting rock drama.
CLEM CATTINI (The Pirates): "Johnny Kidd was tremendously important to British rock 'n' roll. Cliff Richard, Billy Fury and Johnny were the pioneers of rock in this country. They put it on its feet and laid the foundations for what came afterwards."

Remember me this way: That vibrating Pirates' hit and The Who's version 'Live At Leeds'.

SMILEY LEWIS

Died October 7th from stomach cancer. Singer / songwriter and performer who penned 'I Hear You Knockin'. Sadly, though, Lewis never really lived up to his early promise.

Read about it in books:
In the 1950s Smiley Lewis was the unluckiest man in New Orleans. He hit on a formula for slow-rocking small-band numbers like 'The Bells Are Ringing' and 'I Hear You Knockin', only to have Fats Domino come up behind him with similar music more ingratiatingly delivered.
From The Blues From Robert Johnson To Robert Cray by Tony Russell

Remember me this way: Always knocking at that door.

MISSISSIPPI JOHN HURT

Died November 2nd of a heart attack after leading a life of God-fearing country blues playing. Along the way he managed to stay up late with his ode to Java 'Coffee Blues'.

Remember me this way: As featured on the 'Anthology Of American Folk Music' with 'Spike Diver Blues'.

JOE MEEK

Died February 3rd. Meek shot himself in his recording studio after shooting his landlady, following an all-night recording session and numerous strange spiritual happenings. Involved in the monumental production advances which resulted in hits for Johnny Leyton, Heinz and The Tornado's with 'Telstar', Meek was terminally unstable and more than a touch paranoid.

Read it on record sleeves:
When Joe Meek made the ultimate career move on the anniversary of Buddy Holly's death, February 3rd, 1967 - it's unlikely he would have expected to be revered as a legend some 25 years later. Let's face it, he'd been written off as an anachronism by his peers, hadn't registered a substantial hit in many months, and he'd seemed to have lost the plot completely - his paranoia and fantasies having escalated totally out of control.
RW Dopson and D Blackburn from the sleeve of the CD issue of 'I Hear A New World'

Read it in the press:
JOE MEEK GUN DEATH TRAGEDY
Joe Meek, the songwriter/producer who created international smashes like 'Telstar' and hits for artists like The Honeycombs, Heinz, John Leyton and Mike Berry from a home-built studio in his flat in London's Holloway Road, has been found dead from gun wounds to the head on the floor of the same studio.
The evidence suggests suicide, and it is known that Meek had been depressed for some time as he fought to come to terms with the rapidly changing styles that have taken over pop music since his 'Telstar' heyday in 1962.
One of Meek's abiding musical inspirations was Buddy Holly, and it has already been suggested as being no coincidence that February 3 - the day on which he apparently chose to take his own life - was the eighth anniversary of Holly's death. NME

EDWYN COLLINS: "His stuff was so far ahead of its time, but he was completely paranoid. He was a suspect in the sinister gay police investigations, which were dubbed 'The Suitcase Murders', and he was convinced that Phil Spector had bugged his house."

Remember me this way: Seek out the book The Legendary Joe Meek by John Repsch for the full low-down.

JB LENOIR

Died April 29th from a heart attack following a car crash. Lenoir was a Mississippi blues player who hung out with Big Bill Broonzy on the Chicago scene in the Fifties.
IAN ANDERSON (Jethro Tull): "I saw him at the Free Trade Hall in Manchester when I was 16. I didn't think about him again till years later when I heard an album called 'Alabama Blues'. He had a beautiful, clear, high voice, like a bell, and his guitar playing was remarkable."

Remember me this way: The 1953 hit 'The Mojo Boogie'.

JOHN COLTRANE

Died July 17th from cancer. Expressive, avant-

garde jazz saxophonist who inspired generations of rock jamming with his awesome 'A Love Supreme' and numerous improvised classics that took in all musical styles, from jazz through to world music.

Read it on record sleeves: *There is a danger in trying to write about the music itself, a danger in using words to capture such a strong non-verbal experience. Coltrane himself seems to have preferred to release his music without notes, perhaps because he preferred the plain and simple, perhaps because he felt the music was its own best spokesman.*
David A Wild from the sleeve of 'The Complete 1961 Village Vanguard Recordings'

Remember me this way: 'A Love Supreme' still rings the bell, but for haunting, layered improv, try the Village Vanguard sessions.

BRIAN EPSTEIN

Died August 27th from an accidental overdose of sleeping pills and alcohol. Epstein turned The Beatles from leather-clad punks into Mop Top faves, his story and sexuality still remain intriguing today.

Remember me this way: Be-suited, explaining to Brian Matthew just why he thought that The Beatles would probably last longer than a couple of hits.

WOODY GUTHRIE

Died October 3rd from Huntington's Chorea, after a long illness. Oklahoman Dustbowl folkie who inspired the protest song with the exceptional 'This Land Is Your Land' and a string of other roadworthy anthems. It seemed that every time Guthrie got within inches, a handshake or a nod of fame and fortune, he'd get drunk at a showcase and disgrace himself. He ended his life suffering from a debilitating illness having never fully realised his potential.

Read it on the internet: *Woody Guthrie is the original folk hero. It was Guthrie who, in the Thirties and Forties, transformed the folk ballad into a vehicle for social protest and observation. In so doing, he paved the way for Bob Dylan, Bruce Springsteen and a host of other folk and rock songwriters who have been moved by conscience to share experiences and voice opinions in a forthright manner.*
The Rock and Roll Hall of Fame web site at **www.rockhall.com**

Woody Guthrie (taken from Born To Win): "I've heard several pretty smart thinkers tell me that folk songs are on their way out. That folk as we hear it and know it is on its way out the old golden gate of history. That a folk song, to be called a folk song, must wear a snatch of hair and whiskers older than an oily leather skin drum. I say that folk music and folk songs, folk ballads, are just now getting up onto their feet, like Joe Louis after a couple of sad knockdowns."
BOB DYLAN: "When I met him I was there as a servant, to sing his songs. That's all I was, a Woody Guthrie jukebox."

Remember me this way: 'Vigilante Man' by Ry Cooder, 'Pretty Boy Floyd' by The Byrds, 'Tom Joad' by Spingsteen, 'Do Re Mi' by Uncle Tupelo. Or anything by Bob or the man himself.

OTIS REDDING

Died December 10th in a plane crash along with The BarKays (Ronnie Caldwell, Jimmy King, Phalin Jones and Carl Cunningham). Redding was a legendary soul icon who'd headlined at the Monterey Pop Festival and helped coin the term 'rock and soul' music.

DAVID PORTER (Stax Records): "When Otis came on the scene he brought such energy. I remember when he came in and recorded 'These Arms Of Mine'. When you listened through the walls, because they were cutting everything at once, the rhythm, horns and vocals, you knew a great session was going on. He was a great stimulus for Stax Records. He had a kind of positive aggression in his singing and the way he approached music."
BEN CAULEY: (survivor of the crash that killed Redding): "The aeroplane started shaking and I remember the sax player was sitting in front of me and he said, 'What's that? Oh no!'."
ISAAC HAYES: "Everyone at Stax cried. It was such a shock. He was a person that represented so much life. When we got the news we just sat around. It was, like, what do we do now?"
EDDIE FLOYD: "The last time I spoke to Otis I was joking with him about training for a light plane license. I'll never forget that day, he

wasn't flying himself, but he was in his own plane. I can only say that I've lost my brother, we as soul brothers are one."

PAUL HEATON (The Beautiful South): "He used to sing like Little Richard at first until he discovered Sam Cooke and began to sound so much sweeter, singing in a style that suited him. I was a massive Otis Redding fan when I was younger. I always used to spend the morning of December 10 in mourning."

LISA STANSFIELD: "I love 'I've Been Loving You Too Long', especially when it gets to the end and his voice just breaks up."

MICK JONES (fan): "He was a big powerful man with a powerful voice and far too many hits to fit into one set. I saw him at the Astoria in Finsbury Park and he did 'Try A Little Tenderness' with such feeling it wouldn't have mattered if that was his only number."

JIM MORRISON: "Poor Otis dead and gone, left me here to sing his song, pretty little girl with the red dress on, poor Otis dead and gone." (from 'Running Wild' by The Doors).

The classic tunes: 'My Girl', The Rolling Stones' 'Satisfaction', 'My Lover's Prayer', 'I Can't Turn You Loose', 'Fa Fa Fa Fa Fa (Sad Song)', 'Try A Little Tenderness', 'Let Me Come On Home', 'Shake', his biggest UK chart entry, a posthumous number three in 1968 'Dock Of The Bay', 'Happy Song', 'Hard To Handle' and 'Love Man'.

Remember me this way: He's just '(Sittin' On The) Dock Of The Bay'.

LITTLE WALTER

Died February 15th from injuries sustained in a street fight. Louisiana-born legend who's harmonica playing set Muddy Waters' band apart.

Read about it in books: *Walter's voyage into blues legend began when he started playing amplified on sessions with Muddy Waters. One of their earliest collaborations was 'Country Boy'; this was emphatically urban music, a kind that nobody had heard before.*
From Blues Legends by Tony Russell

Remember me this way: With The Rolling Stones' cover of 'Confessin' The Blues'.

Poor Otis, dead and gone...

LITTLE WILLIE JOHN

Died March 26th of a heart attack. At the time he was in prison, convicted of murder. His main claim to fame, prior to his incarcerated demise, was a co-writing credit for 'Fever' and 'Need Your Love So Bad'. Much much later, he was name-checked in the Robbie Robertson song 'Somewhere Up That Lazy River'.

Remember me this way: His 'You Hurt Me' torch song, a King single from 1961, recently re-issued on 'Roc-King Up A Storm'.

DON DRUMMOND

Ska mover and shaker and member of The Skatalites. Drummond was jailed for the murder of his girlfriend, exotic dancer Marguerita Mahfood, on New Year's Day in 1965. Her body was found in his home, she was the victim of multiple stab wounds. After a brief investigation, Drummond was deemed legally insane and sent to Belle Vue Asylum. His death, while incarcerated, was never explained. There was no official autopsy. At Drummond's memorial service, Supersonics drummer Hugh Malcolm ripped up the death certificate and charged the hospital staff with murder.

Remember me this way: The Skatalites' Top 40 UK hit from 1967, 'The Guns Of Navarone'.

FRANKIE LYMON

Died February 28th from a heroin overdose. As the ill-fated and underage singer in the chart-topping Frankie Lymon And The Teenagers, he quickly turned to drugs and thus began his rapid decline. Even in death there was no rest for Lymon, or at least his estate. A huddle of would-be and could-be wives emerged to argue over his royalties. The singer was buried without even a tombstone.

Read about it in books: *Lymon, emerged as a star from the Teenagers and left the group in 1956 to pursue a solo career. He was going on 15. While not unheard of, it was a brave move for a young black singer. But his solo career flopped and Lymon became increasingly dependent on heroin. His girlfriend attempted*

to help, but the relationship collapsed and when Lymon joined the army he was back on heroin. After his discharge he went home to New York. In February 1968, aged 25, he died of an overdose on the floor of his grandmother's apartment - penniless and forgotten.

From Rock 'n' Roll Babylon by Gary Herman.

Remember me this way: 'Why Do Fools Fall In Love?' and the probably misquoted 'I'm Not A Juvenile Delinquent'.

MARTIN LAMBLE

Died May 14th, when Fairport Convention's van crashed after a gig killing the drummer and his girlfriend, dressmaker Jeannie Franklyn.

Read it in the press:

FAIRPORT DRUMMER IS KILLED IN CRASH

Martin Lamble, the 19-year-old drummer of folk-rock act Fairport Convention, was killed in the early hours of Monday, May 12th, when the group's van crashed on the M1 as the group returned to London from a gig in Birmingham.

Also killed in the crash was American clothes designer Jeannie Franklin, while Fairport guitarists Richard Thompson and Simon Nicol, bassist Ashley Hutchings, and road manager Harvey Bramham, were all injured.

The group's singer Sandy Denny was travelling separately in a car and was not involved. NME

Remember me this way: His rattling snare on 'Fotheringay' from the Fairport's 'What We Did On Our Holidays'.

SHORTY LONG

Died June 29th. The man behind such uptempo rock 'n' soul anthems as 'Devil With A Blue Dress' and 'Here Comes The Judge' drowned in a boating accident. Believe it or not, the radio regular 'Here Comes The Judge' only reached number 30 in the charts for the American vocalist in 1968.

Remember me this way: The funky soul brother wisecracks of his court room drama.

BRIAN JONES

Died July 3rd in, some say, mysterious circumstances. The just-ousted Rolling Stones' guitarist was found drowned in his swimming pool, even though he was an accomplished swimmer. Books and documentaries are still being made of the story.

MUSIC CENTRAL SAID: *During 1968, Jones prompted doubts about his availability for US tours and in the succeeding months he contributed less and less to recordings and became increasingly jealous of Jagger's leading role in the group. Keith Richards' wooing and impregnation of Jones'*

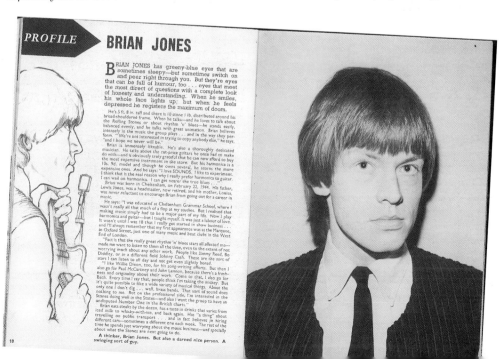

girlfriend Anita Pallenberg merely increased the tension. Matters reached a crisis point in June 1969 when Jones officially left†the group. The following month he was found dead in the swimming pool of the Sussex house that had once belonged to writer AA Milne. The official verdict was death by misadventure.

RED ROOSTER "*The many theories of murder mostly revolve around the many people who were at Brian's home that night, and whose police statements all clash and contradict one another. These theories carry a lot of weight and there seems to be too much proof to be just rumours. To find out more about the murder of Brian, look out for the books: Golden Stone-The Untold Life And Death Of Brian Jones by Laura Jackson or Paint It Black - The Murder Of Brian Jones by Geoffrey Giuliano.*"

KEITH RICHARDS (in Q magazine, 1988): "I don't think, honestly, that you'll find anyone who liked Brian. He wasn't a likeable guy. He had so many hang-ups, he was unreliable, he wanted to be a star. At the same time he had a certain charm. And we all tried to get on with him, but then he'd shit on you."

MICK JAGGER "Brian wasn't really good material to be in the pop business. He was over-sensitive to everything. Some people are born shy."

KEITH RICHARDS: "I wouldn't say murder, I'd say manslaughter. I think he was pretty out of it, he'd let these builders in and they were sort of running his house and having fun with the stoned-out rock star. I think that maybe someone held him under the water for a joke and he didn't come up. Murder? No. I think stupidity."

Remember me this way: Bedraggled and dirty-fingernailed as he struggles with a sitar in Ken Russell's film of the recording of 'Sympathy For The Devil'.

JOSH WHITE

A contemporary of Woody Guthrie who played the folk circuit. White

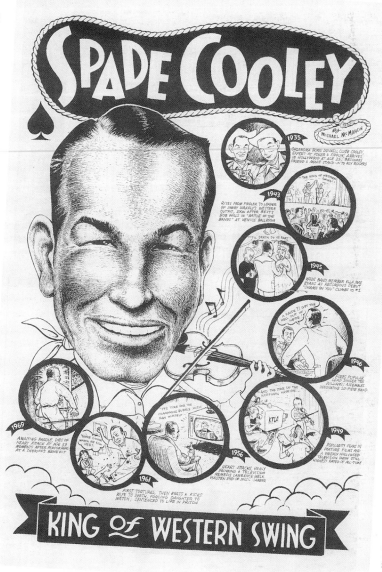

Good Morning Blues

also released gospel songs under the name Joshua White and blues tunes under the moniker Pinewood Tom. He died during an operation to replace a defective heart valve on September 6th.

Read it on record sleeves:
Josh White's music isn't just drawn from the music of the Negro. His music, like that of his great white contemporary Woody Guthrie, drew on the folk heritage of the entire American nation. Songs of the poor white farmers found their way into his repertoire alongside ones from the Negro ghettos of Chicago, Los Angeles, New York and New Orleans; country blues mixed with city blues, songs of love with political songs.

Roger St Pierre, 1957 from the sleeve of 'Good Morning Blues'

Remember Me this way: With Woody in the dustbowl.

SPADE COOLEY

The King Of Western Swing died on November 23rd, aged 59, awaiting parole while in prison after torturing and beating his wife to death. Before he was locked up, Cooley transferred his flowing country sounds to TV in the early '50s. However, his marriage to band member Ella Mae Evans turned sour and he tortured then beat her death in front of his daughter. Banged up in chokey, on the verge of getting out, he was invited to play a policeman's benefit show and expired in the wings halfway through.

Remember Me this way: His seemingly poignant number one 'Shame On You' which charted the week he married Ella Mae.

MEREDITH HUNTER

Died December 6th from stab wounds after Hell's Angels took control of The Rolling Stones' show at Altamont Racetrack in California. The event virtually ended the hippie movement.

Remember me this way: In fits and starts of violence in the film of the doomed concert.

1970's

It is not that I do not want to die, I just do not want to be there when it happens. **Woody Allen**

1970

DARRELL BANKS

Legendary soul singer who was mysteriously murdered. He gave the world the thumping Northern Soul stomper 'Angel Baby' and the perennial 'Open The Door To Your Heart'. 'Angel Baby' was on regular rotation at UK northern soul haunt The Torch in the early '70s. Two versions were playlisted but Banks' remains the benchmark.

Remember me this way: At late nights long gone in Wigan Casino and even earlier at the Torch in Stoke-on-Trent.

JAMES 'SHEP' SHEPPARD

The lead singer with The Heartbeats and Shep And The Limelites died in his car on the Long Island Expressway after being beaten and robbed, before being shot on January 24th. Sheppard was actually a key figure in the creation of rock 'n' roll concept pieces, as we know them today. His songs of tales of love and romance were acclaimed as a precursor to The Beatles 'Sgt Pepper'.

Remember me this way: With the top ten US R&B hit 'A Thousand Miles Away' or the pop crossover 'Daddy's Home'.

SLIM HARPO

Died January 31st of a heart attack. Louisiana blues veteran best remembered for 'Baby, Scratch My Back' and 'Don't Start Crying Now' as well as the R&B crossovers 'I'm A King Bee' and 'Shake Your Hips'.

Remember me this way: The underplayed throb of 'I'm A King Bee' and the minimal one-note solo that's ushered in as Harpo begs, "Sting it, then".

TAMMI TERRELL

Died April 16th from a brain tumour resulting from a contusion. Terrell had been singing since her early teens, she hooked up with the James Brown Revue and duetted with the man before being signed to Motown as a solo artist. Her early sides were R&B ballads – including a hit version of 'This Old Heart Of Mine (Is Weak For You)'. Terrell also worked with Marvin Gaye; the duo developed a close harmony style that fizzed with sexual tension. Sadly their success was short-lived, Terrell was diagnosed with a brain tumour after collapsing in Gaye's arms while the two performed live.

Read it in the press:

TAMMI TERRELL DEAD

Tamla Motown star Tammi Terrell, best known for her series of duets with Marvin Gaye, died at Graduate Hospital in Philadelphia on March 16, after undergoing the last of several brain tumour operations she had over the previous 18 months. During 1967 she collapsed into Gaye's arms during a show at Virginia's Hampton-Sydney College. The collapse was believed to be due to exhaustion, but doctors later discovered a brain tumour.
NME

Remember me this way: With Marvin, singing 'Ain't Nothin' Like The Real Thing', 'You're All I Need To Get By', or 'The Onion Song'.

OTIS SPANN

Died April 25th from cancer. Mississippi-born pianist who recorded 'Keep Your Hand Out Of My Pocket', later covered by Van Morrison. Played with Fleetwood Mac on the UK Blue Horizon label recording a swooping 'The Temperature Is Rising'.

Remember me this way: The belter 'Can't Do Me No Good' or Van's live version of 'Get Your Hand Out Of My Pocket' from the live double 'It's Too Late To Stop Now'.

AL WILSON

Died September 3rd. Mystery surrounded his drug overdose, which happened during the night while he was camping. The falsetto-voiced Canned Heat harmonica player is best remembered for his driving delivery of 'Going Up The Country' which opens the Woodstock film and his love of trees (fact!).

Read it in the press:

CANNED HEAT MEMBER FOUND DEAD

Al 'Blind Owl' Wilson, singer and guitarist of Canned Heat, has been found dead in fellow band member Bob Hite's garden in Topanga Canyon, California. Aged 27, he was discovered with an empty bottle of barbiturates at his side.
NME

Remember me this way: That reeling harmonica.

JIMI HENDRIX

Died September 18th when he asphyxiated on his vomit after ingesting a heavy dose of barbiturates. The Seattle-born guitar legend unleashed three albums in the space of a year as The Jimi Hendrix Experience, and in the process changed the face of rock music. Hendrix lived the rock 'n' roll life at breakneck speed.

Read it in the press:

HENDRIX 'NO JUNKIE' SAYS PATHOLOGIST

A coroner's inquest into the death of Jimi Hendrix, who died at a London, Notting Hill, flat on September 18, has established that the guitarist died of 'suffocation from inhalation of vomit'. Pathologist Professor Donald Teare added that there was no evidence that Hendrix had been a drug addict and he had no needle marks anywhere on his body.
NME

BUDDY MILES [Band Of Gypsies' drummer]: "Jimi was too easy to get along with. He just had a real gentleness and a kindness about him and in my opinion it got him in a lot of trouble in the long run. He would never say no. Not everyone took advantage of him, but then again I saw a lot of people who did."

NOEL REDDING [Experience bassist]: "After he died, it seemed as if everyone knew Hendrix, but he didn't make friends easily, certainly not in public because he was basically very shy. When I first met him, he was very quiet and polite. It was only when we were working that he used to do the wild man bit."

KATHY ETCHINGHAM (girlfriend): "Jimi was very, very funny. He had an amazing sense of humour. He was just a very nice, extremely funny person to be with, especially in the early days before the strains of it all set in. I think his death was all very dodgy. I don't think it should have happened. As Mitch said: 'He was in the wrong place at the wrong time with the wrong people'."

CHAS CHANDLER [manager]: "He wasn't an extrovert at all. He was a very reserved but happy character. Jimi was good fun to be with. I don't think of this brooding, menacing person that we

The star that played with Laughing Sam's dice

hear about now, I think of someone laughing. He was a brilliant mimic. One of my favourite memories of him was doing his Little Richard impersonation. If he was telling a story that had four characters in it, he would slip into the roles of the four characters. He was a highly intelligent guy and he was a good artist, but all he really wanted to do was play his guitar."

MITCH MITCHELL[Experience drummer]: "I found it incredibly easy to work with Jimi. Whether it was eye contact or even in a booth with headphones, if I could hear what he was doing I found it very easy. Whether I played what he wanted, that's a different question! We were fans of the same sort of music, which helped a lot – Curtis Mayfield, Wes Montgomery, people like that – so if you share those reference points, it helps in terms of knowing where a certain sequence is likely to lead."

JEFF BECK: "I went along to see Hendrix. It was amazing. I just went away thinking I better get something else to do. He was doing things so upfront and wild and so unchained. That's what I wanted to do."

CHAS CHANDLER: "He never stopped thinking about music. He'd eat breakfast with his Strat on a strap around his neck."

RICHARD THOMPSON [Folk troubadour]: "He loosened everything up, in the way that John Coltrane made the saxophone's honks and squeaks acceptable."

NOEL REDDING: "We learnt to play as a band as we went along. It was all very short, intense gigs in front of The Beatles or the Stones, which really freaked me out. There were never any set lists, we didn't do soundchecks and there was hardly any rehearsing."

ROBERT CRAY: "Hendrix, man, the first time I heard his music, I was living in Virginia and a kid at school who played the guitar did some songs at assembly. The curtains opened and he played 'Purple Haze'. I didn't know who Hendrix was, but I heard those chords and I had bumps all over. To this day I've never heard anyone as innovative as Jimi Hendrix."

MIKE McCREADY (Pearl Jam): "I fucking love Hendrix. He's all encompassing. His songwriting ability was amazing, his leads were genius - he was so far ahead of his time."

VERNON REID (Living Colour): "He played guitar solos as political statements. His 'Star Spangled Banner' is Martin Luther King's 'I Have A Dream'."

KIRK HAMMETT (Metallica): "Jimi Hendrix invented the Church Of Tone, he had monster technique and soul to spare."

EDDIE VAN HALEN: "Hendrix blew my mind, like he did everybody's. One of my favourite guitar solos is 'All Along The Watchtower'."

LENNY KRAVITZ: "Voodoo Chile' just howls from the soul. It's so intense."

CARLOS SANTANA: "Hendrix learned to paint with another brush, the brush of mescaline, LSD. He didn't play notes anymore."

BRIAN MAY: "Queen came together through Hendrix. Freddie was a complete Hendrix freak - he once saw Jimi 14 nights in a row, in different pubs each time."

VIC REEVES: "My first single was 'Voodoo Chile', that was when I first got interested in Hendrix. I only had two records so I used to play it constantly, and my dad used to say, 'Anyone can play guitar like that'. I always vowed that when I was old enough I'd buy a guitar and make him prove it."

LENNY KRAVITZ: "Hendrix was right out there, way out there in outer space. His music to me is the most modern music, like Miles Davis. They're beyond modern. When you get to that place where you're very primal, just expressing yourself. That's what it's about. It wasn't all sexual charge, it was head music for me."

MICKEY QUINN (Supergrass): "Of all the dead artists, Hendrix is the one I'd have liked to have seen live. I've seen things like his performance at Woodstock and his fingers are just a blur and doing really weird stuff. He was always trying to write pop songs but he was too weird and rough but it's just amazing what he came up with."

ERIC CLAPTON: "It's really sad that he didn't make it through. I don't believe that he burned out. That's bollocks."

JIMI SAID: "I've turned full circle – I'm right back where I started. I've given this era of music everything, but I still sound the same. My music is the same and I can't think of anything new to add to it. When the last US tour finished I started thinking about the future. Thinking that this era of music is finished. Something new has to come and Jimi Hendrix will be there." (From his last Melody Maker interview)

Remember me this way: 'Purple Haze', 'Angel', 'The Wind Cries Mary', 'Voodoo Chile (Slight Return)', 'If Six Was Nine', 'Manic Depression', etc, etc.

JANIS JOPLIN

Died October 4th from a heroin overdose. As the singer in Big Brother And The Holding Company, she took her groggy blues wail into the rock arena, before recording her exquisite solo album 'Pearl'. Her drunken and dosed-up private life became public property and tales of her sexual ambiguity merely enlarged her reputation.

Read it on the internet:

Janis Joplin, one of the most powerful singers of her generation, found her voice as a hard-living, blues-loving diva on the psychedelic San Francisco scene. She sang with feverish power over the high-adrenaline music of Big Brother and the Holding Company, finding a release in their psychedelic blues-rock.
The Rock and Roll Hall of Fame web site at
http://www.rockhall.com

Read about it in books:

What more lonely way to die, than alone in a motel room in Los Angeles, feeling great and being that careless, blowing the whole thing, all alone, quietly before she was ready.
From Janis Joplin, Her Life And Times by Deborah Landau

Read it in the press
JANIS ODS

Janis Joplin was found dead of a drug overdose in a room at Hollywood's Landmark Hotel on October 4. She was discovered laying face down with fresh puncture marks in her arm. The singer had frequently suffered from drink and drugs problems in the past, yet things seemed to be taking an upturn in her career. Earlier this year she had stated, referring to Jimi Hendrix's death: "I can't go out this year because he was a bigger star."
NME

JOHN COOKE (road manager): "People imagine that, because of her drinking and heroin problems, Janis would have been an irresponsible person. That wasn't true at all. So, when Paul Rothchild (the producer) rang me and said that Janis was really late, I thought it must be something serious. I went over to her hotel and I looked up and saw the light was on. It must have been on all day but in the daylight we hadn't noticed. I went straight to the desk and got a key, then went in and found Janis lying on the bed. I knew as soon as I went in that she was dead."

LEONARD COHEN: "There's one thing that I always regretted, that I spoke about Janis and attached it to a song. There's that line, 'giving me head on an unmade bed, while the limousines wait in the street. It was an unforgivable indiscretion. I never speak about women like that. I don't like kiss-and-tell as a form."

SAM ANDREW (Big Brother And The Holding Company): "Her voice was high and edgy like the scratching of an old Victrola spinning out a Bessie Smith tune. She seemed to be on fast forward, with very quick reflexes. She understood the blues tradition intellectually and she had absorbed the blues feeling by osmosis growing up in Texas and listening to a lot of Ma Rainey. Janis had a very authentic sound in her voice that was naturally there."

Remember me this way: Short of one Mercedes Benz.

1971

JIM MORRISON

Died July 3rd from a drug-induced heart attack. You can catch the full story in Oliver Stone's The Doors, where he's portrayed by Val Kilmer, or you could stick with the albums. But certainly look into the story of Elektra Records, Follow The Music, in which Jac Holzman paints a picture of simple excess typified by drunken binges and the stage show in which he exposed himself and was subsequently charged with lewd behaviour.

Read it in the press
THE END FOR JIM MORRISON

Jim Morrison, who ducked out from leading The Doors in order to concentrate on creative writing,

The Lizard King

He could do anything

died in Paris on July 3, aged 27.
On the night of July 2, Morrison regurgitated a
small amount of blood, but claimed he felt fine and
announced his intention to take a bath. Early next
morning, his wife Pamela found him dead in the
water-filled bath, apparently from natural causes.
Morrison had recently consulted a local doctor
concerning respiratory problems.
The singer/poet is to be buried in the same Paris
cemetery as French chanteuse Edith Piaf and
playwright Oscar Wilde.
NME

JOHN DENSMORE [Doors' drummer]: "My first
thought, when I met Jim was, 'I'm in a band with
a psychotic'. My second thought was even more
worrying, I realised 'I'm in the same room as a
psychotic!'."
JAC HOLZMAN [Elektra Records]: "On the tape (of
the show) Jim is taunting and provoking, shouting, crescendo. Now he says that the crowd has-
n't come for music, they want something more -
they want to see his cock - the crowd goes wild."
VAL KILMER: "Jim, in his own way, was very disciplined. He was a very disciplined drunk,
y'know? It didn't matter that an ulcer might be
developing, he just went for it. 90% of the scenes
in the film really happened. He did jump on a
few turkey dinners and he did jump into the
audience and he did many more outrageous
things.
"If you isolate Jim from the rest of the band
around the time of 'LA Woman', it's a beautiful
eerie voice he has, thinned out, just his guts left,
no more vocal chords. You can hear him dying
when you take the music away."
Remember me this way: He was the lizard king, he
could do anything.

KING CURTIS

Died August 13th, he was stabbed to death in a
fight outside his home on West 86th Street in
New York. A former member of The Coasters, he
sang on 'Yakety Yak', before becoming a seasoned saxophone player and appearing on sessions by everyone from Andy Williams to Buddy
Holly.
Remember me this way: His instrumental opus 'Soul
Serenade'.

GENE VINCENT

Died October 12th from an ulcerated wound that he sustained in the car accident that killed Eddie Cochran 14 years earlier. Vincent was born Eugene Vincent Craddock, on February 1935, in Norfolk; he was one of the original bad boys of rock 'n' roll. After he was involved in a motorcycle crash in 1955 his left leg was permanently damaged, which led to often intolerable pain, made worse by alcoholism.

Not content with injuring his leg riding the same kind of hog favoured by Marlon Brando in The Wild One, Vincent's stage antics meant that he'd continually break his cast and make the damage worse. His penchant for the wilder side of life - guns, knives, be-quiffed hairstyles - enhanced his wild image and to combat the pain of his leg, painkillers and booze became his crutch. It was an existence played out on endless tours and attempted comebacks and, even in death, his luck never changed. His funeral slipped into pandemonium when his wife Jackie arrived, then his sister wigged out and gave away all his belongings. At the end there wasn't much left except for a few songs.

PAUL MCCARTNEY: "Gene Vincent's 'Be Bop A Lula' was the first record I ever bought. I got it from Curry's Electrical Appliance shop in Liverpool."

MARK E SMITH: "It's his voice. He can sing real rubbish and make it work, real rubbish lyrics. I've got all his albums, even the psychedelic one. I used to think he was really good, beating up DJs and all that, very impressive. That's why he never got big."

IAN DURY: "There are a few parallels here with Elvis Presley. Just as Elvis was at his best on Sun, Gene was at his peak when he was with the guitarist Gallopin' Cliff Gallup, sort of pre-1958. After then you can forget it. When he started dressing head to toe in black leather, forget it. He'd really lost it. He was better when he was wearing the pale blue bowling shirts.

He was probably the first rocker to smash up hotel rooms. One of the first was this place called the Knickerbocker, which I mention in 'Sweet Gene Vincent'. When the saxophone was introduced to his records, I essentially stopped liking him, same with Elvis. It was 'Lotta Lovin' with Gene and 'King Creole' with Elvis. Two black days in music."

Remember me this way: 'Be Bop A Lula' no less.

Sweet Gene

DUANE ALLMAN

Died October 29th in a motorcycle accident. Southern rock slide guitarist and Allman Brothers mainstay who played that immortal melody on Derek And The Dominos' 'Layla'. Allman also played on sessions for numerous acts from Delaney And Bonnie through to Johnny Jenkins.

ERIC CLAPTON: "His break at the end of Wilson Pickett's 'Hey, Jude' blew me away."

Remember me this way: On the 'Anthology' double released just after his death, which features all sorts of bizarre session pieces as well as some jam-packed Allman moments.

BARBARA ACKLIN

Died November 27th of pneumonia, aged 56. Renowned soul singer/songwriter who co-wrote The Chi-Lites' hits 'Have You Seen Her?', 'Too Good To Be Forgotten' and 'Stoned Out Of My Mind' with husband Eugene Record. Also a well-known cult soul singer whose 'Love Makes A Woman' was a Torch Club northern soul staple.

Remember me this way: Crooning 'Love Makes a Woman'.

1972.

BIG MAYBELLE

Powerhouse vocalist who tripped the live blues circuit before dying on January 23rd aged 51, as a result of constant drug problems. Sadly, the intensity of her legendary live shows was never captured on record, but her song 'Candy' comes closest to capturing her awesome live voice.

Read about it in books: *Big Maybelle was a stentorian blues singer, popular in the 1950s with the same sort of material as Etta James or the young Esther Philips: noisy blues, wide-screen ballads and dance anthems.*
From The Blues From Robert Johnson To Robert Cray by Tony Russell

Remember me this way: With the sweet taste of confection.

MAHALIA JACKSON

Died January 27th from heart failure. The Gospel Granny who gave us 'In The Upper Room With Jesus' just wanted to testify.

Read it on record sleeves:

Many have tried in vain to describe what it is that is so captivating about Mahalia and the songs she sings. And I too have failed, because greatness is seldom describable.
Cal Lampley, from the sleeve of 'Newport 1958'.

Had there been any doubt as to the range of Mahalia Jackson's artistic ability, 'Great Songs Of Love And Faith' is certain to prove it borders on the infinite. For those who have heard Mahalia at religious functions, accompanied only by a piano and organ, this album shows another side of a woman whose talent is abundant.

It has often been said that Mahalia is the world's greatest gospel singer. This recording gives abounding proof of the measure of her greatness.
CBS Records, 1962, from the sleeve of 'Great Songs Of Love And Faith.'

Remember me this way: God knows she's good.

LINDA JONES

Gospel singer who eventually went into the Gamble and Huff writing partnership but not before changing her name to Linda Lane and scoring a hit with 'Hypnotized'. Died March 14 after collapsing from a diabetic shock backstage at a show in New York.

Remember me this way: That hypnotic moment.

LES HARVEY

Died May 3rd when he was electrocuted on stage in Swansea after touching a live microphone. At the time he was a member of Stone The Crows, he'd previously been with The Sensational Alex Harvey Band (he was Alex's brother).

Remember me this way: At the axis of Stone The Crows with Maggie Bell (touted as the UK's answer to Janis Joplin).

THE REVEREND GARY DAVIS

Veteran Gospel-tinged singer who died May 5th from a heart attack aged 76. He exorcised all 'sinful' songs from his repertoire after becoming an ordained minister.

Read it in the press
BLUESMAN DAVIS DIES

Blues, ragtime and gospel performer the Rev. 'Blind' Gary Davis died on May 5th, aged 76. An influence on Ry Cooder and Taj Mahal, he began as a street singer, then became a gospel preacher working camp meetings and country churches. He found national fame via the Newport Folk Festival in 1964.
NME

Remember me this way: Emoting 'When I Die, I'll Live Again'.

CLYDE MCPHATTER

The Drifters vocalist who crooned 'Money Honey', died June 13th from heart, liver and kidney ailments.

Read it in the press
CLYDE MCPHATTER DIES

Clyde McPhatter, the son of a North Carolina Baptist minister, who became one of the world's finest soulmen, has died aged 40. Once lead singer of Ward's Dominoes, he went on to form The Drifters in 1953. Drafted into the airforce in 1954, he became a solo performer on his discharge, scoring several UK hits.
NME

Remember me this way: His solo hits 'Lover Please' or 'Treasure Of Love'.

MISSISSIPPI FRED MCDOWELL

Died July 3rd from cancer. Rural Blues innovator who recorded 'You Gotta Move', which was covered by the Stones on 'Sticky Fingers'. Widely recognised as the middleman twixt blues and gospel.

Remember me this way: The Bonnie Raitt-supported 'I Do Not Play Rock 'n' Roll' album, if you can seek it out.

BOBBY RAMIREZ

Died July 24th after being beaten up in a Chicago bar because he had long hair. Ramirez was a member of Edgar Winter's White Trash. The band added a touch of glitter and mousse to their metal roots.

Remember me this way: Edgar's brief flirtation with success, the single 'Frankenstein'.

BRIAN COLE

Died August 2nd from a heroin overdose. Cole was formerly the bassist and a founding member of The Association; the band produced the Sixties radio-friendly sound of 'Windy' and 'Cherish'.

Read it on record sleeves: *Some people think musicians are weird and many would think The Association are weird. Like Brian Cole who's held 33 jobs in six years and is quite a philosopher. But then it's the creative people who stop the world from being one giant Dow Jones average - people like The Association who are*

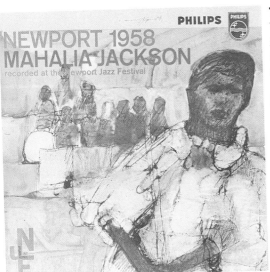

really adding something to today's music scene.

Phyllis Burgess, Teen magazine, 1966, from the sleeve of 'And Then-Along Comes The Association.'

Remember me this way: Even smoothies get hooked.

RORY STORM

Died September 27th from an overdose of sleeping pills in a suicide pact with his mother. As the leader of Rory Storm & The Hurricanes he recorded 'Dr Feelgood'.

Remember me this way: Feeling good...but not for long.

MISS CHRISTINE

Died November 5th from a heroin overdose, this simply named vocalist was a member of the Zappa-inspired GTOs, which stood for Girls Together Outrageously.

Remember me this way: Outrageously.

BILLY MURCIA

Died November 6th from 'accidental' suffocation during another hefty night as a member of the fledgling New York Dolls. The group completed only a handful of shows in the States and were then shipped off to London to play atop of the Biba shop in Kensington and on Bob Harris's Old Grey Whistle Test. During the latter, Whispering Bob vented his spleen on a group he felt just weren't worthy. In the aftermath bassist Arthur Kane and Murcia got down to their habitual drug taking. Later that same night, Murcia was unconscious when his panicking girlfriend decided to pour coffee down his throat to revive him. All to no avail.

Remember me this way: Too much too soon.

The Association, Brian Cole (far right) succumbed to drug addiction

Neil Young's post-Whitten heroin hangover album

DANNY WHITTEN

Died November 18th from a heroin overdose, while he was a member of Neil Young's backing band Crazy Horse. He was the original trigger for Young's harrowing album 'Tonight's The Night'. The album is an intense Tequila-fuelled self-exorcism.

His problems came to a head when he was drafted in to beef up the sound of Young's 'Harvest' album for an upcoming tour. Whitten's addictions meant he couldn't hold the plectrum down and, so the story goes, Young packed him off back to LA with $50 in his pocket. Whitten blew it on heroin and expired, leaving the coroner to inform Young by telephone of his friend's demise.

Remember me this way: He wrote Crazy Horse's emotive 'I Don't Want To Talk About'.

BERRY OAKLEY

Died November 21st in a motorcycle crash. The second member of the Allman Brothers to die in such a way, he was actually three blocks away from where Duane Allman had died when he was injured after coming off his bike. After his tumble, Oakley insisted that he was fine only to die later from a brain haemorrhage. He was buried next to Duane in Rose Hill Cemetery in Macon, Georgia.

Remember me this way: Succumbed to white line fever following brother Duane Allman down the road.

1973

RON "PIGPEN" MCKERNAN

Died March 6th from a stomach haemorrhage. The Grateful Dead keyboard player was a long-term drinker and his body finally gave up. He was the first of three Dead keyboardists to expire. ROBERT HUNTER [Grateful Dead lyricist]: "Pigpen was the best all-round performer around, the only guy (in the Grateful Dead) who could get up on stage and play blues."

Remember me this way: Looking cool on the back sleeve of the Dead's 'Aoxomoxoa', next to an eight-year-old Courtney Love.

CLARENCE WHITE

Died June 14th from a stomach haemorrhage, after being struck by a hit and run driver while loading equipment following a show. Clarence White was a guitarist openly admired by Jimi Hendrix. At the time of his death he was playing with his brothers after his departure from The Byrds.

Clarence's classic Byrds performances: 'Nashville West', 'Drug Store Truck Drivin' Man', 'Oil In My Lamp', 'Tulsa County', 'Truck Stop Girl', Green Apple Quickstep' and 'Farther Along'.

Remember me this way: As the spirit of latter-day Byrds with a heartache vocal.

PAUL WILLIAMS

The Temptations man committed suicide on August 17th, two years after he left the band. All the smart suits and fancy dance steps spiralled out of view for the 34-year-old when he shot himself after years of drug abuse.

Remember me this way: Prancing in the late psychedelia of the '60s with the Temptations doing 'Cloud Nine' and 'Psychedelic Shack'.

GRAM PARSONS

Died September 19th from heart failure following a Tequila and morphine binge. The former member of The Byrds and The Flying Burrito Brothers' body was subsequently stolen by his road manager, Phil Kaufman. Kaufman, it transpires, hijacked Parsons' body in order to cremate it but he, and his accomplice Michael Martin (Gram's on-tour valet), were too pissed to drive too far. They ended up at Cap Rock - a sacred spirit-friendly spot. Much has been written into the legend since. The abduction was greeted with headlines such as 'Rock Star's Body In Ritualistic Burning In Desert' but, according to Kaufman, "it wasn't ritualistic, it was just a couple of piss heads taking care of business for their mate." Gram's step-father, Bob Parsons had the charred remains of his stepson shipped to New Orleans, where, after a small family only service, he was buried in The Garden Of Memories; an unimpressive cemetery on a highway near the airport. A bronze plaque marks the gravesite; it reads "God's Own Singer".

Remember me this way:
In his entire recording career, which effectively amounted to a bit less than a decade and was pursued via five groups and a duet affiliation, Gram Parsons did not enjoy one single hit in the pop charts, nor the country or R&B charts for that matter. Only one album on which he performed, The Byrds' 'Sweetheart Of The Rodeo', entered the Billboard Charts. The great number of radio listeners during the '60s and '70s would not even know that he existed.

Glenn A Baker from the sleeve of 'Warm Evenings, Pale Mornings, Bottled Blues.'

Read it in the press
THE DEATH OF COUNTRY ROCK

Gram Parsons, ex member of The Byrds and The Flying Burrito Brothers, died in California on September 19. Parsons, 26, collapsed in a motel and was rushed to hospital in Uyya Valley, but

was found to be dead on arrival. An initial post-mortem failed to reveal the cause of death and further tests are being made.
NME

ROGER MCGUINN: "I liked Gram fine. We used to play pool together and ride motorbikes. He was a very inspired young man to want to mix country music with rock music like he did. I really like what he did for the Byrds."

PETER BUCK [REM]: "It's amazing how malleable Gram Parsons made country and western music. He took this rigid, conservative art form and sang songs about decadence and drugs, plus no-one's ever written a better song about LA than 'Sin City'."

CHRIS HILLMAN [Byrds/Burritos]: "The Burritos had taken off pretty well but when Gram sought out the Stones during the 'Honky Tonk Women' period, he really got seduced by all the trappings. Here was a kid with a lot of talent but zero discipline. He did not work at his craft. He had one foot in country music and the other in the glamorous world of rock 'n' roll and we started to lose him."

Remember me this way: Keef's good ol' pal, duetting with Emmylou Harris or intoning Dan Penn's classic 'Dark End Of The Street' on the Burrito album 'Gilded Palace Of Sin'.

JIM CROCE

Died September 20th in a plane crash that also claimed the life of his guitarist Maury Meulheisen. Had several posthumous hits, including 'Time In A Bottle' and the treacly 'I'll Have To Say I Love You In A Song'.

Read it in the press
MORE ROCK DEATHS

Following the death of Gram Parsons on September 19, Jim Croce and his guitarist Maury Mulheisen were killed on September 20 when the small plane in which they were travelling from Louisiana to Texas crashed into a tree while attempting to take off.
NME

Remember me this way: A difficult moustache but some great rhyming phrases.

SISTER ROSETTA THARPE

The gospel singer and guitarist died in Philadelphia on October 9th, aged 57.

Read it on record sleeves:
This wonderful revival singer of the Pentecostal or Holiness congregations has taken her music into revival meetings and other church services across the country for years and she has always attracted and held spellbound the packed meeting places. Rosetta Tharpe has proven, a thousand times over, that she has a greater hold on her audience, a deeper feeling for the music and words and a powerful ability to present gospel music than anyone else who has ever played the church circuit.
From the sleeve of 'Gospel Train'

Remember me this way: As an influence on Dylan who brought gospel to the world, chopped and charged by her distinctive guitar style.

JOHN ROSTILL

Died on November 26th when he was electrocuted. Fellow Shadow Bruce Welch, who called at his house to work on some songs, discovered his body.

Remember me this way: As the longest serving bassist in the Shads.

BOBBY DARIN

Died December 20th during heart surgery. He moped through 'Dream Lover' but brought the standard 'Mack The Knife' to life.

Read it in the press
DARIN DEAD AT 37

Bobby Darin, the singer who claimed he would be a legend at 25, died in Los Angeles' Cedars Of Lebanon hospital on December 20, aged 37. The end of a lifelong battle against heart trouble came after a six-hour operation to replace two valves. It was his second bout of open-heart surgery within a short space of time. Said one friend: "He was just too weak to recover."
NME

Remember me this way: The hits 'Splish Splash', 'Lazy River', 'Multiplication' and his version of Tim Hardin's 'If I Were A Carpenter'.

1974

BOBBY BLOOM

Died February 28th in an accidental shooting. The New York-based former Monkees songwriter charted on both sides of the Atlantic with the steel drum-driven 'Montego Bay' in 1970.

Remember me this way: "Oh, oh, oh, oh, oh, oh, oh, oh, oh, oh, it's all on the right side in Montego Bay".

ARTHUR "BIG BOY" CRUDUP

Died March 28th from a heart attack. He wrote 'That's Alright (Mama)', which was covered by Elvis Presley among others, before he moved onto more mellow tunes.

Read about it in books: Crudup's music is lean, sparse, his vocals like field hollers, their edges buffed by a crooning sweetness. His guitar, often sourly

tuned, puts the song in a plain frame.
From The Blues From Robert Johnson to Robert Cray by Tony Russell

Remember me this way: Worried about his cut from the Presley royalty.

GRAHAM BOND

Died May 8th when he fell under a tube train. The former Blues Incorporated and The Graham Bond Organisation man was hugely popular in 1964 with his distinctive Hammond organ sound, but it all went pear-shaped and Bond got into spirituality forming bands called Holy Magick and Magus.

Read it in the press
GRAHAM BOND KILLED IN FALL

Graham Bond, a leading light in the British R&B movement, died on May 8 when he fell in front of a train at London's Finsbury Park station. He was identified by his fingerprints. Bond first gained attention as a jazz saxophonist with the Don Rendell Quintet, later fronting various Sixties bands as a gifted organist, his sidemen including Ginger Baker, Jack Bruce, John McLaughlin and Jon Hiseman. He formed his first band in 1963 and eventually progressed to the renowned Graham Bond Organisation.
On its break up he concentrated on session work before joining Ginger Baker's Airforce. He then formed a band with Pete Brown and his then-wife Diana Stewart, but when his marriage broke up he formed another outfit with Carolanne Pegg called Magus. That group played a few shows, but quickly folded due to financial problems.
Bond, who had quit drugs, was recently hospitalised but was planning a major comeback at the time of his death.
NME

Remember me this way: His interpretations of 'Got My Mojo Working' and 'Wade In The Water' are legendary.

MAMA CASS

Died July 29th from a heart attack after becoming a big star as part of The Mamas And The Papas. She was a pal of Jimi Hendrix, a purveyor of peace and love and a belter of a singer.

Read it on record sleeves: *To end up with, there's Cass. You couldn't really end up with anything else. She collects antiques, talks freely about art and Bob Dylan, loves Whispering Paul McDowell, has travelled the land in satirical revues, wears cute little gold-rimmed glasses and, like the others, she lives for today.*
From the sleeve of 'If You Can Believe Your Eyes And Ears' The Mamas And The Papas'

Read it in the press
MAMA CASS DEAD

Cass Elliot, Mama Cass of The Mamas And The Papas, died in the early morning of July 29th in the London flat of Harry Nilsson, where she was living with her friend and road manager George Caldwell during her stay in the UK.
At a coroner's hearing, held the next day, it was

established that she had died as a result of choking on a sandwich while in bed, and from inhaling her own vomit.
NME

The classic harmonies in full: The Mamas And The Papas: 'California Dreamin' (1966), 'Monday Monday' (66), 'I Saw Her Again' (66), 'Words Of Love' (1967), 'Dedicated To The One I Love' (67) and 'Creque Valley' (67). As Mama Cass: 'Dream A Little Dream Of Me' (1968) and 'It's Getting Better' (1969).

Remember me this way: The solo hits and the misses - like 'California Earthquake'.

CHASE

All the jazz-rock band Chase (Wally York, Walter Clark, Bill Chase and John Emma) were killed in a plane crash.

Remember me this way: Togetherness and a final chorus.

ROBBIE MCINTOSH

Died September 23rd after fatally ingesting heroin at the height of The Average White Band's success. The former Brian Auger's Oblivion Express drummer was allegedly murdered by a promoter, who fed him drugged wine.

Remember me this way: He picked up the pieces, briefly.

NICK DRAKE

Died October 25th. The renowned singer / songwriter committed suicide, by taking an overdose of anti-depressants. An ever-popular figure with students thanks to his beautifully phrased bedsit angst. The full story of his complex life is still unfolding.

Read it in the press
NICK DRAKE FOUND DEAD

Nick Drake, the UK singer/songwriter was found dead in bed at his parent's home in Tamworth, near Stratford-On-Avon, on October 25th. A very private man, who was hardly known even to the people at his record label, he spent a great deal of time in various mental hospitals after the release of 'Pink Moon' in 1972. At the time of his death, resulting from an overdose of anti-depressants, Drake, 26, was recording tracks for a new album with producer Joe Boyd. NME

BEN WATT: "He has the art of understatement. I love his songs as mood pieces as much as anything else, and again the fact that they have influences that are not directly from rock 'n' roll, with an unembarrassed ability to mix almost semi-classical string arrangements with acoustic basses and acoustic guitars. I also like what I've read about him, he was terribly frustrated because he wasn't bigger than he was."

PAUL HEATH (fan): "Though mostly written in the depths of winter under a single lightbulb in a cavernous room in Hampstead, the songs on the wonderful 'Bryter Later' conjure up the timeless feel of summer in the country."

PETER BUCK [REM]: "'Pink Moon' is like an English 'Hellhound On My Trail'."

CLUIVE GREGSON [Folk songwriter]: 'Pink Moon' is my all time favourite record. It's just a timeless music. It all sounds great; just a voice and guitar and a tiny bit of piano on one track."

Remember me this way: The awesome album 'Five Leaves Left'. Find out more in Patrick Humphries' book Nick Drake: A Biography (Omnibus).

1975

PAUL BEAVER

Died January 16th after having a stroke. The veteran electronic composer was also half of Beaver And Krause, the band dragged in Mike Bloomfield and a host of others to make the remarkable 'Ghandarva' in the early '70s.

Remember me this way: 'Ghandarva', the ideal mooged-up head album (with the possible exception of Tonto's Expanding Headband, of course.)

DAVE ALEXANDER

Stooges' bassist, died February 10th after years of drug and alcohol abuse.

RON ASHETON (Stooges' guitarist): Dave Alexander's first job in The Stooges was to take a Kustom guitar amp with a reverb unit in it, pick up the amp head and keep crashing it down, to make weird sounds."

Remember me this way: Thumping through 'I Wanna Be Your Dog'.

T-BONE WALKER

Died March 16th from pneumonia. The Texan Bluesman recorded 'Call It Stormy Monday'. His style influenced BB King, Clapton et al.

Read about it in books: *With his confident swagger, his*

devil may care moustache and his been-there, seen-it-all lyrics, T-Bone Walker was a pin-up of California's blues-loving ladies in the Forties and Fifties.
From The Blues Legends by Tony Russell

Remember me this way: The Bluenote collection of his recordings.

BOB WILLS

Died May 13th from pneumonia. Leader of western swing giants The Texas Playboys, Wills was a well-recognised toughie who stayed on the road until his death, ruling his highly replaceable players with a rod of iron. Wills also ran a venue called The Ranch House where he played with yet another band; he alternated between the two groups. Between the two set-ups he hothoused western swing music and, from 1950 onwards, was a highly sought after performer. When the tireless regime got too much, Wills sold the Ranch House venue to Jack Ruby, who would later turn up to assassinate Lee Harvey Oswald, who in turn allegedly plugged JFK.

Remember me this way: A smile, a swing and a combative approach.

PETE HAM

Died May 23rd. Truly gifted Badfinger songwriter whose mismanaged career and sensitive nature led him to hang himself. Widely acknowledged as a genius and an awesome writer, he went through his time in Badfinger in bedraggled poverty even though his albums sold and every radio station was playing his songs.

Read about it in books: *Tom Evans recalled, "At 7.30 in the morning I was awakened by a call from Anne (Ferguson, Pete Ham's girlfriend). She was screaming for me to come over..."*
Marianne (Tom Evans' wife): "She was yelling into the phone, 'It's Pete, it's Pete..."
Tom left quickly, not really knowing what had happened. When he arrived at Pete's home he could not find anyone. He ran through the different rooms and finally, into the garage.
"That's when I saw Pete," he later stated. "I thought, that's it for me and rock 'n' roll."
From Dan Matovina's excellent Without You, The Tragic Story Of Badfinger.

Remember me this way: Co-wrote 'Without You', loved and lost and lost again. Then again.

TIM BUCKLEY

Died June 29th from a heroin overdose. The father of the late Jeff Buckley was a testing singer/songwriter who mixed folk and blues with jazz to highlight his truly amazing vocal range. Never one to rest on his laurels, he attempted to move into newer and more diverse musical territories. Amid the classic tunes and emotive storylines, he pushed his voice, the music and the boundaries of performance - not always successfully.

CHRISSIE HYNDE (in Mojo magazine): "Put 'Happy/Sad' on now and it sounds like it could've been made last year. It has a unique, timeless sound and feel, and that voice was unlike anyone else's. A lot of people can sing

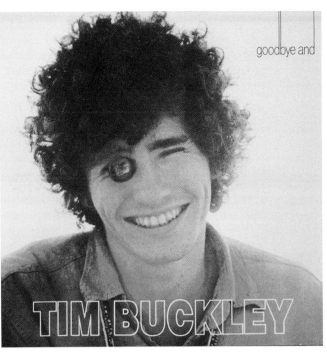

their arses off but they don't sound remarkable, while others sound beautiful but stumble along. He had the lot. He sang from the right place, not just from the heart, but from the diaphragm too."
LEE UNDERWOOD (The Tim Buckley Band): "Tim always wrote about love and suffering in all their manifestations. He felt that underneath love was fear, fear of love and success and responsibility."
THE CLASSIC BUCKLEY BEDSIT ALBUMS: 'Goodbye And Hello' (1967), 'Happy Sad' (1969), 'Blue Afternoon' (1969). The weird out-there ones: 'Lorca' (1970) and 'Starsailor' (1970, rather free-form and including the Cocteau Twins' covered 'Song To The Siren').

Remember me this way: Unsatisfied troubadour and spokesman for a bereft and tattered youth who produced enough gems to make him king of the lonely world.

AL JACKSON JR

Died October 1st when he was shot by two intruders who had entered his home while he was out watching the second Ali-Frazier rematch. The original drummer with Booker T and The MGs.
Remember me this way: When time was just way too tight.

JESSE WHITTEN

One of the original disco hit makers with Heatwave; a group made up of American GIs who'd been stationed in Germany. Whitten was stabbed to death during a fight outside a club. The group's hits were penned by Englishman Rod Termperton, who later went on to write 'Thriller' for Michael Jackson.

Remember me this way: The legendary 'Boogie Nights', which haunted a million dancefloors.

HOWLIN' WOLF

Died January 10th of kidney failure. The legendary R&B guitarist recorded 'Back Door Man' and 'Smokestack Lightning'. Allegedly he was a bitter and angry man who used his hang-ups to play with full conviction.

Read it on the internet:

"Howlin' Wolf ranks among the most electrifying performers in blues history, as well as one of its greatest characters. He was a ferocious, full-bodied singer whose gruff, rasping vocals embodied the blues at its most unbridled. A large man who stood more than six feet tall and weighed nearly 300 pounds, Howlin' Wolf cut an imposing figure, which he utilised to maximum effect when performing. In the words of blues historian Bob Santelli: "Wolf acted out his most potent blues, becoming the living embodiment of its most powerful forces."

The Rock and Roll Hall of Fame web site at **www.rockhall.com**

Read about it in books:

Howlin' Wolf looked exactly the way he sounded. He was built like a brick barrelhouse and when he stamped his feet, the stage rocked.

From The Blues From Robert Johnson to Robert Cray by Tony Russell

ROBERT CRAY: "The thing I dig about the Wolf is, here's this cat that's portraying himself as the Wolf, and his songs start off with some howlin' and he's talkin' and slippin' out the window, and there's always someone chasin' him. I really dig that thing of him thinking of himself as somebody else, livin' out his own mythology. That's the coolest thing in the world."

ERIC CLAPTON: "He was very intimidating. He

taught me to play 'Red Rooster' and it was a hairy experience. He was vehement about doing it right."

JIMMY PAGE "I'd have to say that my main blues influence was Howlin' Wolf. His stuff wasn't just straight groove, playing on the beat. I loved his voice and the sheer intensity of the music as well as the timing of it."

Remember me this way: Janis Joplin's cover of his probably semi-autobiographical 'Moanin' At Midnight' or any of the Wolf's own howling recordings.

CHRIS KENNER

Died January 25th from a heart attack. New Orleans singer/songwriter who created the anthemic 'Land Of 1000 Dances', which became a dancehall standard for pick-up bands the world over. Kenner had some solo success but his main pay cheque came from writing for Fats Domino ('I Like It Like That') and Wilson Pickett.

Remember me this way: Wilson Pickett's 1966 hit with 'Land Of 1000 Dances'.

MANCE LIPSCOMB

Died January 30th from heart disease, aged 77. The Texan Bluesman was only really discovered in the '60s, when he became a folk festival staple renowned for keeping a young head through his music.

BECK: "Mance Lipscomb's voice and guitar are

so perfectly melded; they both have this graceful awkwardness."

Remember me this way: His mix of ragtime, jazz and gospel influences.

FLORENCE BALLARD

Died February 22nd from coronary thrombosis. One of the original Supremes, she left in 1967. She was unhappy when her role in the group began to get smaller in the shadow of Diana Ross's success. Her solo career never really took off and, by the early '70s, she was living in poverty in a Detroit housing project. Her reliance on a lethal cocktail of alcohol and diet pills resulted in her death.

Remember me this way: Chummed with Diana Ross on the likes of 'My World Is Empty Without You', 'I Hear A Symphony' and the stomping 'Love Is Like An Itching In My Heart'.

PAUL KOSSOFF

Died March 19th from a drug-induced heart failure. The Free and Back Street Crawler guitarist was the son of the radio broadcaster David Kossoff. The renowned guitarist had struggled with drugs for some time and died in his sleep during another period of romance with substances unbecoming.

He said: "I'm sick of waking up to see a sack of shit in the mirror. Once you're into drugs you get a morbid interest in death."

Remember me this way: Strutting behind Paul Rodgers on Top Of The Pops as 'All Right Now' scuttled to number two in the charts.

DUSTER BENNETT

Died March 26th in a car crash. Part of the UK blues movement in the late '60s and a member of John Mayall's Bluesbreakers, before he embarked on a healthy solo career.

Remember me this way: His Blue Horizon cut 'I'm Gonna Wind Up Ending Up Or I'm Gonna End Up Winding Up With You'.

PHIL OCHS

Died April 9th. Agit-prop folkie and Greenwich Village troubadour who hung himself while he was in the throes of depression at the music industry's complete lack of conviction and his indifferent sales.

After the protestations and inventive acoustic barrages, Phil Ochs just lost it. He drank. He released a 'Greatest Hits' album with all new material. Then he was strangled while on tour in Africa; this affected his vocal chords and increased his reliance on the bottle. Finally, suffering from schizophrenia, he insisted on being called John Train. He carried weapons, with which he threatened all and sundry, with he went off the precipice completely and hung himself at his sister's apartment. But not before recording his own obituary.

Read it on record sleeves: I realise I can't feel nobility for what I write because I know my life could never be as moral as my songs.
From the sleeve of 'I Ain't Marching Anymore'.

The classic tunes of revolution from the Ochs repertoire: 'Bound For Glory', 'Love Me, I'm A Liberal', 'Too Many Martyrs', 'Here's To The State Of Mississippi', 'Draft Dodger Rag', 'I Ain't Marching Anymore', 'There But For Fortune', 'Cops Of The World', 'William Butler Yeats Visits Lincoln Park And Escapes Unscathed', 'The World Began In Eden And Ended In Los Angeles', 'Jim Dean Of Indiana', and many more. (You can find them all on the essential Ochs box set 'Farewell And Fantasies' (Elektra Records).

Remember me this way: On a makeshift stage in front of today's cause letting his heart bleed and his lyrics do the talking.

KEITH RELF
Died May 14th when he electrocuted himself while playing guitar in the bathtub. Remembered as a member of Renaissance (who scored big with 'Northern Lights') and The Yardbirds.
Remember me this way: As the man who turned down the Robert Plant role in Led Zep.

JIMMY REED
Died August 29th from respiratory failure. Mississippi Bluesman whose best known song is 'Ain't That Lovin' You Baby'. Groovy, bluesy, swampy player whose mid-tempo material was as soulful as hell.

Read it on record sleeves: *One of the most fascinating and successful among today's blues artists is Jimmy Reed. His singing and playing techniques may seem somewhat mysterious not only to persons accustomed to popular and classical music, but even to jazz aficionados. As a matter of fact, we are dealing here with a world of its own. The blues world has always lived by its own rules - parallel to, yet clearly distinct from*

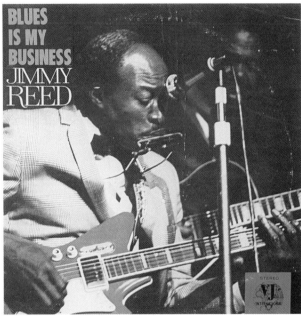

the world of jazz.
Marcel Chauvard and Jacques Deemtre, 1964, from the sleeve of 'Boss Man Of The Blues'.

Jimmy Reed has often been referred to as a 'legend in his own time'. His records have sold in millions both here and abroad; most notably in England, where lately they have been using our basic folk-blues form as the basis of the 'English Rock Sound'.
From the sleeve of 'Blues Is My Business'.
Remember me this way: 'How Long, How Long Blues', 'High And Lonesome' and a load of straggling others.

VICTORIA SPIVEY
Died October 3rd from an internal haemorrhage. Spivey was a blues interpreter from Texas who brought in a young Bob Dylan to play harmonica on her early '60s albums.

Remember me this way: Pictured with Bob on the sleeve reverse of 'New Morning'.

LEONARD LEE
Half of Shirley And Lee, who's best known for their million-selling 'Let The Good Times Roll', Leonard Lee died on October 23rd. The duo had started as an R&B act before their huge 1956 hit took advantage of their hugely different voices. The partnership failed to repeat that success and they went their separate ways in the early '60s. Lee pursued a bluesy solo career, which came to nothing. Shirley resurfaced in the mid-'70s fronting Shirley And Company, who hit the Top Ten in the UK with 'Shame, Shame, Shame'.
Remember me this way: That crossover monster.

TOMMY BOLIN
Died December 4th from a heroin overdose. The James Gang and Deep Purple guitarist joined the latter for 'Come Taste The Band', after the departure of original guitarist Ritchie Blackmore. His jazz/soul playing didn't cut it with Purple's straightforward metal of the '70s and when they split he headed out on the road in the States with his new band Sailor. His girlfriend found him dead from an overdose in a hotel room in Miami, Florida.
Remember me this way: 'Funk 49' (by The James Gang) was just a better place to be. Much better than the photograph of him on page 55 of Rock 'n' Roll Babylon. There a tragic Easy Rider-shades-wearing Bolin sits bare-chested holding a plastic dog turd like some kind of sacrificial icon. The caption reads: "Heroin consciousness equals a man in a frock with a plastic dog turd". Enough said.

FREDDIE KING
Died December 28th from bleeding ulcers and heart failure aged just 42. Blues guitarist who's remembered for 'Lonesome Whistle Blues' and crossing the path of blues and rock.
Remember me this way: As a Clapton-influence and for his collaborations with Leon Russell.

BUKKA WHITE

Delta blues artist Booker T Washington White died February 26th of cancer. A contemporary of Robert Johnson who failed to do the deal with the devil and lived to a ripe old age instead. For the music buyer there are two distinct camps of Bukka material. The original cuts from the late '30s are his most impressive although many others were recorded from the mid-'60s onwards, when he was rediscovered. Second time around White was less focused but his skills as a raconteur and a throaty crooner served him well.

Remember me this way: The Led Zep-friendly 'Shake 'Em On Down'.

HELMUT KOELLEN

Died May 3rd of carbon monoxide poisoning. The German Prog rocker and member of Triumvirat inhaled exhaust fumes while listening to tapes in his car in his garage.

Remember me this way: That's prog rock for you.

WILLIAM POWELL

Part of The O'Jays multi-harmony sound that saw them turn their '60s R&B popularity into crossover hits in the early '70s. Died from cancer on May 26th.

Those OJays hits pre 1976: 'Back Stabbers' (1972) and 'Love Train' (1973).

Remember me this way: Climbing on board the 'Love Train'.

SLEEPY JOHN ESTES

Died June 5th following a stroke. The Tennessee Bluesman was a late developer, even though he cut sides earlier with Sam Philips.

Read it on record sleeves:

"One day the boss kept on giving signs to us and we all just stood still and didn't move from the track. So the boss got mad and walked up to us and said, 'What's the matter with you damn Negroes?'. We couldn't say nothing, so he looked at John Estes and said to him: 'What's wrong?'. But John Estes didn't say nothing, then the white man hitted him. John woke up and started to sing and we all started to work, too. So, after that we all called John Estes the sleeping track caller and that's how he got his name."

Bill Broonzy, from the sleeve of 'Stone Blind Blues'.

I have always been fascinated by the blues that Sleepy John Estes has written about the people and places of his home, Brownsville, Tennessee. It was there that Big Bill Broonzy was led, as he described

SLEEPY JOHN ESTES' BROWNSVILLE BLUES with HAMMIE NIXON

in his autobiography, by Big Joe Williams to meet Estes. Williams was not hesitant in praising John's abilities or singing his songs. John's crying-blues and blues-writing style dominates the Tennessee blues of the era. And, in recent years, isolated by blindness, John Estes further improved his guitar technique.

From the sleeve of 'Brownsville Blues'.

Remember me this way: Seek out the vintage pre-'60s stuff for his full moaning glory and his duet with Yank Rachell on 'Expressman Blues' from the 'Anthology Of American Folk Music' set.

PETER LAUGHNER

Pere Ubu man died June 22nd from acute pancreatitis. Laughner quit Ubu after just two singles to work on a solo career, which produced some austere acoustic strums before he opted to work as a journalist.

Remember me this way: He played guitar on '30 Seconds Over Tokyo' and 'Final Solution'.

ELVIS PRESLEY

Died August 16th from a drug overdose while sitting on the toilet, a larger-than-life shadow of his former self. A bag of dirt from Graceland and numerous paperweights are now available amongst the plethora of The King commemorative items. The Elvis industry and sightings go on and the legendary recordings and epic tunes often get forgotten.

Read it in the press

"That boy," drawled Tex Ritter, "sure gits audiences worked up, and he sure gits himself worked up, getting 'em worked up."

The object of cowboy Ritter's remarks was 20-year-old Elvis Presley, who has risen to record fame in the space of a few months as a rocking and rolling hillbilly.

Presley's weird western bop has startled many more people besides the old cowboy Ritter. It has startled adults who hear nothing more than a mumble jumble when Elvis sings. But teenagers are ecstatic over Elvis. So ecstatic that they rip the seats from the floor and the shirt from his back.

From Your Record Stars, 1957.

ELVIS IS DEAD...

Elvis Presley was found lying on his bathroom floor at his Memphis home in the early hours of August 16 and, despite efforts to resuscitate him, was pronounced dead at Memphis Baptist Memorial Hospital.

Within hours thousands of people gathered outside the gates of Graceland and the scene was set for the biggest media event of the decade. 75,000 people were present for his funeral two days later, when he was laid to rest in a white marble mausoleum near his mother.

Speculation over the cause of Presley's heart attack is rife. His health had been deteriorating for the past four years. He was hospitalised five times for intestinal problems, eye trouble, recurrent 'flu and fatigue. No amount of skilful tailoring could disguise the fact that he was overweight, and there were incessant rumours of drug abuse.

NME

Presley, the windmilling warbler from Tupelo, Mississippi, flails his way through his songs with a maximum of effort.

TROY HOLLIDAY (fan): "I saw him play in Calhoun County high school just before he went on the Ed Sullivan Show. When we walked in he was on stage. His gyrations and singing had set the girls screaming. They were wanting to get up on the stage, they were fainting. We'd never seen any young people swooned over. It was unbelievable. The men couldn't believe it, they were all saying, 'I wish I could do that.'"

ESTELLE LAMAR (fan): "I thought Elvis was very poor taste. Very poor taste. All I could figure was that all this rockin' and shakin' and buggin' was him looking for attention."

Remember me this way: Vegas? The army years? The black jumpsuit? The TV show? In Jailhouse Rock? His primal lip curl? Need we go on?

MARC BOLAN

Died September 16th in a car crash. The former member of John's Children, Tyrannosaurus Rex and T Rex, was being driven by his girlfriend, singer Gloria Jones; she swerved and drove into a tree in Barnes, London.

Read it in the press
MARC BOLAN KILLED IN CAR CRASH

Marc Bolan, the pixie in T Rex who spanned Psychedelia and Glam Rock and was on the verge of a solo comeback, has been killed in a car accident.

He was a passenger in the yellow mini being driven by his girlfriend, singer Gloria Jones, when the car spun off a wet road on Barnes Common, South West London, and crashed into a tree. Bolan was killed instantly, and Gloria was rushed to hospital with a broken jaw.

Bolan scored a string of hits in the early Seventies but failed to repeat this success in America where he became a tax exile. He'd just started his British comeback, touring with The Damned and filming a TV series.
UPI

SIMON NAPIER-BELL: "Marc was a tremendous fraud. His guitar playing was really bad, but I just loved that voice."

JOHN PEEL: "I've always liked extreme voices and Marc's Larry The Lamb stuff was really great."

MIKE LEANDER [producer]: "He started the whole Glam rock thing. He put glitter on his eyelids, then added pencil and mascara."

GLORIA JONES: "He could never understand it if one of his records didn't sell well. When things weren't going well he'd go quiet and try to figure out things to win his audience back."

HOLLY JOHNSON: "After listening to Marc Bolan's 'Electric Warrior' I was fascinated by the surrounding stories - that Bolan had flown to the North Pole with the tapes and they became distorted - and it made me pick up a guitar and tease my hair."

The classic tunes: As Tyrannosaurus Rex: 'Debora', 'One Inch Rock', 'King Of The Rumbling Spires'. As T Rex: 'Ride A White Swan', 'Hot Love' (a UK number one), 'Get It On' (ditto), 'Jeepster' (only number two), 'Telegram Sam' (back on top spot), 'Metal Guru', 'Children Of The Revolution', 'Solid Gold Easy Action', '20th Century Boy', 'The Groover', 'Truck On (Tyke)', 'Zip Gun Boogie', 'Light Of Love', 'New York City',

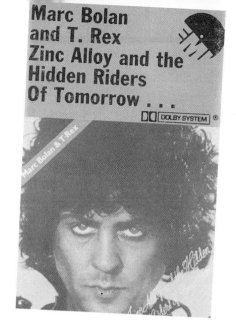

'London Boys', 'I Love To Boogie', 'Laser Love' and 'The Soul Of My Suit'. As Marc Bolan And T Rex: 'Teenage Dream'. As T Rex Disco Party: 'Dreamy Lady'.

Remember me this way: He was the 'Metal Guru'.

LYNYRD SKYNYRD MEMBERS RONNIE VAN ZANT, STEVEN GAINES AND HIS WIFE CASSIE

Died October 20th in a plane crash, the aeroplane they were flying in ran out of fuel. The band was named after their former school teacher, did you know? And, of course, they rocked!

BILLY POWELL [crash survivor]: "Our pilot had been drinking the night before and, for all we know, may still have been drunk. They jettisoned the fuel by mistake when one of the engines went down and then the other one went. We hit the trees at approximately 90mph. It felt like being hit with baseball bats when you're inside a garbage can. Ronnie was catapulted into a tree and died instantly, the co-pilot was decapitated and Cassie was bleeding to death. Artimus Pyle had three of his ribs sticking out of his chest but he somehow made it to a farmhouse three quarters of a mile away to get help."

Remember me this way: With someone always playing 'Free Bird' in a music shop or more appropriately unleashing 'Sweet Home Alabama' as a reply to Neil Young's 'Southern Man'.

1977

STACY SUTHERLAND

The 13th Floor Elevators' man was shot by his wife, after surviving years of playing with Roky Erickson in this bizarre pop psyche outfit. The Elevators split when Erickson decided to plead insanity rather than face a long prison term for possession of drugs.

Remember me this way: 'You're Gonna Miss Me' on 'Nuggets'.

TERRY KATH

Died January 23rd after he accidentally shot himself in the head with a gun. He was a songwriter and original member of Chicago from their rootsy, from the time of their brass-laden psyche pop such as '25 Or 6 To 4', through to their dreadfully insipid global chart topper 'If You Leave Me Now'.

TIMOTHY M WOOD [Chicago]: "He was at the home of a Chicago crew member, Don Johnson, cleaning his guns. Kath enjoyed shooting at targets and was a gun collector. The crew member expressed some concern over what Terry was doing, but Kath told him that because the clip was not in the automatic pistol, there was no need to worry. However, a round was already chambered before he removed the clip."

Remember me this way: With 'Does Anybody Really Know What Time It Is?' from the first album.

SANDY DENNY

Died April 21st from a brain haemorrhage from falling down the stairs at her home. Denny was a member of Fairport Convention, Fotheringay and The Strawbs, and a gifted folk balladeer and songwriter with several fine solo albums to her name.

SIMON NICOLL [Fairport Convention]: "We were auditioning singers for Fairport Convention and when she came in, the room got louder and brighter."

RICHARD THOMPSON [Fairport Convention]: "She made us audition for her, to see if she wanted to join us. She was just incredible, such a classy singer it made the rest of us sound much better."

Remember me this way: Her 1971 solo album 'The North Star Grassman And The Ravens'.

KEITH MOON

Died September 7th. His excessive lifestyle climaxed with an overdose of the drug that was designed to wean him off the booze. A fine book by Tony Fletcher is available to flesh out the space between The Who's violent live performances and their sweet mod pop.

Stories of Moon's wild ways are legendary. The story goes that Keith Moon drove a Lincoln Continental into a hotel pool, thus setting himself up as the number one rock 'n' roll animal of all time.

It all started when Moon decided to hold his 21st birthday party on his 20th birthday, while The Who were on tour in the States. The shindig took place in a Holiday Inn in Flint, Michigan. Moon livened up the evening by throwing cakes at people. In a fit of tomfoolery, he then leapt over a table and broke his front two teeth, exited the party and jumped in a beach buggy, which he proceeded to steer into the swimming pool. So, it wasn't a Lincoln? But the Holiday Inn manager was still a bit upset and the group were from the hotel chain.

Read it in the press:
KEITH MOON TAKEN AWAY

On the cover of The Who's new album, Keith Moon is sitting on a chair inscribed 'Not to be taken away'. But the seemingly indestructible drummer has died - from the drug he was taking to get him off the drug that was most likely to kill him: booze.

After an evening with his girlfriend Annette Walter-Lax at the premiere of the Buddy Holly Story movie and a party with Paul McCartney, Keith went home to his Mayfair flat. Annette found

LES KUMMEL

Vocalist and songwriter with '60s blue-eyed soul pop band New Colony Six, who opened their 'Revelations' album with his Ron Rice-co-written 'I'll Always Think About You'.
Remember me this way: Moodily harmonising in a truly downbeat style.

CHRIS BELL

Founder member of Big Star, Bell died December 27th in a car crash after years of depression, drug-dabbling and general failure to come to terms with rock's inadequacies. His awesome solo album 'I Am The Cosmos' is a must.

Chris Bell was hanging around a Memphis studio, Ardent, where he doubled as an engineer and session guitarist. He also played the local circuit with his group Ice Water. After The Box Tops split up, Alex Chilton tried to lure Bell into a folk duo set-up in New York but to little avail. Chilton's solo work dried up so he moved back to Memphis and the two formed Big Star, named after Big Star Foodmarkets. The duo wrote a brace of Beatles / Badfinger / Byrds-styled songs and released 'No1 Record'. The press latched on to the former Box Top and Bell left the group feeling he'd been overshadowed.

His drug problems escalated and his embittered solo album, 'I Am The Cosmos' struck a bitter-sweet note, sadly Bell never got it together to follow that up.
Remember me this way: The title track of that solo album will shake you to the ground.

him dead the next morning. A post-mortem revealed an overdose of Heminevrin. NME

PETE TOWNSHEND: "After we'd recorded 'Substitute', Keith phoned me up and said, 'How dare you record without me!' He was convinced that he hadn't been at the session. Actually, he was drunk and he just couldn't remember it."
ROGER DALTREY: "Keith had no fear of authority. He took the piss out of me. Of course it created friction."
PETE TOWNSHEND: "Keith dying made me realise that this wonderful music that I loved, that I thought was divine, was capable of diabolical excess. And that was really hard to accept."
Remember me this way: DJ'ing on Radio 1, filling in for John Peel who was on holiday, and deciding to play the whole studio with his drum sticks.

CHRIS BELL i am the cosmos

1979

CHARLES MILLER

Original War member who also teamed up with Eric Burdon in 1969. A multi-instrumentalist who specialised in sax and clarinet for the group, Miller was murdered during a robbery.
Remember me this way: Got down and funky with 'Low Rider' and 'Me And Baby Brother'.

ANGUS MCLISE

Original Velvet Underground drummer, died of malnutrition. McLise left the group before it became the toast of Warhol's Plastic Inevitable when he disagreed with concept of being paid to perform.
Remember me this way: He took Mo Tucker's seat and was immortalised when his long distance phone call was pressed up as a seven-inch single in the '80s.

DONNY HATHAWAY

Died January 13th when he either jumped or fell from a 15th floor hotel window in New York. Best remembered for duetting with Roberta Flack on 'The First Time Ever I Saw Your Face' from the soundtrack of Clint Eastwood's Play Misty For Me. He also penned tunes for Aretha amongst others.
BEN WATT: "His voice is amazing, he has a fantastic range and he's a fantastic arranger and musician. He didn't think he got the praise he deserved, like Nick Drake."
Remember me this way: Roberta's squeeze.

SID VICIOUS

Died February 2nd from a heroin overdose, while awaiting trial for the alleged murder of his wife Nancy Spungen. The drug was given to him by his mother. Oh, yes, he was also in The Sex Pistols. He did it his way.

Read it in the press
SID VICIOUS DIES IN DRUGS DRAMA

Sid Vicious, the tormented star of punk rock, died of an overdose of heroin yesterday. He was found naked in the arms of his latest girlfriend in her New York flat less than 24 hours after he was released on bail from jail. His mother, Mrs Ann Beverley, took the couple a cup of tea in bed and frantically tried to wake Vicious. The girlfriend, Michelle Robinson, was completely unaware that he had died while they slept.
The Daily Mirror, February 3rd.

DRUGS KILL PUNK STAR SID VICIOUS

Punk rock star Sid Vicious, the inadequate youth that turned a tasteless pop gimmick into pathetic real life, died of a heroin overdose yesterday. His body was found after a party in his new girlfriend's apartment in Greenwich Village, New York, held to celebrate his release from jail on bail - he had been accused of murdering his previous girl friend 'Nauseous Nancy' Spungeon, with a knife.
The Daily Mail, Feburary 3rd.

SID DID IT HIS WAY

The predictable death of Sid Vicious came on February 2nd from a heroin overdose. He was at a party given by his current girlfriend Michelle Robinson and his mother Ann Beverley, to celebrate his release from jail pending a hearing of his murder trial.
While in prison, Sid was put on a detoxification course and, as a result, his tolerance to heroin was lowered. Sid collapsed after being given the drug, but recovered before the party broke up and went to bed at 3am. Ann Beverley found him dead in his bed the following morning. A syringe and spoon were found near the body. Sid would have been 22 in May.
NME

Read it on the internet:
SID VICIOUS IS GOD!

RÈsumÈ: Eat Mohawk, Mofo! I am a punk rocker. Fuck you! Green Day sucks! I'm so hardcore, I'll turn your eyebrows green. I've got 23 liberty spikes on my head. The chains on my leather jacket could break your neck twice. I'll skank your ass so hard you'll think it's the Misfits. Fuck
www-personal.umd.umich.edu/~ntm/punk.html

JOHN LYDON: "He took it all too far and, boy, he couldn't play guitar."

REMEMBER ME THIS WAY: Thwacking an American fan of the Pistols during a Limey-baiting show on the group's final tour.

LESTER FLATT

As half of strident bluegrass pioneers Flatt And Scruggs Lester Flatt hit paydirt. The duo had previously been part of the hard working and feebly paid Bill Monroe outfit. Flatt died on May 11th after infiltrating the rock world with his high-powered picking. Dylan covers aplenty.
Remember me this way: Faster than your average cat.

LOWELL GEORGE

Died June 29th from a drug overdose. The sad story of the unfulfilled George, saw him struggle with drugs and falling in and out of Little Feat's country rock creative circle. He finally turned his songwriting skills to good use with some beautifully poignant solo tracks but he was cursed by drink, drugs and God knows what. His demise was only a matter of time.
BONNIE RAITT: "The best singer, songwriter and guitar player I've ever heard."
Remember me this way: '20 Million Things To Do' from his solo album 'Thanks I'll Eat It Here'.

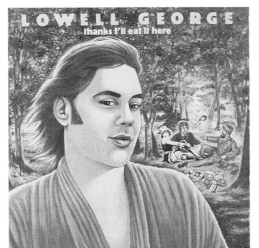

VAN MCCOY

Veteran soul and R&B producer turned instrumental pop star with the success of 'The Hustle' in 1975. Not content to unleash one annoying dance trend on the world, he followed it up in 1977 with 'The Shuffle'. He died July 6th of a heart attack.
Remember me this way: Pontificating on just how annoying the melody line to 'The Hustle' would prove to be in years to come and forgetting about all the cool sub-funk production jobs that should really have made his name.

MINNIE RIPERTON

Died July 12th from cancer. Former Rotary Connection vocalist turned solo and subsequently charted with 'Loving You', which reached number two in 1975. Much later the track was given the full ambient treatment by The Orb.
Remember me this way: The drifting lifelessness of 'Loving You' in the hands of The Orb.

JIMMY MCCULLOCH

Died September 27th. A former member of Wings, Joe Cocker's Grease Band, Thunderclap Newman, Stone The Crows, The Bluesbreakers, Blue and a reformed Small Faces, McCulloch was a musical journeyman destined for a demise in true rock style.
Read about it in books:
The Small Faces project was short-lived and unspectacular and McCulloch left the band to form his own band, The Dukes. But a few days after announcing the formation of The Dukes, Jimmy Went missing. Jimmy was found in his Maida Vale, London flat on the floor, killed by an overdose of morphine on top of booze and pot.
Rock 'n' Roll Babylon.
Read about it in books: Playing any town at anytime.

JOHN GLASSCOCK

Jethro Tull man (who'd previously played in Toe Fat and Chicken Shack) died November 27th from endocarditis resulting from a tooth abscess. His tenure in Tull began in 1976 and included the 'Heavy Horses' album.
Read about it in books: No smiles there.

80+90's

Love makes us poets and the approach of death
should make us philosophers. George Santayana

1980

PROFESSOR LONGHAIR

Louisiana R&B performer, died January 30th. His various line-ups produced cheeky Mardi Gras sounds with a rock 'n' roll slant and were said to have inspired everyone from Fats Domino to Dr John.

Richard Thompson "He was a fantastic innovator of the piano. They say his hands were too small to play octaves so he developed a rolling left hand style that gave him a Latin pulse and a strange syncopation. Did you know that they have Professor Longhairburgers at the New Orleans Jazz Festival?"

Remember me this way: With the song 'Ball The Wall'. No cheese, please.

AMOS MILBURN

Renowned alcohol-imbiber, responsible for 'One Bourbon, One Scotch, One Beer', 'Good Good Whisky' and, as a contrast, 'Bad Bad Whisky'. He died January 3rd after his drinking and his penchant for unfiltered cigarettes resulted in two strokes.

Remember me this way: None for the road.

GEORGEANNA TILLMAN

As part of one of the earliest Motown signings, The Marvelettes, Tillman enjoyed a US number one in 1961 with the group's version of 'Please Mr Postman'. More hits followed but the line-up was fluid and eventually Tillman quit the band in 1965. She died January 6th from the skin disease lupus.

Remember me this way: Delivering 'Please Mr Postman'.

LARRY WILLIAMS

Died January 7th. The rock 'n' roll singer and songwriter shot himself. He wrote 'She Said Yeah', which was covered by the Stones, and had some wild R&B times when he teamed up with Johnny 'Guitar' Watson on the pumping 'Two For The Price Of One'.

Remember me this way: As the man who loved ladies like 'Dizzy Miss Lizzy'.

BON SCOTT

Died February 19th when he choked on his vomit while drunk. Scott was a famed hellraiser, who's inebriated performances gave AC/DC's anthems extra ooomph.

Bon Scott, when asked about recording new AC/DC songs by Sounds: "I can't remember that, it was two days ago."

Scott Ian (Anthrax): "I first heard AC/DC in 1978. It was a song called 'Let There Be Rock'. And I have to admit that I didn't like Bon's voice. But then I went out and bought the album and within a week he was my favourite vocalist."

Robb Flynn (Machine Head): "I'm a huge fan of Bon Scott era AC/DC. He always came across to me, even on record."

Remember me this way: Singing 'Dirty Deeds Done Dirt Cheap' or 'Highway To Hell'.

JACOB "KILLER" MILLER

Reggae band Inner Circle singer, died February 21st in a car crash. In the late '70s he was bigger than Marley in his native Jamaica, but it was several years before the group scored big in Europe with the album 'Everything Is Great'.

Remember me this way: The album's hit 45 'Stop Breaking My Heart'.

IAN CURTIS

Died June 18th. The Joy Division singer hung himself on the eve of the band's first US tour and the release of their second album 'Closer'.

Read it in the press
JOY DIVISION GRIEF AT SINGER SUICIDE

Ian Curtis, the lead singer with Manchester quartet Joy Division, committed suicide today on the eve of their first US tour. He was 23. Though devastated it seems likely that the band will continue under another name.
NME

Read it on the internet: His lyrics and voice are largely responsible for both the band's success and its underground status. He joined the band just before they changed their name from Stiff Kittens to Warsaw. Later, they changed their name again to Joy Division, to avoid any confusion with the band Warsaw Pakt.

Let's get one thing straight: Ian did not die as

"Let's get one thing straight. Ian did not die as some sort of a martyr."

some sort of a martyr for the rest of mankind, as a music journalist wrote a few months later. Whatever the reason was, Ian did it for himself. He was becoming more and more epileptic, the band had been playing intensively for six months and had done radio, TV, and recording-sessions. The stress started to show on Ian and, during the spring of 1980, he collapsed several times on stage. Many people say that Ian was bound to kill himself because of all the depressing lyrics he wrote.

No matter who writes the final biography on Ian the real reason will always remain hidden. Ian had a very complex personality and nobody can ever claim to know exactly what he thought and what triggered the suicide.

The Official Unofficial Joy Division/Ian Curtis home page at
http://members.xoom.com/joy_division/

BERNARD SUMNER: "I first met Ian at the Electric Circus. It might have been the Anarchy tour, or the Clash. Ian was with another lad called Ian and they both had donkey jackets on. Ian's had 'HATE' written on the back but I remember liking him."

NIGEL GUY (fan): "All of us angst-ridden souls of the time latched on to the unearthly voice of Ian Curtis. He wrote so well about his darkness that listening to Joy Division was quite cathartic."

MARTIN RUSHENT (producer): "I'd demo-ed some of their material as part of my production deal with Radar through WEA, but when the label heard it they really hated it. They said I should be recording The Angelic Upstarts, which says something about where WEA were at the time."

ANDY CAIRNS (Therapy?): "ìI saw them on the Old Grey Whistle Test. Ian impressed me and I bought 'Unknown Pleasures'. They had an awful impact on my life when I was 14 or 15."

COURTNEY LOVE "Joy Division's 'She's Lost Control' meant so much to me when I was younger."

MARGI CLARK (actress): "My band supported Joy Division at Eric's. I thought Ian was the ultimate punk because he never smiled. He had the air of a poet, completely damaged, instantly consumptive,"

PETE SHELLEY: "I have no unhappy memories of Ian, except that he killed himself. I was under the impression that a bottle of whisky was involved. If you drink a bottle of whisky, don't have a gun

or ropes. You feel like death the next morning anyway."

BERNARD SUMNER: "I can't imagine what Ian would be doing if he hadn't died. He once threatened to go off and open a corner shop in Bournemouth, an off-licence that sold books. I think that was his plan."

TONY WILSON (Factory supremo): "I think Ian Curtis deserves to be treated as a myth because he was a wonderful character. Most rock deaths aren't romantic."

Remember me this way: "I've been waiting for a guide to come and take me by the hand…"

CARL RADLE

Renowned session player, died June 30th from chronic kidney problems. Originally the bass player for Gary Lewis And The Playboys, he played with Delaney And Bonnie, Eric Clapton, Derek and The Dominoes and a host of others.

Remember me this way: Playing bass on 'Bell Bottom Blues' by Derek And The Dominoes.

MALCOLM OWEN

Ruts vocalist and South London wide boy, died July 14th from a heroin overdose. The Ruts' brief career invited comparisons with The Clash, largely because of their use of reggae and dub, but if anything they leaned closer to the Jamaican sound. Their debut 45 'Babylon's Burning' - with the aid of a John Peel radio session ñ hit the Top Ten and they subsequently charted with 'Something That I Said'. Their album 'The Crack' cemented their fan base. Owen's untimely departure scuppered the band's success and, even through they continued as Ruts DC, they were never able to repeat their early promise.

Remember me this way:
Babylon burn out.

The Ruts with Malcolm Owen (right)

Zep at their hariest (Bonham, second from left)

KEITH GODCHAUX

Died July 23rd in a car crash, the second Grateful Dead keyboard player to expire. A trend was developing.
Remember me this way: Plinking and plonking at the 'Mars Hotel'.

JOHN BONHAM

'Bonzo' Bonham, the Led Zeppelin tub-thumper died September 25th when he asphyxiated on his own vomit after 40 shots of vodka. Don't mention 'Moby Dick'.
Remember me this way:

BONZO'S LAST BASH THE END FOR ZEP?

The sudden death of drummer John Bonham on September 25 has cancelled Led Zeppelin's US tour, scheduled to open on October 16, and thrown the whole future of the group into jeopardy.
The drummer was in residence at Jimmy Page's Windsor mansion, where the group were rehearsing for the tour. The cause of death was thought to be Bonham's choking on his own vomit, but this could

not be confirmed by the post-mortem.
NME
Remember me this way: Absolut hero or bit-part player in Hammer Of The Gods.

PAT HARE

Died September 26th in prison after being convicted of murdering his girlfriend and a policeman. Ironically, the blues player is best known for his 'I'm Gonna Murder My Baby'.
Remember me this way: Life imitating music.

STEVE PEREGRINE TOOK

The other half of the original Tyrannosaurus Rex, who quit the group before they became T Rex. Took was found dead in his flat in West London on October 27th, aged just 21, he had choked to death. Took - real name Steve Porter - played on the group's first three albums before being replaced by Mickey Finn.
Remember me this way: Splitting after 'King Of The Rumbling Spires' in 1969 to join The Pink Fairies.

OV WRIGHT

Died November 16th as a result of long-term drug abuse. The deep soul crooner from Memphis had previously sung with The Harmony Echoes and The Sunset Travelers, but it was his solo sides during the sixties that confirmed his melancholy sound and tear jerking popularity. A period in jail for drug offences in the '70s didn't alter his intake and his later material consisted of tales of self-pity, broken hearts and lost love. He finally died of heart failure, as ever, on the verge of another comeback.
Remember me this way: In the Sixties, in a smoky club, tearing at your tear ducts.

DARBY CRASH

Crazed vocalist from LA combo The Germs, committed suicide on December 7th by overdosing on heroin, aged 22, a week after the band had reformed.
Remember me this way: Too fast, too young.

JOHN LENNON

Died December 8th when he was shot by a fan on the steps of his New York home. Mark Chapman, Lennon's assassin, has vowed to kill himself rather than spend the rest of his life locked up. During an interview for ITV, in his flat Georgian drawl, Chapman confesses: "There was no emotion on my part. There was no anger. There was nothing. It was dead silence in my brain. Then Lennon looked at me and I heard a voice in my head say, 'Do it! Do it!'"

Remember me this way: Still in a creative frenzy, the couple were already at work on their next project when, coming home late from a session, Lennon was hailed by a fan to whom he'd given an autograph earlier that day, Mark David Chapman. Lennon turned and Chapman shot him five times with a .38 revolver. Lennon was rushed to the hospital but pronounced dead on arrival from a massive loss of blood. Chapman later claimed it was Lennon's remarks in 1966 on Jesus that drove him to his act, but more likely he was just a schnook in search of fame. He found it.

Jeff Pike from Death Of Rock 'n' Roll

Read it in the press:
LENNON MURDERED - WORLD MOURNS

December 8th: John Lennon, ex-Beatle and working class hero to millions, gave his last autograph today - to the man who killed him.

Lennon signed the proffered copy of 'Double Fantasy', his acclaimed comeback LP of 1980 and Mark David Chapman, a 25-year-old Hawaiian, repaid the compliment with five .38 calibre bullets to John's upper body, severing a major artery. His victim was dead on arrival at New York's Roosevelt Hospital.

Crowds gathered to pay their respects, both outside the Dakota apartment building on New York's Upper West Side, and in Lennon's native Liverpool. His wife Yoko Ono, who was at his side at the time of the shooting, requested a ten-minute silent vigil be

held on December 14, in which millions more fans could participate and mourn the untimely death of a major rock talent.
NME

NOEL GALLAGHER: "Lennon would be shite if he were alive today."
KURT COBAIN: "John Lennon was definitely my favourite Beatle, hands down. Lennon was obviously disturbed. So I could relate to that."
GEORGE HARRISON (in 1988): "Yeah, we miss him. We miss him because he was so funny."
LENNY KRAVITZ: "I was never really a Beatles fan but when I heard 'John Lennon And The Plastic Ono Band', I loved the way that John Lennon expressed himself so freely. He was doing that primal therapy and he was just letting it out."
Remember me this way: Working class hero.

TIM HARDIN

Died December 12th from a heroin overdose. Hardin was a hugely talented and immensely wasted folkie who penned 'Reason To Believe' and 'If I Were A Carpenter'.
Read it on record sleeves:
He was usually filed under folk, but Tim Hardin

was not a folk singer. There are no paeans to long-forgotten causes here, no anthems, none of the naive political earnestness of the era. Tim went on record as saying that he was too involved in his personal life to write about what was going on in the world. Instead, his work was a road map of life's highs and lows, both awfully familiar to him.
Colin Escott, 1993, from the sleeve of 'Hang On To A Dream - The Verve Recordings'.

If ever a life was lived to a set of alternate co-ordinates, it was Tim Hardin's. The heart-stopping beauty and simplicity of his best songs, and the almost embarrassing intimacy with which he sung them, stood in stark contrast to an often chaotic life that always threatened to spin out of control. Colin Escott, 1996, from the sleeve of 'Simple Songs Of Freedom - the CBS Recordings.'
Remember me this way: 'It'll Never Happen Again'.

STEVE CURRY

Another T Rex man dies. Bass player Curry headed for the Glam resurrection in the sky. Glitter and stack heels optional.
Remember me this way: Pumping out 'Jeepster' to rows of screaming teens.

BILL HALEY

The acceptable face of rock 'n' roll cashed in his chips on February 9th. He rocked but never really rolled and denounced the devil's music later.

Read it in the press:
CLOCK RUNS OUT FOR HALEY

Bill Haley, who died in Texas on February 9th age 55, ensured his place in rock 'n' roll history on just one day back in 1954. On April 12th that year, he cut 'Shake Rattle And Roll' and 'Rock Around The Clock', two tracks which will always be remembered for launching rock 'n' roll on an unsuspecting world.

Even so, he remained a quiet unassuming idol. "I'm just an ordinary guy making a living the only way I know how." he said of himself.
NME
Remember me this way: See you later, alligator.

MIKE BLOOMFIELD

Found dead in his car on February 15th of an accidental drug overdose, the former Paul Butterfield Blues Band and Electric Flag guitarist is best known for his incisive guitar playing. His ringing guitar tone echoed back to the blues and before and the addition of his electric zip earned him the reputation "the finest white blues guitarist America had so far produced".

ELVIN BISHOP: "Michael Bloomfield was consumed with music, just burning up. On a good night Bloomers would have an endless stream of shit that would come out of that fingerboard."

AL KOOPER: "He'd eat fire on stage. It was as exciting as Hendrix setting his guitar on fire or Townshend smashing his guitar."

Remember me this way: Rolling down 'Highway 61 Revisited' with Bob.

TAMPA RED

Georgian Bluesman, credited with inventing the slide guitar, died March 19th. He was the purveyor of 'Turpentine Blues', part of the Tampa Red legacy, which started way back in the '20s.

Remember me this way: Playing the Chicago Blues houses with a host of would-be legends in support.

BOB 'THE BEAR' HITE

Face fungus-friendly Canned Heat frontman died April 15th from a heart attack. Hite epitomised white blues hollering, worked with John Lee Hooker and turned Canned Heat into a hard rock-a-boogie proposition. A serious beard man too.

FITO DE LA PARRA (Canned Heat drummer): ìWe were dragged to play Woodstock, we were really tired, exhausted, at the end of an 83 date tour.

Bob: Not Mick Jagger thankfully

At the airport there was a fight to get on the helicopter but no-one would argue with us because we had Bob Hite with us and nobody was gonna fuck with the Bear!"

Remember me this way: Unleashing 'Let's Work Together'.

BOB MARLEY

The man who took reggae to the masses died May 11th from brain cancer. Marley had suffered from cancer for some time and had previously lost a toe to the disease. The Village Voice dubbed him the "Jagger of reggae". To which he replied: "Me have a laugh sometimes when dem scribes say me like Mick Jagger or some superstar like that. Dem have to listen close to the music because the message not the same."

A Bob Marley theme park was recently opened at Universal Studios in Florida. Marley is commemorated in a two-level venue entitled A Tribute To Freedom, which includes a restaurant serving Jamaican food and a live outdoor sound stage where reggae is performed. The design of the park is based on Marley's home and garden in Kingston, Jamaica.

JOHNNY MOORE (Wailers' trumpet player): "When The Wailers started they were more like The Impressions, but they were dissuaded from going along those lines and influenced to go inside themselves."

ALTON ELLIS: "Bob was always ragamuffin on stage. Everyone else was trying to appeal to the American audience but him was a rebel, jumping up, throwing himself about on stage."

Chris Blackwell (Island Records): "Bob came into my office at the right time when I had an idea in my head that a rebel type character could emerge."

RICHARD WILLIAMS (Island Records): "I was prepared to find someone talented, but it soon became clear that Bob was Marvin Gaye or Bob Dylan. Or both."

VIVIEN GOLDMAN (Island Records' press officer): "'Catch A Fire' altered the landscape of reggae completely."

CARLOS SANTANA: "The first album I bought was 'Catch A Fire' and from there on I was hooked."

Remember me this way: Through the movement of Jah people.

Hubert Johnson

Mainstay of Detroit vocal outfit The Contours, who tore up dance floors in the early '60s with their version of 'First I Look At The Purse' for Motown. Johnson's cousin Jackie Wilson had to fix them up with an audition for Motown, even though the band had already released the hugely inspirational 'Do You Love Me', which became

Remember me this way: Their brewing soul as interpreted by The Beatles and New York Dolls.

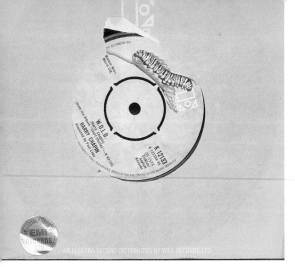

HARRY CHAPIN

Much-touted singer / songwriter, died July 16th in a traffic accident. He was the local DJ on 'WOLD', not to mention the writer of 'Cat's In The Cradle'. Chapin was a strange cove who was sought out by Elektra boss Jac Holzman; he hoped Chapin was the first of a new kind of singer / songwriter. Indeed he was, but his commercial potential was not as great as Holzman had originally believed and Chapin soon moved on.

Remember me this way: With the bizarre and lengthy 'Sniper'; a song about the stuff that goes through a sniper's mind.

FURRY LEWIS

Lamented blues man, died September 14th. His greatest recordings were made back in the '20s, before he changed horses and became a character actor on US TV and finally a lacklustre comedian.

Remember me this way: Singing 'Kassie Jones' on the 'Anthology of American Folk Music'.

1982.

LIGHTNIN' HOPKINS

Died January 30th from cancer. Hopkins was a late starter; he'd been playing a good 20 years before he recorded a note.

Read about it in books: Surveying the world through is tinted glasses, he noted the games men and women play, picked up his guitar and spun out his thoughts. From The Blues From Robert Johnson to Robert Cray by Tony Russell

Remember me this way: As the man who was inspired by Blind Lemon Jefferson and handed the torch on to a new generation.

ALEX HARVEY

Scottish pre-punk malcontent and founder of the Sensational Alex Harvey Band, died February 4th from a heart attack. Following a rare European tour, Alex Harvey was stricken down in the port of Zeebruggen in Belgium with two heart attacks. He died the night of his 47th birthday in a hospital in Brugge.

Read it in the press:
GOODBYE FAITH HEALER

Alex Harvey, affectionately known as Britain's oldest punk, died on the eve of his 47th birthday on February 5th. Glasgow born Harvey's influence on British rock music dated back to the late Fifties, but it was his work with The Sensational Alex Harvey Band for which he'll be best remembered. NME

Zal Cleminson: "He was very organised when it came to putting ideas down but he had a wild side. He'd take sheets from hotels and wander around airports dressed as an Arab, carrying huge slices of Camembert."

Remember me this way: Hooped shirts, Jacques Brel and 'Delilah'.

SAMUEL GEORGE

Mainman of The Capitols, who'd previously turned out as a rock 'n' roll outfit called The Three Caps. Their new incarnation hit the dance floors with 'Cool Jerk' in 1966. George died on March 17th as a result of stab wounds inflicted in a fight.

Remember me this way: "I know a cat who can really do the cool jerk."

RANDY RHOADS

Gifted young guitarist who died on March 19th when the wing of the plane he was in nicked Ozzy Osbourne's tour bus. Rhoads was the guitarist who helped put Ozzy Osbourne back on the road in the early 1980s after he'd moved on from Black Sabbath.

Apparently Rhoads and a make-up girl were on board the plane when the pilot, high on cocaine, seemingly aimed the aircraft at the empty tour bus in an attempt to scare the passengers on the bus. The stunt went horribly wrong and everyone on the plane was killed.

Remember me this way: Blizzard Of Ozz's 'Diary Of A Madman'.

DANIEL BEARD

Latter day member of The Fifth Dimension (post '76) who died in a fire in his apartment block.

Remember me this way: Singing one of the group's only late '70s hits 'Love Hangover'.

The Alex Harvey Band, with Alex centre (blearily)

JAMES HONEYMAN SCOTT

Original member of the Pretenders, who died June 16th after a period of drug abuse. Found dead two days after fellow member Pete Farndon had been fired from the band for habitual drug use.

Remember me this way: The last single he played on was 'I Go To Sleep'.

JOE TEX

The Atlantic soul legend died August 13th from a heart attack. His hits included the moody, emotional, life-re-affirming ballad 'Hold On To What You've Got' and more uptempo numbers such as 'Show Me' and 'SYSLJFM (The Letter Song)', which enjoyed a new lease of life courtesy of The Commitments movie. Tex later turned disco and had his biggest hit ever with 'Ain't Gonna Bump No More With No Big Fat Woman'.

Remember me this way: Not bumping no more.

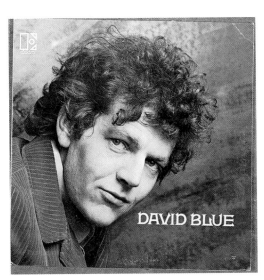

DAVID BLUE

Died December 2nd from a heart attack while out jogging. Blue was a revered contemporary of Dylan's; the maudlin singer / songwriter produced a handful of truly great albums.

THE BEST OF THE GREAT DAVID BLUE LEGACY: 'David Blue' (1966, sounds like a natural brother-in-law to Dylan's 'Highway 61 Revisited'), 'These 23 Days In September' (1968, he's getting moody and thought provoking now), 'Stories' (1972, and he's doom-laden), 'Nice Baby And The Angel' (1973, and his sadness is complete). Beware of the smooth and over contemporary 'Com'n Back For More' from 1975.

Remember me this way: With 'These 23 Days In September' or his eponymous 'Highway 61'-sounding platter.

BIG JOE WILLIAMS

The Mississippi Bluesman died December 17th. He wrote '(Baby) Please Don't Go', made famous by Them and 'Crawlin' King Snake', likewise for The Doors.

Remember me this way: By trying to track down the Big Joe originals.

BILLY FURY

Died January 28th from heart disease. Fury was the UK's answer to Elvis, he swaggered into rock 'n' roll on the British show circuit and charted with 'Halfway To Paradise' and 'Jealousy' in the early '60s.

Read it in the press:
BILLY FURY: HALFWAY TO PARADISE?

Billy Fury, one of Britain's foremost rock stars of the late Fifties and early Sixties, died on February 28th after a long history of heart trouble. He had undergone three major operations, including open-heart surgery. He collapsed at his London flat and was found to be dead on arrival at hospital. He was 41. Although Fury had 19 Top 20 hits during the period 1959 to 1965, he never quite made the top spot. Before The Beatles, Billy Fury (real name Ronald Wycherley) was the nearest thing to Elvis Britain had. His death marks the end of an era. NME

IAN DURY: "There's only ever been two English rock 'n' roll singers - Johnny Rotten and Billy Fury."

The sound of Fury: 'Maybe Tomorrow' (1959), 'Margot' (59), 'Colette' (1960), 'That's Love' (60), 'Wondrous Place' (60), 'A Thousand Stars' (1961), 'Don't Worry' (61), 'Halfway To Paradise' (61), 'Jealousy' (61), 'I'd Never Find Another You' (61), 'Letter Full Of Tears' (1962), 'Last Night Was Made For Love' (62), 'Once Upon A Dream' (62), 'Because Of Love' (62), 'Like I've Never Been Gone' (1963), 'When Will You Say I Love You' (63), 'In Summer' (63), 'Somebody Else's Girl' (63), 'Do You Really Love Me Too' (1964), 'I Will' (64), 'It's Only Make Believe' (64), 'I'm Lost Without You' (1965), 'In Thoughts Of You' (65), 'Run To My Lovin' Arms' (65), 'I'll Never Get Over You' (1966) and 'Give Me Your Word' (66).

Remember me this way: With 1964's 'It's Only Make Believe'.

LAMAR WILLIAMS

Bassist with The Allman Brothers, who died January 28th from Agent Orange-related cancer. He'd joined the group in 1973 to replace the just-departed Berry Oakley.

Remember Played on the 'Brothers And Sisters' album and the instrumental 'Jessica'.

They long to be close to you...

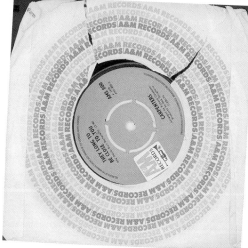

More (1973), 'Top Of The World' (73), 'Jambalaya' (1974), 'I Won't Last A Day Without You' (74), 'Please, Mr Postman (1975), 'Only Yesterday (75), 'Solitaire' (75), 'Santa Claus Is Coming To Town (75), 'There's A Kind Of Hush' (1976), 'I Need To Be In Love' (76), 'Calling Occupants From Interplanetary Craft' (1977) and 'Sweet Sweet Smile (1978).

Remember me this way: With the compilation 'If I Were A Carpenter' and covers by Matthew Sweet, Sonic Youth and pals or by her own fair vocal on 'Goodbye To Love'.

DANNY RAPP

Shot himself on April 5th. The singer in the band Danny and The Juniors briefly found fame with 'Rock And Roll Is Here To Stay' but just couldn't hang around any more.

Remember me this way: Charting in the UK with 'At The Hop' in 1958.

PETE FARNDON

The second Pretenders member to die in drug-related circumstances. Farndon died April 14th, less than a year after James Honeyman Scott. He'd left the band the year before.

Remember me this way: Playing bass on 'Stop Your Sobbing'.

FELIX PAPPALARDI

The Mountain man was shot by his wife Gail Collins on April 17th. Pappalardi had played in the reformed Mountain and then recorded two solo albums before relocating to Japan.

Remember me this way: Riding the 'Nantucket Sleigh Ride', a pretty tedious vehicle for Mountain guitarist Leslie West, but remembered because the heaviest bit was used as the intro music for television's World In Action.

MUDDY WATERS

Died April 30th from a heart attack. The Mississippi blues guitar player who hit Chicago in the '40s, spawned a string of heroic players from his group. Along the way, he also delivered a brace of standards including 'Hoochie Coochie Man' and 'Mannish Boy'.

ROBERT CRAY: "I played six dates with Muddy and got to go backstage. He adopted me, you know, and he would tell me all these incredible

KAREN CARPENTER

Died February 4th from heart failure, after a long battle with anorexia nervosa. Drummer turned emotive vocalist and latter-day icon. She'd only just begun.

Read it in the press:
KAREN CARPENTER DEAD AT 32

The brother and sister duo of Karen and Richard Carpenter swept all before them in the Seventies, selling over 60 million albums of high-gloss American pop. But the dream ended on February 4th when Karen was found by her parents on the floor of her bedroom in the family's Downey, California home.

Her mother believes that it was her inability to overcome anorexia nervosa, the so-called slimming disease that caused her death. Back in 1975 it caused the cancellation of a British tour, following which she was confined to bed for two months. NME

RICHARD CARPENTER: "I think she was one of the greatest pop vocalists who ever lived. She had perfect intonation, perfect diction, remarkable breath control, that 'time and time again' line in 'Goodbye To Love', amazing."

Those Carpenters' hits in full: 'They Long To Be Close To You' (1970), 'We've Only Just Begun' (1970), 'Superstar' (71), 'Merry Christmas Darling' (1972), 'Goodbye To Love' (72), 'Yesterday Once

stories about the old band and Little Walter. He'd get me up to play encores and I got pictures at home of me and him. That to me is one of the highlights of my life."

DAVID WAS: "A jazz critic of the '50s had a definition of the blues that I thought was pretty apt. He said it was a perfect balance of passion and detachment. I think that Muddy Waters is the most sympathetic figure in blues, the most approachable, the warmest - one of the most generous spirited of performers."

JOHN LEE HOOKER: "His 'Got My Mojo Working' just sticks in my mind. There's a lot of people who say they got their mojo working but it just ain't right, they just think that they got it workin'. I never could get my mojo to work till way later than when I first heard the song."

Remember me this way: 'You Shook Me', 'Got My Mojo Workin' and a whole lot more.

JOBRIATH BOONE

Died July from an AIDS-related illness. The glamster failed to hit it big, despite his fancy outfits and the backing of a major label.

ìI'm a true fairy!" he proclaimed when he signed for a staggering $300,000. It was not money well spent. Two albums failed to get noticed and he even fluffed an audition to play Al Pacino's lover in Dog Day Afternoon.

Remember me this way: Turning down an offer to come out of retirement and support Morrissey.

CHRIS WOOD

An original member of Traffic member and occasional Hendrix co-player, Woods died July 12th from liver failure. Wood supplied the woodwind and brass to the band and helped craft Traffic's new psychedelic sound on singles like 'Paper Sun' and 'Hole In My Shoe'. The going proceeded to get weirder and the band came up with an epic reworking of English folk called 'John Barleycorn Must Die' along with their jam-friendly workouts, 'Low Spark Of The High Heeled Boys' and 'Shoot Out At The Fantasy Factory'.

Remember me this way: Searching for 'Mr Fantasy'.

MERLE TRAVIS

Country star that took his working roots ('Sixteen Tons') into the charts. Died October 20th from heart failure. His career had been riddled with drink and drug problems and his unreliable reputation reduced the number of potential live opportunities.

Remember me this way: Tennessee Ernie Ford: "He could write songs that would knock your hat off, but he was a chronic alcoholic and when those binges came, there was nothing we could do about it."

TOM EVANS

Badfinger's second songwriter followed Pete Ham's lead and hung himself. Died November 23rd with the group's career and business affairs still in disarray.

Read it in books: Tony Kaye (Badfinger keyboard player) was in Los Angeles, "I had been sleeping and I woke in a cold sweat. I bolted upright. My wife was next to me and I said, 'Something terrible has happened and I think it's Tommy." Then Marianne (Tom's wife) phoned. At 8:45am Marianne had looked out of the rear window. Recognising Tom's clothing, she saw him, suspended from a backyard tree...

From Dan Matovina's excellent Without You, The Tragic Story Of Badfinger.

Three classic Badfinger moments: 'Come And Get It' (1970), 'No Matter What' (1971) and 'Day After Day' (1972).

Remember me this way: 'It's Over' from the band's 'Straight Up' album.

DENNIS WILSON

The pretty one in The Beach Boys, who trifled with Charles Manson and even surfed, Wilson drowned after swimming from his yacht on December 28th. Drugs, booze and all sorts of narcotics were in the frame for the skinny kid who played dumb in Two Lane Blacktop before filling out in later years.

Cut out all the Dennis Wilson-penned tunes from The Beach Boys albums, add the slow ones from his solo stuff and behold a C90 of sheer morbid beauty, bedsit loss and drug-addled intensity. Relationships, huh?

Remember me this way: Singing the sad ones from 'Pacific Ocean Blue', especially track six 'Thoughts Of You'.

Early, innocent and the in the middle: Dennis Wilson

1984

ALEXIS KORNER

Blues fan-come-performer and DJ, died January 1st from cancer.

Read it in the press:

BYE BYE BLUES - KORNER DIES AT 55

Alexis Korner, the founding father of British rhythm and blues, died on January 1st after a short illness. At the time of his death Korner was working on a television series covering the history of rock. NME

Read it in the press: Croaking through 'Tap Turns On The Water' with CCS.

JACKIE WILSON

Died January 20th. Wilson had suffered a massive heart attack and stroke on stage eight years earlier. He remained in a coma until he died in 1984, his demise triggering a posthumous hit and instant, if-belated, crossover fame.

Read it in the press:

FAREWELL TO JACKIE

Soul star Jackie Wilson died on January 22nd at the age of 49. He had been in a coma since a heart attack eight years ago. Born in Detroit in 1934, *he began his singing career in the early Fifties and scored a hit with 'Reet Petite', which was penned by future Motown boss Berry Gordy. Wilson graced the US top 20 more than a dozen times and even when the hits dried up his all action performances - rivalled only by James Brown - ensured that he could work wherever and whenever he pleased.*

His name is probably best known to British music fans as the subject of Van Morrison's tribute song 'Jackie Wilson Said'.

NME

Remember me this way: Reborn with 'Reet Petite' and a claymation cartoon, or perhaps think of him more sentimentally with 'The Sweetest Feeling'.

TOM JANS

The folk singer-songwriter teamed up with Mimi Farina for a couple of albums before embarking on a successful solo career and an even more worthy songwriting path. Died of a drug overdose on March 25th.

Remember me this way: His well-spiked harmonies with Farina.

MARVIN GAYE

Motown stalwart turned reborn social commentator, Gaye eventually became a super-slick, sensual crooner. He was shot by his father on April 1st on the eve of his birthday.

Read it in the press:

WHAT'S GOING ON? MARVIN GAYE SHOT

Marvin Gaye, the soul music legend, was shot dead on April 1st, the eve of his 45th birthday. His 69-year-old father, a retired minister, has been charged with his murder.

Father and son allegedly argued over an 'insurance matter' and 'a letter', the contents of which are unknown. The argument continued overnight and when he refused to leave his room, Gaye Jr shoved him into the hallway. His father apparently returned with a gun and shot his son twice in the chest.

In his 32-year career, Gaye was instrumental in bringing black music to a new and prosperous white audience with albums like 'What's Going On?', his 1971 masterpiece which mixed soul with social comment, and 'Let's Get It On', an LP dedicated totally to the sexual act. NME

Read it on record sleeves: Marvin Gaye's extraordinary career matched his extraordinary life, a mixture of blessings and banes, dazzling success and inscrutable pain. David Ritz from the sleeve of 'The Very Best Of Marvin Gaye'

MARVIN GAYE: "The only thing between me and Beethoven is time."

SHARLEEN SPITERI: "On the album 'Love Starved Heart (Rare And Unreleased)' he sings like he's crying. He had this big thing about being a real man so maybe these tracks were just too emotional for him, too helpless for him to cope with at the time. But, for a Marvin Gaye fan, this really is heaven."

MARVIN GAYE: "I like these cigarettes. I like Courvoisier. I like women, I like good food. Human emotions, passions - I must say... Oh, give it a shot, that's all I can say."

LISA STANSFIELD: "I was in America doing a radio interview and the DJ played 'Just To Keep You Satisfied' from 'Let's Get It On' and I just couldn't help but cry."

NIGEL KENNEDY: "Marvin Gaye's 'What's Going On' is my favourite for playing late and lying on the floor."

Remember me this way: Doing the soundtrack, before his time, of 'Trouble Man'.

ZZ HILL

Seasoned soulman died April 27th from injuries sustained in a car crash. Hill epitomised the relaxed crooning sound of deep soul and used Lamont Dozier and Allen Toussaint to flesh out his mellow groove.

Remember me this way: His best album? 'Keep On Lovin' You', originally on United Artists.

PHILLIPE WYNNE

The former Detroit Spinners vocalist, died on stage in California during a solo set in a nightclub on July 14th. He was 43.

Remember me this way: Crooning 'Could It Be I'm Falling In Love' or the old Motown chestnut 'It's A Shame'. The latter includes a wineglass shattering high note that just can't be beat.

Marvin: Parents, they screw you up

'BIG MAMA' THORNTON

Died July 25th. An R&B legend who originally did 'Ball And Chain', which was later made famous by Janis Joplin, and 'Hound Dog', similarly popularised by someone called Elvis.

Remember me this way: Hogging the ball and chain for sure.

ESTHER PHILLIPS

She was originally billed as Little Esther when she recorded, but eventually matured into a more soulful mode. Born in Texas, Esther became a popular blues and jazz singer before eventually capturing the soul market with 'What A Difference A Day Makes'. She died August 7th.

Remember me this way: Her emotional croons like 'And I Love Him'.

STEVE GOODMAN

Singer/songwriter of the Greenwich Village variety, died September 20th from leukaemia. He wrote 'The City of New Orleans', which was popularised by Arlo Guthrie.

Remember me this way: His fine 'Somebody Else's Troubles' album on Buddha.

NICHOLAS 'RAZZLE' DINGLEY

Razzle was an Isle Of Wight rock fan who became part of the Swedish Glam rock revivalists Hanoi Rocks. The group pre-empted the success of Guns n' Roses with their brash mix of punk and metal and it seemed that nothing could stop them. However, their ill-fated US tour of '84 ended in tragedy when Razzle died on December 8th in a car accident. The car's driver, an intoxicated Vince Neil from Motley Crue was accused of manslaughter.

Remember me this way: Obviously 1983's 'Malibu Beach Nightmare'.

1985

DAVID BYRON

Uriah Heep vocalist who formed the band with Mick Box and Ken Hensley in 1970 and quit five years later. Died February 28th from a heart attack.

Remember me this way: Being very 'eavy but very 'umble.

THE SINGING NUN

The Belgian nun, died March 31st from an overdose of sleeping pills in a suicide pact with her friend / gay lover. Rum stuff indeed. The nun had been brought into the public eye through her habit-forming single 'Dominique', which was all sweetness and light. However her sexual preferences saw her drummed out of the church and even a disco version of her radio-friendly 45 couldn't resuscitate her singing career.

MOTHER TERESA: 'A beautiful death is for people who have lived like animals to die like angels."

Remember me this way: At number seven in the UK in 1963 with 'Dominique'.

KLAUS NOMI

The eccentric pan-sticked German crooner died from an AIDS-related illness on August 6th. Discovered by David Bowie in a New York nightclub, Nomi fashioned his operatic vocal and released a string of Teutonic albums. He looked pretty darn odd too.

Remember me this way: Covering Donna Summer's 'I Feel Love' in a unique electronica style.

LORRAINE ELLISON

Gospel singer turned soul and R&B chart topper, died August 17th.

Remember me this way: Reaching the highest of high notes on her magnificent 'Stay With Me'.

RICKY WILSON

Died November 13th from AIDS, although it was initially claimed that cancer was the cause. The B-52s guitarist had played with the group from day one, fashioning their quasi-'50s groove.

THOSE KITSCH EARLY B52'S TRACKS IN FULL: 'Rock Lobster' (1978), 'Planet Claire' (1979), 'Give Me Back My Man' (1980), 'Private Idaho' (80), 'Dirty Back Road' (80), 'Deep Sleep' (1982) and 'Song For A Future Generation' (1983).

Remember me this way: Doing the 'Rock Lobster'.

GARY HOLTON

Died November 25th as a result of drugs and alcohol abuse. Member of The Heavy Metal Kids who turned actor in the award winning Auf Wiedersehen, Pet.

Remember me this way: Tattooed and earinged in tight, tight drainpipes and wellington boots.

BIG JOE TURNER

Died November 24th from a heart attack. A truly innovative performer who forged a boogie woogie and rock 'n' roll crossover and scored with 'Corrina Corrina' and 'Shake Rattle And Roll'.

Remember me this way: Rolling his fingers across the keys, impressing an impressionable Bob Dylan.

IAN STEWART

Originally recognised as the sixth member of The Rolling Stones, Stewart was "pushed to the back" by their manager Andrew Loog Oldham. He died December 12th from a heart attack.

Remember me this way: Banging it out on 'Let's Spend The Night Together'.

D BOON

Motor-obsessed vocalist with San Pedro trio Minutemen, who died December 22nd in a car accident. Careering into a crescendo of short, sharp anthems, his best work is heard on 'Double Nickels (On The Dime)' and 'Three Way Tie (For Last)', both of which perfected their mini-epic style. Alongside the likes of The Meat Puppets and Husker Du, they typified the hardcore thrash and psychedelic possibilities of new guitar music as distributed by the SST label.

Remember me this way: Cramming the facts into the shortest space of time possible.

RICKY NELSON

Died December 31st in a plane crash, along with his country rock crew The Stone Canyon Band (Andrew Chapin, Bobby Neal, Pat Woodward and Ricky Intveld). The reborn country-tinged

Phil Lynott: Don't believe a word...

crooner had previously been a rock 'n' roll balladeer. Rumours still persist that when the chartered DC3 caught fire and crashed near De Kalb, Texas, the fire had been started by the passengers free-basing cocaine, as they travelled between concerts at Guntersville and Dallas.

Remember me this way: At the 'Garden Party'.

raw emotion into his music, and how to weave a story that would hold the listener to the end. From his interpretation of 'Whisky In The Jar', to 'Still In Love With You' and right up to the rocking 'Thunder and Lightning', he never betrayed himself musically, always writing and performing what his heart told him to.

Unfortunately, the same could not be said about his personal life. Phil Lynott is probably one of the most tragic figures in recent times. Why this articulate, intelligent, and compassionate soul self-destructed will never be answered.

From A Tribute To Phil Lynott at **www.suresite.com/nh/t/thnlizzy/**

I often felt Thin Lizzy to be highly under-rated. Phil's lyrics touched you in the heart, he spoke of feelings, but most of all, togetherness. We are all together in this world. He had great imagery. The twin guitar sound was ahead of its time. I think the 'Jailbreak' era band was the best. 'Live and Dangerous' is the band at its peak though.

Written by Doug, a Lizzy fan, on Bobby Shred's Lizzy Tribute Site

I have been a fan since I was about ten-years-old when Pat Curtis introduced me to some of Phil Lynott's records. You may recognise his surname; he is the brother of Gus Curtis, Phil's personal assistant.

For the last few years I have been attending all the vibes for Philo, at the Point, the Tivoli and the Temple to name a few and have enjoyed them tremendously. Phil's music and vibes will always be with my friends and me.

Written by Keith McDonnell, a Lizzy fan, on Bobby Shred's Lizzy Tribute Site

PHIL LYNOTT

Thin Lizzy mainman, a rock 'n' roll hero and drink and drugs expert, died from liver disease on January 4th. His distinctive vocal and wild lifestyle made him an icon in rock and metal.

Read it on the internet:

From the first day I bought and listened to "Bad Reputation", I knew there was something that separated Lynott and the boys from other bands. Twenty years later I still feel that way.

Phil was a masterful songwriter, both musically and lyrically, he always seemed to know how to interpret

Remember me this way: Throbbing his bass (and his moustache) on 'The Boys Are Back In Town'.

GEORGE MCCRAE

One hit wonder, who scored a major number one with the Jayboy single 'Rock Your Baby', which he recorded when his sister Gwen failed to turn up for the session. Died January 24th from cancer.

Remember me this way: With the mid-tempo groove of 'Rock Your Baby'.

RICHARD MANUEL

A gifted songwriter and an original member of The Band, Manuel hung himself on March 6th during a Band comeback tour. Manuel's fragile state was continually exposed through The Band's albums, every emotional vocal tugged at the heartstrings.

The Manuel Legacy: He co-wrote 'Tears Of Rage' with Bob Dylan and contributed 'In A Station', 'We Can Talk' and 'Lonesome Suzie' to The Band's 'Music From Big Pink'. And on 'The Band' he co-wrote 'When You Awake', 'Whispering Pines' and 'Jawbone' with Robbie Robertson. He did the same with 'Just Another Whistle Stop' and 'Sleeping' from 'Stage Fright'.

Remember me this way: Intoning the unfolding drama of 'Whispering Pines'.

SONNY TERRY

Died March 11th. Famed harmonica player recognised for his partnership with fellow blues legend Brownie McGhee. The duo were omnipresent from their meeting in the late '30s and lasted through till the Eighties. Terry's input to the relationship was a gruff vocal and unequalled acrobatics on the harmonica. When the two finally went their separate ways, Sonny Terry's solo efforts were by far the most engaging.

Remember me this way: Parping the blues.

O'KELLY ISLEY

One of the original trio of Isley Brothers who went from R&B to soul and eventually to psychedelic funk. Died March 31st from a heart attack.

Remember me this way: Syncopating to 'This Old Heart Of Mine (Is Weak For You)'.

TRACY PEW

The founding member of Birthday Party who died on July 5th, after suffering an epileptic seizure while in the bath.

Read about it in books: *The outspoken, leather-clad, hard drinking bassist of Australian alternative rock band* *The Birthday Party.*

From The Encyclopaedia Of Rock Obituaries by Nick Talevski.

Remember me this way: 'Drunk On The Pope's Blood' should be fine.

CLIFF BURTON

Original Metallica bass player, died September 27th in a bus accident while the band were en route to a show in mainland Europe. The rest of the group struggled to come to terms with Burton's death and on their next tour they trashed their hotel in honour of their departed bass player.

Read about it in books: Venom and Motorhead paved the way, but early Metallica took all the cues, rather than mere templates. Their first release 'Kill 'Em All' overbrimmed with snarling spit and snot, but most importantly that guitar sound, stoked the fires of Thrash Metal. Two albums on and an Ozzy Osbourne US tour under their belts, Metallica were on the road to Copenhagen when their tour bus crashed and flares-loving bassist Cliff Burton was killed." From The Kerrang! Direktory Of Heavy Metal

Remember me this way: Demonically driving 'Creeping Death'.

LEE DORSEY

Died December 2nd from emphysema. The Soul King is best remembered for 'Working In A Coal Mine', however the follow up 'Holy Cow' got far higher in the chart. An ex-boxer Dorsey was always a showman and an opportunist and when one of his early '60s sides 'Ya Ya' achieved R&B chart success, it wasn't long before 'The Ya Ya Twist' was on the market.

Remember me this way: "Going down, down, down".

1987

ALEX CAMPBELL

The folk singer died in January of alcohol-related problems. A busker on both sides of the English Channel, Campbell recorded more than 100 albums during his career.

Read it on record sleeves: *The Scottish cowboy they call him in France, but there's nothing belittling about that expression. For although Alex is as full-bloodedly Scottish as a glass of his favourite spirit, there's something of the cowboy about him too, a tumbling*

tumbleweed restlessness one associates with the west, a determination to take life as it comes and wring a smile or song out of it come what may.

Fred Dallas, 1962, from the sleeve of 'Way Out West'.

Remember me this way: His version of 'And The Band Played Waltzing Matilda'.

PAUL BUTTERFIELD

Electric Blues innovator and harmonica patron from Chicago, who led the innovative Butterfield Blues Band, died May 4th aged 44. His demise was attributed to alcohol and drug abuse.

Read it on record sleeves: Paul Butterfield, an intense, wryly-humorous 23-year-old Chicagoan, is by all odds the most consistently stimulating, unaffected, committed and thoroughly satisfying of all young Bluesmen on the current scene. He is a consummate, powerful singer who phrases with ease and natural swing, wholly without artifice or the hip posturing of his contemporaries.

Pete Welding, 1965, from the sleeve of 'The Paul Butterfield Blues Band.'

Remember me this way: With 'Love March' as featured on the soundtrack to Woodstock.

CURT BOETTCHER

Seasoned producer and mainman/songwriter for both Illusion and Sagittarius, died on June 23rd from a liver complaint. Boettcher worked closely with producer Gary Usher and created a unique style of production for their uplifting songs. Both The Illusion and Sagittarius albums were re-issued in 1999 on Revola and Sundazed respectively (and both with extra tracks).

Remember me this way: 'The Truth Is Not Real' from Sagittarius's 'Present Tense' album.

SNAKEFINGER

Occasional Residents member and seasoned guitarist, Snakefinger died July 1st as the result of a heart problem. Under his real name, Phil

Lithman, the 'finger had also served his time in Chilli Willie And The Red Hot Peppers. However his love of the blues led him to tour the UK in 1983 playing blues standards by the likes of BB King, Furry Lewis, Muddy Waters and Elmore James.

During the tour, Edwin Pouncey (Sounds) asked, If you could recommend any one blues record which one would it be? Snakefinger replied, ìIt would have to be 'King Of The Delta Blues' by Robert Johnson."

Remember me this way: Standing next to four blokes with eyeballs for heads.

PETER TOSH

The reggae star who crossed over into the rock world was shot by burglars on September 11th. He was an original member of Bob Marley's Wailers and a big mate of Mick Jagger's.

The Wailers man was notorious for getting into scrapes with the law. Being caught with a spliff in his native Jamaica he was beaten up by police, who smashed his ribs and abdomen on two separate occasions. His anti-police anthem 'Mark Of The Beast' was banned, as was his ode to free dope 'Legalise It'. Perpetually stoned, Tosh was an easy target. So thought four burglars who entered his apartment and demanded that he and his friends lay face down and hand over some cash. When no money materialised, Tosh was threatened with an axe and, as one of his friends tried to intervene both he and Tosh were shot.

Confusion continued even after Tosh's shooting when two different men claimed to be his father and disputes over his estate ensued.

Remember me this way: His anthemic choon 'Legalise It'.

WILL SHATTER

Died December 9th from a heroin overdose. He was the frontman, singer and bass player with primal punk grungesters Flipper; a well kept secret but true innovators of what later became grunge.

Remember me this way: On 'Generic Flipper' or on the excellent 'Gone Fishin'.

MEMPHIS SLIM

Died February 24th from kidney failure. Slim was a blues traditionalist who relocated to France where he became incredibly popular. Prior to heading for France in 1961, Slim released the much-praised album 'At The Gate Of Horn', which featured his ebullient live show. Once settled in Europe, he became an accepted part of traditional blues heritage and a local hero to boot.

Remember me this way: One of his early ones, maybe 'Beer Drinking Woman'.

ANDY GIBB

Died March 9th from an inflammatory heart virus. Brother of The Bee Gees' Gibb clan, Andy couldn't cope with his siblings' success and developed a serious cocaine problem.

Remember me this way: The 1978 hit 'An Everlasting Love'.

DAVE PRATER

Died April 9th in a car crash. Half of legendary soul duo Sam And Dave who produced uptempo dance anthems like 'Hold On (I'm Coming)' and 'Soul Man', which mixed Prater's lower range with Dave Moore's wispy rasps. Their call-and-response style made them hugely popular

on the live circuit.
Remember me this way: Singing the hits, not to mention 'Soul Sister, Brown Sugar'.

CHET BAKER

Rock 'n' roll-styled jazz trumpeter and vocalist, died May 13th when he either fell or was pushed through a window.
Read it on record sleeves: Chet Baker's name was suddenly revealed to the jazz world in 1952 with his first recordings of the original Gerry Mulligan Quartet. Many jazz critics of that time acclaimed Chet Baker as Bix Beiderbecke's reincarnation and considered him as one of the leading personalities of the "Cool Jazz".
From the sleeve of 'Chet Baker Sextet And Quartet'.
Remember me this way: With Chet's moody blues.

JESSE 'ED' DAVIS

Session guitarist (played with Lennon, Stewart, Dylan) who also released several nicely strummed solo albums. Died from a heroin overdose on January 23rd.
Remember me this way: Soulfully sliding into a bottleneck solo.

HILLEL SLOVAK

Original Red Hot Chili Peppers' guitarist, died June 27th from a heroin overdose.
Remember me this way: Walking across the crossing at Abbey Road, naked with only a sock for protection.

NICO

Died July 18th from a brain haemorrhage, following a fall from her bicycle. Nico was an Andy Warhol icon who appeared with the fledgling Velvet Underground before forging her own career specialising in moody ballads.

Read it in the press:
NICO NO MORE

Nico, cult figure and Velvet Underground collaborator of the '60s died last month in hospital after suffering a heart attack whilst riding her

bicycle in Ibiza.
Manager Al Wise: "It's so ironic. People expected that when she went it would be an overdose, not a cycling accident."
Once called "the most beautiful woman in the world" and the influence for Lou Reed's 'Femme Fatale', Nico had been a long time heroin addict but stopped using the drug 18 months ago, although she was still on a methadone course at a Manchester rehabilitation centre. She had been based in England, living with poet John Cooper Clarke for some time, and is survived by her 25-year-old son Air.
Q Magazine, September 1988.

READ IT ON RECORD SLEEVES:

Nico's speech is slow; she makes sudden leaps of thought jettisoning the bridging word. Like a movie camera her thoughts keep cutting, instead of panning, from one to another; only feeling linking them up and leading her on. Pat Patterson, In magazine, New York from the sleeve of 'Chelsea Girl'.
NICO: "I like sad songs, tragic ones... I like to improvise with the notes, with the feeling I have at the time about the song."

TRACEY THORN: "Nico's 'Chelsea Girl' album really influenced me when I made my solo record. It's a mood record, you either feel like listening to it or you don't. Her singing is very flat and I found it quite natural to sing like that. And the actual sound of the record with strings, harmonium and guitar has a lot of richness to it."
LEONARD COHEN: "I was madly in love with her. I was lighting candles, chanting incantations and wearing amulets, anything to have her fall in love with me. The years went past and it never came to anything."
Remember me this way: Doing 'The End'.

ROBERT CALVERT

Space rock innovator with Hawkwind, died August 14th at his home in Margate from a heart attack, aged 43, but not before writing 'Silver Machine'.
Remember me this way: Lemmy: "To me he will always be 'Raving Rupert'."

ROY BUCHANAN

The blues rock guitarist hung himself on August 14th in his prison cell in Fairfax, Virginia. He was found hung by his shirt after being arrested for public drunkenness.
Remember me this way: As the man who turned down an offer to join The Rolling Stones.

SCOTT LA ROCK

Early hip-hop casualty, the Boogie Down Productions' DJ was murdered on August 27th. An unknown assailant shot him while he was sitting in his car in the Bronx, New York.
Remember me this way: Scoring big-time with the album 'Criminal Minded'.

SON HOUSE

Legendary Delta Bluesman, from Mississippi, whose later performances saw him struggle to be coherent, lapsing into flashes of lucid excitement. House had been an influence on a fledgling Robert Johnson and possessed a rich, deep voice accompanied by his ringing bottleneck playing, that's best heard on the Alan Lomax-compiled field recordings still available from Arhoolie. He died October 19th aged 86.

Remember me this way: Howling on 'Preaching The Blues'.

ROY ORBISON

Died December 6th from a heart attack amid a second coming with The Travelling Wilburries. Best remembered as the man who delivered 'Pretty Woman' and a host of tempered rock 'n' roll. Orbison's life was littered with tragedy and this was amply reflected in his music. Not only did his wife die in a motorcycle crash, but his two sons were killed in a fire in their family home in Hendersonville.

Read it in the press:
ROY ORBISON'S WIFE DIES IN CRASH

Claudette Orbison, 26-year-old wife of singer Roy (and the inspiration behind 'Claudette', the song he wrote for The Everly Brothers in 1958), died on June 7, two hours after her motorcycle was in collision with a truck on the road between Nashville and the Orbison's home in Hendersonville, Tennessee.
Roy and Claudette were riding together on separate machines when the crash occurred, and he witnessed the tragedy. The couple reunited a few months ago after and earlier separation, had just begun a holiday at home following a lengthy bout of overseas touring.
NME, June 1966.

IT'S OVER FOR ORBISON

"Roy Orbison was the finest singer on the planet." claimed U2's Bono on hearing of the Big O's death following a heart attack.
Orbison, who was greatly admired by many other artists, was a rare phenomenon, a first generation rock 'n' roller who never degenerated into self-parody or tarnished his credibility.
He will be remembered not only for his Sixties hits like 'Only The Lonely' and 'Oh Pretty Woman' but also for his new recordings like 'You Got It'. NME

Roy Orbison: Tragic in life, love and song

Read it on record sleeves:

When a person has achieved success in the field of endeavour, it's customary to say that they have "arrived". I feel sure that you are already aware of this tid-bit of information, but as my next remarks hinge on the expression, you will please forgive my mentioning it. When I wrote the notes for Roy's first album, he was "on the way". Now, at that point, the shish kebob had not been skewered, but the onions were sliced and the charcoal was lit, which is to say that although Roy had not yet actually arrived, he was most certainly expected.

As you must know by now Roy has made it. Roy HAS ARRIVED and the party is going on now. Shall we join him?

Boudleaux Bryant from the sleeve of 'Crying'.

Read it on the internet: *Roy Orbison possessed one of the great rock 'n' roll voices: a forceful, operatic bel canto tenor capable of dynamic crescendos. He sang heartbroken ballads and bluesy rockers alike, running up a formidable hit streak in the early Sixties. From the release of 'Only The Lonely' in 1960 to 'Oh! Pretty Woman', a span of four years, Orbison cracked the Top Ten nine times.*

Orbison's most memorable performances were lovelorn melodramas, such as 'Crying' and 'It's Over', in which he emoted in a brooding, tremulous voice. The melancholy in his songs resonated with listeners of all ages, but especially heartsick teenagers who knew how it felt to lose in love.

The Rock and Roll Hall of Fame web site at **www.rockhall.com**

Remember me this way: The way he intones: "Mercy!"

SYLVESTER

Died December 16th from an AIDS-related illness. A disco oddity who'd previously fronted outrageous live shows, Sylvester was discovered by an ex-Motown producer who took him to a much wider audience with the timeless anthem 'You Make Me Feel (Mighty Real)' and the equally successful 'Dance (Disco Heat)'. Both tracks featured his reeling falsetto vocal and driving rhythms that would later fuel the Hi-NRG movement.

Remember me this way: Revamped by Jimmy Somerville.

PAUL AVRON JEFFREYS

Original member of Cockney Rebel member who died December 21st in the Lockerbie plane crash. Avron Jeffries was recruited through a music paper ad to join this new, innovative outfit at the start of the '70s. The band immediately got noticed (Steve Harley claimed they would topple Bowie and Roxy) and the hit single 'Judy Teen' ensured the band remained a contender.

Remember me this way: On 'The Human Menagerie' and its standout track 'Sebastian'.

DONNIE ELBERT

R&B singer turned soulful chart-topper with 'Little Bit Of Leather' and a handful of covers of

Sylvester: Feeling mighty reel

Motown and Motown-styled material. Died from a stroke on January 26th.

Remember me this way: His sweet falsetto on Holland / Dozier / Holland's 'Where Did Our Love Go?'

VINCENT CRANE

The doomy keyboard player and Atomic Rooster mainstay committed suicide on February 1st. Having split from The Crazy World Of Arthur Brown with drummer Carl Palmer, Crane formed a power trio. The hits followed, including 'The Devil's Answer' and 'Tomorrow Night', but Palmer left to form Emerson, Lake And Palmer and the group collapsed in 1974. The intervening years saw revivals, regroupings with Arthur Brown and sessions with Dexy's Midnight Runners but Crane's long term problem with depression finally led to his demise.

Remember me this way: With the group's number four UK hit 'The Devil's Answer' from 1971 (things were pretty different back then!).

KING TUBBY

Tubby was the dubmaster general and former electronics repairman who dissolved sound to invent new recording techniques. He was murdered during an armed robbery at his home in Jamaica on February 6th.

Remember me this way: In full echo.

TREVOR LUCAS

The former Fotheringay man joined Fairport Convention as a guitarist in 1971. He died from a heart attack on March 4th.
Remember me this way: On 'Rosie', 'Nine' and 'Live Convention'.

JOHN CIPOLLINA

Died May 29th from a respiratory ailment after suffering from chronic asthma. Cipollina was a guitarist in the '60s acid rock outfit Quicksilver Messenger Service, he powered their jamalong sessions.
Read about it in books: The group made only one noteworthy record, 'Happy Trails', which catches them live at their peak, on versions of 'Who Do You Love' and 'Mona'. Both tracks feature guitar extravaganzas by John Cipollina that are among the best instrumental work any San Francisco band did. The Rolling Stone Record Guide.
Remember me this way: Doing the deed on Bo Diddley's 'Who Do You Love?'

BeachBeachBeachBeachBeachBeachBeachBeachBeachBeach

PETE DE FREITAS

The Echo And The Bunnymen drummer who played on their string of classic albums, which culminated in 'Seven Seas'. De Freitas died June 14th in a motorcycle accident.
Remember me this way: Sailing off in the 'Seven Seas' video.

COWBOY

A member of Grandmaster Flash And The Furious Five's original hip-hop team. Cowboy died September 8th from an undisclosed illness, after slipping into a crack habit.
Remember me this way: His part in 'The Message'.

EWAN MACCOLL

Legendary folk interpreter and father of Kirsty MacColl, whose innovative work produced hundreds of albums of traditional and self-penned material. He died October 22nd. His hand over the ear stance and succinctly pitched vocal are classic British folk traditions and his inventiveness (check out the 'Radio Ballad' series on Topic) was truly impressive.

Ewan MacColl was born Jimmie Miller in Salford, Lancs in 1915. He changed his name during the movement of the Lallans poets in the 1940s. He left school and went on the dole. Later he went on to form theatre workshops with his wife Joan Littlewood and to father two children by the actress. He eventually left the workshop, as he felt it had betrayed its politics, and turned his attention to traditional music. He met Peggy Seeger in 1956 and together they wrote and sang for films and television and, in had three children.

Remember me this way: Hand on ear, reaching the right note.

Pattie Santos

The It's A Beautiful Day vocalist, died December 14th in a car crash.
Read it in the press: *Much of their set consisted of material from their upcoming debut album. 'Hot Summer Day' and 'White Bird' utilised the voices of La Flamme and Santos as solos, in counterpart, as duet, and with organist Fred Webb.*
Billboard magazine, 31st May 1969.

They rocked, but with softer elements too. Two good lead vocalists, David La Flamme and Pattie Santos, are the key for It's A Beautiful Day.
LA Free Press, 25th April 1969
Remember me this way: Holding it together on the wayward rock opus 'Bombay Calling'.

1990

BRANDON MITCHELL

Hip-hop and rap star whose death was surrounded by confusion. Local knowledge is split over whether Mitchell died in a fire or was shot first. He was a member of Wreckx-N-Effect.
Remember me this way: Too real and too quick.

ROGER RUSKIN SPEAR

The Bonzo Dog Band man died January 18th. Spear was the eccentric inventor and pageboy

haircut-sporting loon of the team who became the first man to play a trouser press on record on the track 'Trouser Press'.
SOME BONZO DOG BAND SONG TITLES (Just for a lugh): 'WE ARE NORMAL', 'CAN BLUE MEN SING THE W H I T E S ? ', MOUSTACHIOED DAUGHTERS', 'MY PINK HALF OF THE DRAINPIPE'.
Remember me this way: Was he the 'Urban Spaceman'?

PUMA SANDRA JONES

Black Uhuru singer, died January 28th from cancer just as the group seemed on the verge of major success.
Remember me this way: Singing about 'Sensimilia'.

DEL SHANNON

One of the few post doo-wop male vocalists to find musical credibility. Shannon died after being shunted onto too many unfulfilling rock 'n' roll revival tours, which finally took their toll on the 8th of February. A severely depressed Shannon pointed a .22 calibre rifle at his head and pulled the trigger, ending the misery echoed in his catalogue of hits.
Those classic Shannons in full: 'Runaway' (1961),

'Hats Of To Larry' (61), 'So Long Baby' (61), 'Hey Little Girl' (1962), 'Cry Myself To Sleep' (62), 'Swiss Maid' (62), 'Little Town Flirt' (1963), 'Two Kinds Of Teardrops' (63), 'Two Silhouettes' (63), 'Sue's Gonna Be Mine' (63), 'Mary Jane' (1964), 'Handy Man' (64), 'Keep Searchin' (1965) and 'Stranger In Town' (65).
Remember me this way: Shedding 'Two Kinds Of Teardrops'.

JOHNNIE RAY

Hailed as the 'Prince Of Wails', Johnnie Ray died on February 24th from liver failure. One of the earliest heart throbs, he greatly influenced the style of Morrissey.
Read it on record sleeves:

"Man, I just love pickles," munched Johnny Ray at one of the cocktail receptions that have studded his career in these past years. "Hand me another dish of those gherkins, will you?"
Johnnie Ray - if you need reminding - arrived during the middle of the "gimmick" era after the Second World War. British listeners were hearing him when they didn't realise when DJ Jack Jackson started slipping his crying routine into his show. "I did it for a laugh but quickly realised that Johnnie was bigger than both of us - the public and me."
Mr Ray, from that moment, was on his way to capturing British fans in the same way that he had taken America.

From Your Record Stars, 1957.

ROBERT PLANT: "I remember Johnnie Ray, his voice and Presley's had a great similarity. In fact Presley was influenced by him and did his song 'Such A Night'. Ray's masculine whimper was remarkable, nobody was making that noise."
Peter Jones (fan): "Live at the Palladium you just couldn't hear him above all the screaming. His movements were astonishing almost spastic, very gangly and awkward and every shift provoked more screams. It was frightening, almost incomprehensible. When he died the fans cried too."
Remember me this way: The number ones 'Such A Night' or 'Yes Tonight Josephine'.

RICK GRECH

Transient bassist died March 17th in drug-related circumstances. Played with Gram Parsons, Family and Blind Faith and was reported in Q magazine in 1989 as having taken up employ as a carpet salesman.
Remember me this way: Throbbing behind Roger Chapman singing 'Strange looking band are weeeeeeeeeeeeee'.

ANDREW WOOD

Short-lived superstar, died March 19th from a heroin overdose while a member of Mother Love Bone. Wood's legacy of Seattle grunge with a touch of humanitarian brashness is still being developed elsewhere.

Wood had created a new sound and, although a known drug user, his band were keen to stick with him. Once Mother Love Bone had recorded their debut album 'Apple' Wood decided he would kick smack and checked into rehab. Clean for four months Wood dabbled one night, cranking up to his pre-rehab dose only to find he couldn't handle it anymore.
Remember me this way: Bringing to life the tribute band Temple Of The Dog.

STIV BATORS

Died June 4th after being hit by a car. The Dead Boys vocalist went on to join The Wanderers and Lords Of The New Church.

PAUL GRANT (Bomp Records): "I worked with Stiv after The Dead Boys split up and I got pretty used to his sense of humour. He was my kind of joker. When he went on tour abroad you could guarantee that he'd make a point of calling me between 3am and 5am to make sure that I was asleep. And, when catalogue books like Gunfighters Of The Old West, 100 New Ways To Prepare Chicken and Home Plumbing arrived at the office, I knew it was him sort of being thoughtful. The best memory I have, though, is in those early CBGBs days. He was wild, uncouth and frenetic. A true gentleman."
From an interview in Scram magazine.
Remember me this way: The Dead Boys' tell-all album 'Young, Loud And Snotty' any of his pranks and his general lack of good dress sense!

RICHARD SOHL

The pianist with the Patti Smith Group, died June 5th of heart failure.
Remember me this way: Holding court for Patti's beat poetry on 'Piss Factory'.

JIMMY HODDER

The 42-year-old Steely Dan drummer drowned on June 15th.
Remember me this way: Paradiddling in the early '70s on 'Can't Buy A Thrill', 'Countdown To Ecstasy' and 'Pretzel Logic'.

BRENT MYDLAND

Another Grateful Dead keyboard casualty, died July 1st in a drug-related incident.
Remember me this way: On the single 'Touch Of Grey' that went top ten Stateside.

STEVIE RAY VAUGHAN

Blues guitarist Stevie Ray Vaughan died on August 27th when the helicopter he was travelling in collided with a ski slope. The chopper was less than a mile from the Alpine Valley Music Theatre where Vaughan had just played his last concert, sharing a bill with Eric Clapton and Robert Cray.

Read it in the press:
STARS MOURN VAUGHAN

Stevie Wonder, Bonnie Raitt and Jackson Browne sang 'Amazing Grace' at the graveside of blues guitarist Stevie Ray Vaughan. The funeral attracted over 1,000 people to Dallas including Ringo Starr, ZZ Top, Nile Rodgers and Delbert McLinton. Vaughan, 35, was killed in a helicopter crash in East Troy, Wisconsin, along with four members of Eric Clapton's touring party. He first came to the public's attention as the guitarist on David Bowie's

'Let's Dance' album in 1983, and was building a very large following which looked set to lead to superstardom.
NME

KENNY WAYNE SHEPPARD (Stevie Ray Vaughan Band) "Stevie Ray Vaughan could grab everyone's attention and hold it in the palm of his hand."
BB KING: "Most of us play a 12-bar solo with two choruses and the rest is repetition. With Stevie Ray, the longer he played, the better."
Remember me this way: Playing 'Scuttlebuttlin'.

TOM FOGERTY

The Creedence Clearwater Revival guitarist died September 6th, from respiratory failure as a result of TB, on his ranch in Scottsdale, California.
Remember me this way: Brother of John, with five solo albums to his credit after he left the superb Creedence Clearwater Revival.

XAVIER CUGAT

Lounge instigator and Cha Cha champion, often seen holding his pet dog as he began the beguine, died October 27th.
Read it on record sleeves:
Cugat's contribution to Latin-American music goes far beyond the popularisation of the Cuban dance steps. Always on the look out for new musical talent, he has brought many of Cuba's outstanding instrumentalists to this country. Some of these, like Desi Arnaz, Luis del Camp and Miguelito Valdes, went on to make their own mark as interpreters of Afro-Cuban music.
From the sleeve of 'Viva Cugat!'
Remember me this way: Bongo-handed on 'Cugat A-Go-Go'.

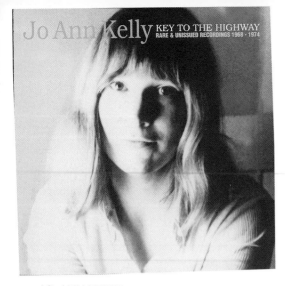

Jo Ann Kelly KEY TO THE HIGHWAY
RARE & UNISSUED RECORDINGS 1968 - 1974

JO-ANN KELLY

British blues scene staple in the '60s, collaborator with John Lee Hooker and other US imports and a fine belting vocalist to boot. Dabbled in jazz and folk before she died during surgery for a brain tumour.

Remember me this way: Out walking the dog.

TOM CLANCY

Tom Clancy was a member of Celtic folkies The Clancy Brothers. He died on November 7th. The group were early Greenwich Village cohorts of Dylan, who took their Irish roots to the masses when they teamed up with Tommy Makem.

Remember me this way: Belting out 'The Leaving Of Liverpool'.

STEVE CLARK

The Def Leppard guitarist, died January 8th after an alcohol and drugs binge as the band were readying to follow up their multi-million selling 'Hysteria' album.

Read it in the press:
LEPPARD DEATH

Def Leppard look certain to continue despite the death of guitarist Steve Clark. Clark, who had studied classical guitar before helping form the

multi-platinum group in 1978, was found dead at his home on January 8th. Singer Joe Elliott said: "He was a really quiet, shy, humble, nice sort of bloke. He was a master of riffs and wrote some of the best we've done. We'll definitely miss his creative input." NME

Remember me this way: Riffing on 'Pour Some Sugar On Me'.

SERGE GAINSBOURG

The moaning pop guru, died March 2nd, aged 63. His effect on pop music and French culture was extensive. In fact he can be credited for introducing sex to pop, taking the piss out of the Eurovision Song Contest and officially 'coming on' to, well, just about anyone.

Just prior to his death, Gainsbourg uttered the immortal chat up line "I would like to fuck you" to Whitney Houston live on French TV during a mild-mannered chat show. He also went out with Brigitte Bardot, Jane Birkin and a host of other beauties. In his spare time Gainsbourg produced a brace of strange, sensual albums which mixed dialogue and oddball storytelling with songs.

RUSSELL MAEL (Sparks): "Both Ron and I are real Francophiles and we loved him. He was an alcoholic, he chain smoked, went on TV not giving a fuck, and was a real womaniser. In the middle of a TV show with Catherine Ringer he said he wanted to go down on her. He also did the French national anthem blasphemously in a reggae style. It caused a huge stir, went to number one and sold two million copies."

Remember me this way: Crooning 'Je T'aime Moi, Non Plus' with Jane Birkin.

THE REBA MCINTIRE BAND

The whole of McIntire's band (Chris Austin, Kirk Cappello, Joey Cigainero, Paula Kaye Evans, Terry Jackson, Michael Thomas and Tony Saputo) died on March 16th when their plane crashed shortly after take off.

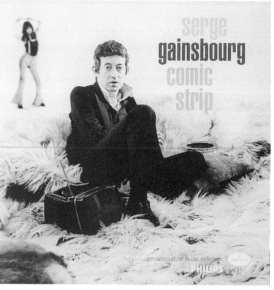

serge gainsbourg comic strip

PHILIPS

Remember me this way: Taking country to the masses with covers of 'Respect' and 'Sunday Kind Of Love'.

STEVE MARRIOTT

The former Small Faces' mainman and Humble Pie instigator died April 20th in a house fire started by a stray cigarette. Marriott had one of the most distinctive voices in British pop, he's best remembered for his late '60s hits 'Itchycoo Park' and 'Lazy Sunday'. Marriott was immortalised in many ways: As the cheeky cockernee in The Small Faces, the robust rocker with Humble Pie and the never-say-die institution with Packet Of Three. At the height of his popularity in 1966 he was bestowed the great honour of having a Marriott wig created in his image.

Read it in the press:
STEVE MARRIOTT DIES

Steve Marriott, the best known Face in the successful Sixties group The Small Faces, has died tragically at his home, in a fire believed to have been started by a cigarette. Marriott was a reluctant star during his teens when The Small Faces had a string of hits. He eventually left

IMMEDIATE

the group to form Humble Pie with Peter Frampton, where he spent the best part of the Seventies after Frampton departed in 1971. Just days before his death, Marriott had been working with Frampton again in America.
NME

JIM LETTERTON (latter-day bassist): "He had this character inside him called Melvin, who he called 'The Enemy Within'. Melvin wasn't very nice, but he could be funny. There were times when you felt like grabbing him and saying, 'Leave it out', but if he hadn't been like that he wouldn't have been half the performer he was."
Remember me this way: Giving 'All Or Nothing'.

DOC POMUS

Legendary R&B and pop songwriter, died aged 65. His partnership with Mort Shuman produced numerous memorable songs.
Remember me this way: Laying down 'Teenager In Love', 'Save The Last Dance For Me' and 'Viva Las Vegas'.

JOHNNY THUNDERS

Died April 23rd from a drug overdose aged 38. Thunders was the founder of Glam rock legends The New York Dolls, and a prime mover in the punk scenes with The Heartbreakers who toured with The Sex Pistols on the aborted Anarchy Tour in 1977. He later worked with Patti Palladin.
Remember me this way: Singing 'Born Too Lose'.

WILL SINNOTT

Drowned May 23rd, while under the influence of liquid Ecstasy, during the filming of a video for his band The Shamen's single 'Move Any Mountain'.
Remember me this way: On the video that killed him, singing 'Move Any Mountain'.

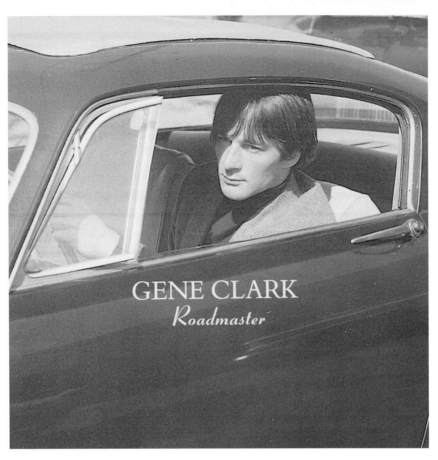

GENE CLARK
Roadmaster

GENE CLARK

Original Byrds member, country rock player with Dillard And Clark and solo crooner who penned numerous classic songs. Died May 24th from a heart attack.
Remember me this way:

Gene Clark was quite simply one of the greatest songwriters of the rock 'n' roll era, one of that era's finest male singers and one of its most visionary and influential musicians. He wrote several all-time classic compositions which are regularly heard on oldies radio world-wide, performed as a member of two legendary bands and lived a full, exciting life in his all too brief 49 years. Yes, there is a deep sadness that Gene Clark is no longer with us but there is a great joy for all that he achieved and shared and blessed. The man is gone, but the legend continues and the music grows.
Sid Griffin. From the sleeve of 'Flying High.'

EDDIE TICKNER (Byrds co-manager): "Gene was handsome, a good songwriter and a frontman. We saw him as a possible '60s Elvis! But his record didn't sell, we couldn't get him onto the radio - no-one, but no-one, could get Gene on the radio for the next 25 years."
CHRIS HILLMAN (The Byrds) "Gene was a really sweet soul who got waylaid by everything negative and just had the fight taken out of him. Sometimes I think it might have been better if he'd stayed at home in Missouri, raised some kids and never come to Hollywood."
Remember me this way: Singing 'She Don't Care About Time'.

DAVID RUFFIN

Temptations mainman and younger brother of Jimmy, died June 1st from a drug overdose aged 50. He'd just completed a tour with Eddie Kendricks and Dennis Edwards as Tribute To The Temptations. A few weeks after the last performance he overdosed on crack.

Read it in the press:
TEMPTATION REMOVED

50-year-old David Ruffin, a founder member of soul supergroup The Temptations, has died in Los Angeles following a reaction to cocaine. The funeral, paid for by Michael Jackson and attended by a galaxy of stars including Stevie Wonder, Aretha Franklin and Diana Ross, was disrupted when fellow Temptation Eddie Kendricks was arrested for non-payment of child support. NME

Remember me this way: Singing 'Get Ready' and 'Ain't Too Proud To Beg'.

ROB TYNER

The MC5 vocalist died September 17th from heart failure aged 46. Tyner was found dead at the wheel of his parked car at his home in Ferndale, Michigan.
Remember me this way: Fronting the '5 with guitar heroes Wayne Kramer and Fred 'Sonic' Smith.

Miles: Broodin'

MILES DAVIS

After several bouts of serious illness, the legendary jazz trumpeter, fusion innovator and jazz rock Godhead (not to mention funky maestro) died aged 75 on September 28th. During his life he survived a car crash, drug problems and a shooting incident and still found time to produce some monumental music. Starting out with Billy Ecsktine's Orchestra, he played alongside Charlie Parker, Dizzy Gillespie and Dexter Gordon, before unleashing the super fine 'Birth Of The Cool' and the awesome mood pieces 'Kind Of Blue' and 'Sketches Of Spain'. Not content to sit still, Davis then embraced rock music and from 'Bitches Brew' moved on to jazz-rock fusion on 'Pangea' and 'Angharta'.

Remember me this way: Anything from 'Kind Of Blue' through 'Bitches Brew' and way, way beyond.

VINCE TAYLOR

British rocker who liked being wheeled on stage in a cage. Taylor failed to make it big in the UK and moved to France in 1962, where he was hugely successful and just as wantonly eccentric.

Remember me this way: Insisting he was American and claiming that "It should have been me, not Elvis!"

Queen (left to right)
Roger Taylor, Brian May,
Freddie and John Deacon

FREDDIE MERCURY

The legendary Queen vocalist, died November 24th from AIDS. But not before producing some awesome videos, histrionic live performances and breathtaking music that ranged from rock to novelty - with opera thrown in for good measure.

Read it in the press:
QUICKSILVER FREDDIE LOSES AIDS BATTLE

Superstar Queen vocalist Freddie Mercury's death from AIDS has prompted industry rumours that the group's Number One hit, 'Bohemian Rhapsody', is to be re-released, and will be followed by a marketing blitz of Queen material over Christmas.
Years of speculation over whether Mercury was suffering from the debilitating virus ended with a statement to the press by the star, and within 24 hours another statement announced that he had died of bronchio-pneumonia brought on by AIDS.
NME

Those Queen Hits In Full: 'Seven Seas Of Rhye' (1974), 'Killer Queen (74), 'Now I'm Here' (1975), 'Bohemian Rhapsody' 9750, 'You're My Best Friend' (1976), 'Somebody To Love' (76), 'Tie Your Mother Down' (1977), 'We Are The Champions' (77), 'Spread Your Wings' (1978), 'Bicycle Race' / 'Fat Bottomed Girls' (78), 'Don't Stop Me Now' (1979), 'Crazy Little Thing Called Love' (79), 'Save Me' (1980),
'Play The Game' (80), 'Another One Bites The Dust' (80), 'Flash' (80), 'Under Pressure' (1981), 'Body Language' (1982), 'Radio Ga Ga' (1984), 'I Want To Break Free' (84), 'It's A Hard Life' (84), 'Hammer To Fall' (84), 'Thank God It's Christmas' (84), 'One Vision' (1985), 'A Kind Of Magic' (1986), 'Friends Will Be Friends' (86), 'Who Wants To Live Forever' (86), 'I Want It All' (1989), 'Breakthru' (89), 'Invisible Man' (89), 'Scandal' (89), 'The Miracle' (89), 'Innuendo' (1991), 'I'm Going Slightly Mad' (91).
Remember me this way: "Mamma mia, mamma mia, could
he do the fandango?"

ERIC CARR

Kiss drummer, who joined for the band's concept piece 'The Elder'. Died November 24th from cancer.

Read about it in books: "When Eric Carr joined the band one of the first things he had to do was change his name because Paul Caravello just wouldn't work. One of the names he came up with was Rusty Blade and we told him to think about it a bit more. Also, his original idea for make-up was The Hawk. The outfit had a padded feather front that made him look like one of those baseball mascots. The only thing missing were big webbed feet."
From Kisstory

Remember me this way: Made up and thumping.

1992.

JOHN CAGE

Intriguing avant-garde composer who inspired Eno, Bowie, Can and Stereolab with his treated piano pieces and tape manipulations.
Remember me this way: Conducting the three movements of '4' 33''', a silent piece for anyone who'd like to attend.

JERRY NOLAN

Died January 14th from a stroke while being treated for meningitis, aged 40. Former sticksman with The New York Dolls and The Heartbreakers.
Remember me this way: Powerhousing through his kit, bedraggled and playing host to Sid Vicious the night he died from an overdose.

CHAMPION JACK DUPREE

Louisiana Bluesman who became a boxer en route to recording some excellent hybrid blues / boogie tracks. Died January 21st.
Dupree: "I'd rather have the piano than a wife... the piano ain't gonna leave me."
Remember me this way: Playing with Clapton and Alexis Korner.

WILLIE DIXON

Died January 29th from heart failure. Mississippi Blues stylist who penned 'Back Door Man', 'Big Boss Man, 'Spoonful' and 'Little Red Rooster'.

Read it in the press:
When asked by Brutarian Magazine what he thought of people covering his songs Dixon said, "frankly I like all of them, because they all come from a different angle. I've heard all different types of versions in different languages and all. The first person to do 'Wang Dang Doodle' was Howlin' Wolf, but they kept it on the shelf a long time. Then Koko Taylor released it. She is nice people. I like her.

Willie Dixon died in a California hospital aged 76, not before summing up his position in the scheme of things with the album and book 'I Am The Blues'.

His songs made a lasting impression on the British R&B scene in the '60s, with The Rolling Stones recording 'Little Red Rooster' and 'I Just Wanna Make Love To You', Cream covering 'Spoonful' and worthy efforts from Jeff Beck, The Pretty Things and Savoy Brown. Later he accused Led Zeppelin of plagiarising his material and got an out-of-court settlement. His other achievements included working as an A&R scout for Chess Records and fathering 11 children, who went on to bring in 30 grandchildren. Q Magazine
Remember me this way: With his pork pie hat and a moaning riff for every occasion, doing 'Ain't Misbehavin' or 'Wang Dang Doodle'.

DEE MURRAY

The bass player for Elton John's band for many years and a seasoned session player with the likes of John Prine, Murray was diagnosed with skin cancer and died during treatment on January 15th.
Remember me this way: Doing a thing like the 'Crocodile Rock'.

STEFANIE SARGENT

A 7 Year Bitch member, Stefanie Sargent had been with the Seattle group until her untimely death on June 27th from an alcohol and drug†overdose, just one month before the release of their debut album. The record eventually surfaced a year later and was dedicated to Sargent.
Remember me this way: The posthumous 'Sick 'Em'.

MARY WELLS

Died July 26th from throat cancer. Motown belter best remembered for her 1964 number one 'My Guy', which was specially written for her by Smokey Robinson and Ronnie White. What went on between her time at the top of the charts and her destitute state prior to her death is a long and sorry tale.
Remember me this way: Singing that hit.

JEFF PORCARO

Died August 5th from a heart attack. The 'great West Coast session drummer' played with Toto and Steely Dan and died in mysterious circumstances aged 38. It's believed his heart attack was caused by an allergic reaction to a pesticide he was using on his garden (immediately sparking Spinal Tap parallels). No mention was initially made of drugs but subsequent investigation revealed that Porcaro's body / drug ratio might have had something to do with his outdoor demise.
Remember me this way: Playing with Springsteen, Michael Jackson et al.

JACKIE EDWARDS

Reggae singer died August 15th aged 52. Having teamed up with Millie Small of 'My Boy Lollipop' fame, Edwards headed for the UK where he found fame as a songwriter.
Remember me this way: The Spencer Davis Group's hits 'Keep On Running' and 'Somebody Help Me'.

EDDIE KENDRICKS

Former Temptations man and solo groovemaster with 'Keep On Truckin'. Died October 5th from lung cancer. Kendricks' solo breakthrough with 'Keep On Truckin' came in 1973 and provided a creative bridge for Motown to meld psychedelia, soul and new funk. The length of the song meant that the single cut had to be split in two parts, however it still reached number 18 in the UK charts. In less than a year Kendricks had repeated the formula with 'Boogie Down', but by then his new funk efforts had been surpassed. From there on in his releases became less and less chart-friendly.
Remember me this way: With the Tempts in all their synchronised glory.

EARL VAN DYKE

The Motown pianist and Soul icon that penned 'Six By Six' died September 18th from prostate cancer.
Remember me this way: On the dance floor at the Torch (Stoke-On Trent) with 'Six By Six' doing cartwheels and the splits.

PAUL RYAN

Half of Paul And Barry Ryan. Died December from lung cancer, aged 44. Paul and Barry were twins who had eight Top 40 hits. Paul also wrote a host of hits for Barry's solo effort.

THOSE HITS IN FULL: As Paul And Barry Ryan: 'Don't Bring Me Your Heartaches' (1965), 'Have Pity On The Boy' (1966), 'I Love Her' (66), 'I Love How You Love Me' (66), 'Have You Ever Loved Somebody' (66), 'Missy Missy' (66), 'Keep It Out Of Sight' (1967) and 'Claire' (67). Just Baz: 'Eloise' (1968), 'Love Is Love' (1969), 'Hunt' (69), 'Magical Spiel' (1970), 'Kitsch' (1970) and 'Can't Let You Go' (1972).
Remember me this way: Singing the pop belter 'Eloise'.

ALBERT KING

Died December 21st from a heart attack aged 69. An trulydistinctive R&B guitarist from Mississippi, he moved to Chicago in the early '60s and fashioned a sound that was highly influential in the UK.
JOHN LEE HOOKER: "Albert King, Boy, now he played the blues. He's my favourite guitar player."
Remember me this way: Writing 'Born Under A Bad Sign', which was later covered by Cream and John Mayall.

1993

MICK RONSON

The guitarist who was the muscle in Bowie's Spider From Mars died April 29th from liver cancer. Following the group's break up in 1972, he recorded a couple of solo albums and turned out on Lou Reed's 'Transformer' album before playing with Dylan, Van Morrison, Roger McGuinn, Ian Hunter and Morrissey.
MORRISSEY: "I don't think he had the respect he

deserves."
DAVID BOWIE: "He provided this strong, earthy, simply-focused idea of what a song was all about. And I would flutter around the edges and decorate."
REMEMBER ME THIS WAY: In full 'Ziggy' regalia or instrumentally handling 'Slaughter On Tenth Avenue'.

MARV JOHNSON

Soulman who launched the Tamla

Motown label with 'Come To Me' in 1958, died May 16th in South Carolina aged 54.
Remember me this way: Singing his biggest tune 'I'll Pick A Rose For My Rose'.

ARTHUR ALEXANDER

Songwriter who penned 'You Better Move On', died June 9th from heart and kidney failure. Aged 53, he was a huge influence on the British beat boom.
Remember me this way: His 'Sally Sue Brown' covered by Bob Dylan on 'Down In The Groove'.

GG ALLIN

Extreme purveyor of the punk rock ethos and self-styled scum rocker, died June 28th from a heroin overdose. Allin's extreme live shows mixed performance art with music; during the show he would mutilate his body. Allin's descent into drug abuse was almost inevitable.

Read it in the press:
The self-proclaimed 'most violent man in rock 'n' roll', Kevin Michael (GG) Allin, died June 28th in New York City at age 36, apparently of a heroin overdose. Allin, whose antics included hurling his faeces at audiences, punching out crowd members, and holding women at knife-point (to bring back "the danger of rock 'n' roll, which is dead," he said), always claimed his death was destined to come on stage.
At a show at Manhattan's Gas Station, an art gallery on the Lower East Side, where the set lasted about 10 minutes a particularly violent crowd spilled onto the street and commenced a bottle-hurling battle with police while GG made his escape to an Avenue B apartment. He was found dead the next morning at 9am. Allin was buried in New Hampshire. At his request, he was laid to rest in his favourite outfit: a dog collar, a leather jock-strap and boots.
Variety, July 6th, 1993.
Remember me this way: As the punk performer who defecated during his act.

EURONYMOUS

The notorious Norwegian Black Metal guitarist with Mayhem, was stabbed to death on August 10th by rival band member Count Grishnacht. The bands had taken more and more extreme stances and Grischnacht, who is now languishing in a Norwegian cell for a rather long time, took the argument to extremes.
Remember me this way: Face painted and hooded.

RONNIE BOND

Died on November 13th from an alcohol-related illness after being ill for some time . The star of The Troggs' tapes who couldn't get the right beat, Bond immediately went into Tap-esque legend.
Remember me this way: Unable to realise the paradiddle.°

ALBERT COLLINS

The blues guitarist, who died November 24th from liver cancer was one of a handful of greats from the BB King era. Taught by Lightnin' Hopkins, he was inspired by BB and T-Bone Walker and went on to inspire Johnny Winter and Hendrix.

JOHNNY LANG: "The way that Albert Collins chooses his notes, the way he attacks the guitar - he can be sweet and gentle at the same time."

Remember me this way: In the fallow years he worked as a labourer on Neil Diamond's house, sure gave him the blues.

RAY GILLEN

Died December 3rd from AIDS-related complications, dying at his home in New Jersey. In a career that spanned nearly a decade, Gillen had played with Black Sabbath, Badlands and George Lynch.

Remember me this way: In Badlands with Jake E Lee's six string.

FRANK ZAPPA

Died December 4th from prostate cancer. Once diagnosed, he spent his time making sure he completed as many projects in as many styles as he could.

Read it in the press:

Mad genius Frank Zappa and his latest batch of Mothers wound up a short run at the Roxy and proved once again that they're not just another band from LA. Zappa, the counter culture's John Cage, assembled a remarkable group of musicians and produced music that is almost impossible to classify. He seems to have successfully invented his own."
Los Angeles Herald, 1973.

Chief freak and bull goose loony of the rock world, Frank Zappa is one of the most complex artists working in rock music. He integrates thematic statements and restatements on many levels, juxtaposing them for special effect
San Francisco Chronicle, 1974.

MATT GROENING: "Frank was my Elvis. As soon as Bart Simpson is able to shave, he'll have a little moustache and goatee."

Mark Volman [Turtles/Mothers]: "Frank was truly a Renaissance man. As a writer of classical

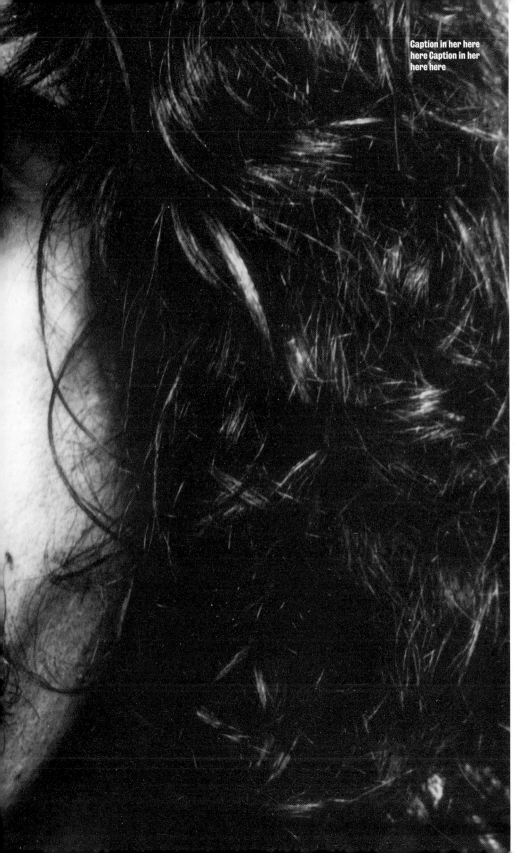

Caption in her here here Caption in her here here

and jazz, as a conductor, as a director of feature films. He didn't wait for people to like it or review it; the minute we finished one thing we were on to something else."

ARTHUR BARROW [Mothers]: "He was pretty much Frank Zappa all the time. It wasn't like he'd put on the beard and moustache just when we went on stage."

SOME BIZARRE ZAPPA SONG TITLES JUST FOR OLD TIME'S SAKE: 'I Promise Not To Come In Your Mouth', 'Penis Dimension', 'Why Does It Hurt When I Pee' and, of course 'The Illinois Enema Bandit'.

Remember me this way: Playing 'Peaches On Regalia' and in the film 200 Motels, with Ringo Starr as a lookalike Zappa.

DOUGLAS HOPKINS

Committed suicide on December 5th after leaving a detox unit. Formerly a member and songwriter with The Gin Blossoms who was asked to leave the band after his behaviour became "questionable".

Remember me this way: With the hits 'Hey Jealousy' and 'Found Out About You'.

MICHAEL CLARKE

The original Byrds' drummer died from liver disease brought about by alcohol abuse in Treasure Island, Florida. After playing on the first four Byrds albums, he moved on to Dillard And Clark, The Flying Burrito Bros and, eventually, Firefall before forming a version of The Byrds, which caused no end of trouble with his old compadres.

Remember me this way: With that foppish fringe.

1994

HARRY NILSSON

Died January 15th from a heart attack brought on by alcohol and excessive living. Nilsson was famous for two hits and his friendship with John Lennon.

Read it on record sleeves: *Slanted-patterned parking lot and the children in the cars of many colours were whining "Why" and "When" and stout and bouncing bobbing frozen-food-faced ladies in wobble-pink capris were roller-curling their basket-way to the fat and hungry Riviera trunks and we, store-sullen men, waited in the scorching smog-stained sun on various vinyl-shining seats when I button-pushed into a 17-bar song-snatch and Timothy, eight and bright, said, "Oh. You're smiling now. Why? Oh why?"*
The song disturbed my Saturday Safeway stupor. Hayes, who rides the discs like Joel McCrea said, "1941, folks, by Nilsson". Nilsson. And Hayes told us it was good and that's why we smiled, Timothy.
Radio Corporations Of America, 1968, from the sleeve of 'Aerial Ballet'.

MARIANNE FAITHFULL: "Harry died in the dentist's chair and he was put in a coffin and left in a funeral home. That night, one of the big Californian earthquakes happened, it went right through the building, and Harry's rather large body fell down a fissure and was lost forever. So they buried another coffin that was filled with stones. I heard it from someone who heard it from someone who was there."
Remember me this way: Singing 'Everybody's Talkin' At Me' or 'Without You'.

PAPA JOHN CREACH

The eccentric Hot Tuna violinist and occasional dabbler with Jefferson Airplane and Starship died of natural causes in LA on February 22nd.
Remember me this way: Mixing jazz and rock with a classical flutter.

DAN HARTMAN

Quirky singer/songwriter, died March 22nd from an AIDS-related illness. Hartman first came to prominence as the bassist in the Edgar Winter Group, before writing a couple of catchy disco hits.

Remember me this way: With 'Instant Replay' rattling around the disco ball.

KURT COBAIN

Died April 8th when he shot himself. Drug problems and his own success weighed down Cobain. He will be remembered as the leader of Nirvana, the inventor of grunge and the man who killed cock rock and married Courtney Love.

Read it in the press:
Friday, April 8. 8.40am. Electrician Gary Smith, employed by Veca Electrical Company, arrives at the Lake Washington Boulevard house to begin work on a security system. Tracing wires from the garage to the upstairs apartment, which had once been occupied by the Cobain's former nanny, Callie, Smith glances through a window and sees what he initially takes to be a dressmaker's mannequin on the floor. Nearby lies an upturned pot plant. Then he sees a body dressed in jeans, a long-sleeved sweatshirt and black trainers. There is blood on the floor.
Q magazine

KURT COBAIN: ARTIST OF THE DECADE.

"The drama played out in Kurt Cobain's performance was a drama of surplus population, be it that of a solitary nobody who nobody liked or a generation the economy didn't need and the culture it didn't want."
Greil Marcus in Rolling Stone, May 13th, 1999

Read it on the internet:
NIRVANA RULES.

KURT will be back. Trust me. I should know. I am a Kurt Cobain Lover and Follower so I should know. I will bring Kurt back and we will rule the world together. Nirvana is a legacy. And Legacies NEVER die. Will Kurt be back? Yes. Why? Cause I said so. When's he coming back? Sooner than planned. Actually Tomorrow Night when the sun goes down. Kurt's married to Courtney Love. Kurt was killed. He didn't kill himself. Unlike some people. Quotes: The sun is gone- Kurt Cobain. I'm not the only one- Kurt Cobain. I'm not like them but I can pretend - Kurt Cobain.
www.angelfire.com/me/ComeAsYouAre/

KURT SAID: "I wish I could have taken a class

Nirvana (left to right): Chris, Dave and Kurt

To **BoddAH** pronounced

Speaking from the tongue of an experienced simpleton who obviously would rather be an emasculated, infantile complainee. This note should be pretty easy to understand. All the warnings from the punk rock 101 courses over the years, since my first introduction to the, shall we say, ethics involved with independence and the embracement of your community has proven to be very true. I haven't felt the excitement of listening to as well as creating music along with really writing for too many years now. I feel guilty beyond words about these things. For example when we're backstage and the lights go out and the manic roar of the crowd begins It doesn't affect me the way in which it did for Freddy Mercury who seemed to love, relish in the love and adoration from the crowd which is something I totally admire and envy. The fact is, I can't fool you. Any one of you. It simply isn't fair to you or me. The worst crime I can think of would be to Rip people off by faking it and pretending as if im having 100% fun. Sometimes I feel as if I should have a punch in time clock before I walk out on stage. I've tried everything within my power to to appreciate it (and I do, God, believe me I do, but its not enough). I appreciate the fact that I and we have affected and entertained a lot of people. I must be one of those narcissists who only appreciate things when they're gone. Im too sensitive. I need to be slightly numb in order to regain the enthusiasm I once had as a child. On our last 3 tours I've had a much better appreciation for all the people Ive known personally and as fans of our music, but I still can't get over the frustration, the guilt and empathy I have for everyone. There's good in all of us and I think I simply love people too much. So much that it makes me feel too fucking sad. The sad little, sensitive, unappreciative, pisces, Jesus man! why don't you just enjoy it? I don't know! I have a goddess of a wife who sweats ambition and empathy and a daughter who reminds me too much of what I used to be. full of love and joy, kissing every person she meets because everyone is good and will do her no harm. And that terrifies me to the point to where I can hardly function. I can't stand the thought of Frances becoming the miserable self destructive, death rocker that I've become. I have it good, very good. and Im grateful, but since the age of seven I've become hateful towards all humans in general. Only because it seems so easy for people to get along and have empathy. Empathy! Only because I love and feel sorry for people too much I guess. Thank you all from the pit of my burning nauseous stomach for your letters and concern during the past years. Im too much of an erratic, moody, baby! I don't have the passion anymore and so remember, its better to burn out than to fade away. peace, love, Empathy. Kurt Cobain

Frances and Courtney, I'll be at your altar.
please keep going Courtney
for Frances
for her life which will be so much happier
without me. I LOVE YOU, I LOVE YOU!

on becoming a rock star. It might have prepared me for this."

NEIL YOUNG: "One of the absolute best of all time."

LIAM GALLAGHER: "He was a sad cunt who couldn't handle the fame."

MARTIN CARR (The Boo Radleys): "He probably hadn't even reached his creative peak."

BILLY CORGAN (Smashing Punkins): "After what happened to Kurt, opening yourself up to the press seems even more ridiculous than ever."

KURT SAID: "I can't decide whether I like playing music enough to put up with all the shit that's written about us."

Remember me this way: In the video for 'Smells Like Teen Spirit', all tattoos and cheerleaders.

KRISTEN PFAFF

Died June 16th from a drug overdose. The Hole bassist died in the bathroom of a friend's house and was discovered the next morning. Her death came as the band's album 'Live Through This' was released. Pfaff joined the band when original bassist Jill Emery quit and has since been replaced by Melissa Auf Der Maur.

Remember me this way: She lived through this. Almost.

JESSE BOLIAN

Singer for close-harmony soul act The Artistics who hit the Northern Soul circuit with 'Hope We Have' and entertained the R&B circuit with 'I'm Gonna Miss You'. Died June 8th.

Remember me this way: Hamming it up at breakneck, stomping speed.

MAJOR LANCE

Legendary Chicago soul singer, died September 3rd from heart failure in Decateur, Georgia aged 53. Co-conspirator with Curtis Mayfield, Lance eventually charted with a slew of soul hits. Signed to Okeh, Lance released a series of upbeat dance material including 'The Matador' and the anthemic soul belter 'Ain't No Soul (Left In These Old Shoes)', before he began his journey through independent soul labels and eventually hit the cabaret circuit.

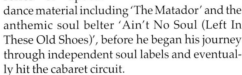

Remember me this way: Stomping through Mayfield's 'The Monkey Time' or 'Um, Um, Um Um, Um'.

NICKY HOPKINS

Revered session keyboard player and occasional Rolling Stone died September in San Francisco, aged 50. Played with Screaming Lord Sutch, Quicksilver Messenger Service, The Small Faces, Jefferson Airplane and many more.

Remember me this way: Being introduced by Grace Slick at Woodstock.

WILBERT HARRISON

Purveyor of Jump Blues whose 'Kansas City' became a standard. Died October 26th.

Remember me this way: Singing his other one, 'Let's Stick Together', which was covered by Canned Heat and Bryan Ferry.

FRED 'SONIC' SMITH

MC5 guitar stalwart and husband of Patti Smith, died November 5th following a heart attack. Having formed the band in 1964, Fred led the group's live assaults and proto political activism. When the group burnt out he married Patti and, just prior to his death, taught her to play guitar.

PATTI SMITH: "Instead of focussing on the loss of individuals, I've found that it's very helpful to

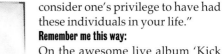

consider one's privilege to have had these individuals in your life."

Remember me this way: On the awesome live album 'Kick Out The Jams'.

JERRY EDMONTON

Canadian drummer with prime rock/metal movers Steppenwolf, died in a car crash on November 28th.

Remember me this way: Tub-thumping on 'Monster' or revving it up on 'Born To Be Wild'.

DINO VALENTE

Truly eccentric Quicksilver Messenger Service and later solo songwriter. Died November 16th in abject confusion and poverty. After starting out playing the Greenwich Village Folk Circuit occupied by Fred Neil, Dylan et al, Valente formed Quicksilver Messenger Service but quit when he got into trouble over tax payments. He later rejoined the band but wrote under a different name, before leaving again to record just one awesome solo album.

Read it on record sleeves: *You take the electrical power out of the wall and you send it through the guitar and you bend it and shape it and make it into something, like songs for people and that power is a wonderful thing.* From the sleeve of 'Dino Valente'.

TOM DONAHUE (San Francisco DJ): " If every chick that Dino's slept with buys the album, it will be number one."

Remember me this way: Lost and bereft on his masterful self-titled solo album.

1995

DAMON EDGE

Integral member of the influential US electronic outfit Chrome who dabbled in the industrial arena and released a batch of obscure albums during the '80s. Edge eventually quit and embarked on a lengthy solo career.

Remember me this way: In ambient mode with Chrome's 'Alien Soundtracks'.

TED HAWKINS

Busking blues player, died January 1st from a stroke just as his career was undergoing a revival. Hawkins' born-again blues had become contemporary following the recording of a new album, but the success proved to be too little too late.

Remember me this way: With 1971's 'Watch Your Step' album.

PHILIP TAYLOR KRAMER

Iron Butterfly bass player who died in a car crash on February 12th. His body was missing in dense woodland for four years.

Remember me this way: In a Gadda Da Vida-style (but not on the actual original record), baby.

MELVIN FRANKLIN

One of two original Temptations men who were still performing with the group in the '90s, Franklin died February 23rd from heart failure after suffering with diabetes and rheumatoid arthritis for years.

Remember me this way: In a suit, side-stepping and in harmony.

BOB STINSON

Replacements member, died February 18th from complications resulting from drug and alcohol abuse. Stinson had been sacked from the group, he was found with a hypodermic next to his body.

Remember me this way: On half a dozen Replacements' platters.

VIVIAN STANSHALL

Died March 5th in a fire at his home in Muswell Hill, London aged 52. The singer with the Bonzo Dog Band, the vocalist on 'Tubular Bells' and an eccentric performer and writer of various solo projects.

Read it on record sleeves:

I was pleased to see that a full-grown Plecostumus is 18 inches long. I have one at home. He is only two feet at present and is called Blinky. I also have two bullfrogs called Roly and Poly that I intend to amplify. And a hedgehog.

Viv Stanshall from the sleeve of 'The Doughnut In Granny's Greenhouse'.

VIV SAID: "I like shouting and declaiming and using my voice and playing the tuba and painting loudly..."

ROGER RUSKIN-SPEAR (The Bonzo's): "Viv was obviously very fond of the Bonzos, but he was so schizophrenic and unstable that it couldn't continue as a viable commercial proposition. There was always a crate of champagne in the dressing room and we were always completely pie-eyed. When he'd finished singing he'd usually just throw the microphone away. We actually stopped on one occasion and left the stage, left him to it. We just couldn't cope with him."

NEIL INNES: "He was like a 14th century fool who'd just breeze into your life with a lute."

Remember me this way: Introducing "Adolf Hitler on vibes".

Bonzo Dog singer 'died without pain'

By Sean O'Neill

VIVIAN STANSHALL, founder of the Bonzo Dog Doo-Dah Band, was drunk and under the influence of drugs when he died in a fire at his home, an inquest was told yesterday.

Stanshall's body was so badly burned that he had to be identified from dental records.

The blaze was started either by a lamp next to a pile of papers or by a discarded cigarette.

Prof David Bowen, a pathologist, said the 52-year-old performer probably suffered no pain.

"It seems likely that Mr

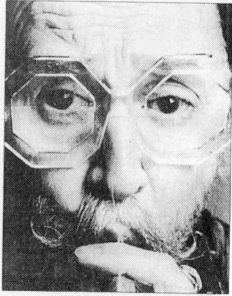

Stanshall: colourful

ple of bottles of vodka on the

NWA: Eazy (centre)

DELROY WILSON

Reggae singer, and one of the formative vocalists in Jamaica, died March 6th, aged 46 after years of alcohol abuse. In his career he released in excess of 100 singles and was name checked in The Clash's 'White Man In Hammersmith Palais'.

Remember me this way: As the inspiration for Dennis Brown and Gregory Isaacs.

EAZY E

NWA rapper and Ruthless Records' boss, died March 27th from an AIDS-related illness.

EAZY E: "I would like to turn my own problem into something good that will reach out to the homeboys and their kin, because I want to save their asses before it's too late."

Remember me this way: Coming 'Straight Outta Compton'.

SELENA QUINTANILLA PEREZ

Died March 31st when she was shot by the president of her fan club.

Read it in the press:

FAN CONVICTED OF MURDERING SINGING STAR

The founder and former president of the fan club of the Grammy-winning singer Selena has been convicted of murdering the 23-year-old Tejano music superstar.

Yolanda Saldivar, 35, who also managed the singer's boutiques, sobbed after being told she could face a maximum of life imprisonment for the shooting in a motel in Selena's home town, Corpus Christi, Texas. John Hiscock in Los Angeles Times

Remember me this way: Much loved in life and death.

LEE BRILLEAUX

Singer in UK R&B combo Dr Feelgood, died April 7th from lung cancer. Since 1971, when they emerged from Canvey Island and championed the pub rock circuit with their white R&B, the Feelgoods' pub rock struck a chunky chord in the hearts of many a pre-punk pub goer. Critically acclaimed from the outset, it wasn't until they took their music out on the road that people really cottoned on to Brilleaux's soulful strut and the quirky shuffling of guitarist Wilko Johnson.

Remember me this way: The mono version of 'Down By The Jetty'.

JOHNNY GUITAR WATSON

Blues guitarist and latter-day crossover pop soulster, died May 17th from a heart attack. Much sampled in recent years and a big influence on Prince and Snoop Doggy Dogg.

Remember me this way: Twanging on 'I Need It', his big hit in 1976, and its follow up 'A Real Mutha For Ya'.

RORY GALLAGHER

Died June 14th from a chest infection following a liver transplant. Blues guitarist and former main-man in Taste.

Read it in the press:

"His music was informed by an erudite appreciation of the Anglo-Celtic folk stylings of Martin Carthy and the pre-war Mississippi Delta country blues of Son House and Robert Johnson; it was also influenced by the electric Chicago blues of Buddy Guy, Freddie King and Hubert Sumlin, Howlin' Wolf's great guitarist."

Gallagher's obituary in The Telegraph

GALLAGHER: "I'm serious about the blues and I study it."

LENNY KAYE (Patti Smith Group): "The workingman's guitarist. That constant attack appealed to all other guitar players."

NICK HORNBY (author): "I had a picture of Rory Gallagher on my wall when I was 14."

Colin Harper (journalist): "In terms of the voice / guitar chemistry, he was a one-man Led Zeppelin."

Remember me this way: Taste's 'On The Boards' or his face gurning solos throughout his career.

EDDIE HINTON

Oddly rockabilly-esque gone country songwriter, died July 28th. Hinton's strange torch vocals and disjointed guitar gave him a drawl that's well worth the admission price. Numerous recent recordings have crept out on the UK indie label Zane.

Remember me this way: 'Hard Luck Guy' or any of the Dan Penn-like later tunes.

STERLING MORRISON

Founder member and guitarist with The Velvet Underground, died August 30th of non-Hodgkin's lymphoma one day before his 53rd birthday.

Read it in the press: Holmes Sterling Morrison was born in Long Island on Aug 29 1942, and studied English at Syracuse University, where he met Reed. The Velvet Underground was founded in 1965, its name was taken from the title of a pornographic novel.

Morrison's obituary in The Telegraph

STERLING MORRISON (on playing with The Velvet Underground): "It was real fun."

LOU REED: "The Velvet Underground would have been impossible without his guitar playing. He had an incredibly acute mind - very, very incisive."

Remember me this way: Exchanging riffs with Lou.

JERRY GARCIA

Died August 9th from a heart attack. The seemingly tireless Grateful Dead guitarist played country, folk, rock, experimental and all points between with a host of bands. An exceptional guitar player and stylist, Garcia powered the Dead through many years and just as many incarnations.

Read about it in books:

Jerry Garcia was the lead guitarist, vocalist, and spokesman for the seminal '60s rock 'n' roll band the Grateful Dead who became one of the most famous figures in the history of rock 'n' roll. Garcia pursued an eclectic array of side projects, ranging from the bluegrass group Old And In The Way to his folky solo recordings.

Late in the summer of 1995, he entered Serenity Knolls, a drug rehabilitation facility in Forest Knolls, California after slowly sinking back into heroin addiction. While he was attempting to recover, Garcia died in his sleep of a heart attack on August 9, 1995. Several months after his death, the Grateful Dead announced that they were disbanding.

Stephen Thomas Erlewine in the All-Music Guide

Read it in the press:

Jerry Garcia, the American musician who has died in California aged 53, was the lead guitarist and chief inspiration of the psychedelic group The Grateful Dead.

The Grateful Dead came to fame as a live group, known for its long improvisational performances at the major festivals of the 1960s, as well as for its connections with the laid-back, LSD-infused culture of the West Coast, and the Haight-Ashbury district of San Francisco in particular.

Garcia's obituary in The Telegraph.

Death, as Jerry Garcia so mournfully warbled on his memorable 'Live/Dead' album, don't have no mercy, and as 1995 ends Garcia's own death still seems to me to be the saddest and most significant rock death of the year. Who now will be the standard bearer of that often derided but, to so many of us, endearing and seductive vision of a spaced-out world of love and peace?

Charles Spencer in The Telegraph.

Sterling Morrison

STERLING MORRISON, who has died suddenly at his home at Poughkeepsie, New York, aged 53, was a founder member of the The Velvet Underground, one of the most influential rock groups of the 1960s.

Though the band is now accorded almost mythical status, it failed to win any commercial success during the few chaotic years of its existence.

This was partly due to the subject matter of its songs (heroin addiction, sado-masochism, street violence and transvestitism) which alienated mainstream radio stations, and partly because the band was at odds with the West Coast ideals of peace, love and LSD.

The band's line-up was Lou Reed, as poetic lyricist and dead-pan vocalist; the classically-trained John Cale on *avant garde* electric viola; and Maureen Tucker on the drums. Morrison contributed a wall of guitar noise and a notably out-of-tempo bass-

The Velvet Underground in 1966. Left to right: Tucker, Morrison, Reed, and Cale

line. The nominal producer was Andy Warhol. The band recorded only four albums but proved a favourite with critics and such musicians as David Bowie, Iggy Pop, Bryan Ferry, Patti Smith and the "punk" movement.

Holmes Sterling Morrison was born in Long Island on Aug 29 1942, and studied English at Syracuse University, where he met Reed.

The Velvet Underground was founded in 1965, its name taken from the title of a pornographic novel. The next year it featured in Warhol's multi-media extravaganza *The Exploding Plastic Inevitable* and became the in-house band at his studio The Factory.

By the time the first album, *The Velvet Underground & Nico*, was released in 1967, divisions within the band were apparent. After three more albums, Morrison and Reed left in 1970.

With long, dark hair, sunglasses, and black clothes, Morrison looked the quintessential depraved rock musician, though he was in fact a serious academic and had completed a second degree. He taught at Texas University, and completed a Phd in mediaeval literature.

In 1993, when The Velvet Underground reformed for a European tour, Morrison was working as a tug-boat captain in Galveston, Texas. The band's planned tour of America did not go ahead.

He was married and had two children.

Founder of Grateful Dead dies of heart attack at 53

By John Hiscock in Los Angeles

JERRY Garcia, grey-bearded leader of the 1960s cult rock band the Grateful Dead, died yesterday in a drug rehabilitation centre.

The 53-year-old erstwhile hippie who founded the band 30 years ago was discovered dead by a counsellor at Serenity Knowles, a residential drug treatment centre near his home in Marin County, California.

A nurse and sheriff's department staff tried in vain to revive him.

Dennis McNally, the band's spokesman, said last night that Garcia died of a heart attack, but he did not know why he was at the centre. He said: "It was news to me. thought he was going to Hawaii. Apparentl he was paying increased attention to hi health."

The Grateful Dead's most recent perfor mance was on July 9 in Chicago.

The shaggy-haired guitarist had a long his tory of drug use involving cocaine, heroi and LSD.

Ten years ago he went into a diabetic com for several days and then three years ago h again lapsed into a near-fatal coma sufferin from obesity-related diabetes. At the time h weighed more than 21st and smoked 60 cig rettes a day.

Doctors reported that his heart w enlarged and his lungs congested.

McNally said at the time: "It was a me down. Too many cigarettes, too much ju food and too little exercise."

Since then Garcia said he was attempting to lose weight and cut down on his smoking and drug use. He said recently: "I feel much younger and have a lot more vitality."

He married his third wife, film-maker Deborah Koons, last year. He has three grown-up daughters from his previous marriages.

The Grateful Dead had its roots in San Francisco's 1960s psychedelic scene and combined rock, bluegrass and folk influences. It has long been one of the most popular acts in the United States, grossing tens of millions of dollars each year.

Garcia's death will be mourned by "Deadheads" around the world — the vast following of devoted fans who attend every concert, trade tapes of shows and flood the group's two hotlines with 1,000 calls a day.

At the time of Garcia's death he was planning an autumn concert tour of the US.

Born Jerome John Garcia, he was the son of a bandleader. He dropped out of high school and worked as a salesman and a teacher before forming the Warlocks rock group in 1965. The following year the Warlocks became the Grateful Dead.

Among their best known songs were Truckin', Casey Jones and Friend of the

SAM ANDREW (Big Brother And The Holding Company): "Not long before Jerry died I went to see the film Smoke and I loved the atmosphere in the story, the relationship between the characters played by Harvey Keitel and William Hurt, the languid emotional pace of the plot, and not least the choice of music. The tunes by Tom Waits were really well chosen, but another song played under the closing credits really intrigued me. It was a reading of that beautiful old ballad 'Smoke Gets In Your Eyes' and to my knowledge I had never heard the people who were playing. It was difficult to tell if the artists lived then or now and the rendition was so moody, sulphuric and rich. The singing voice was rough yet in tune and very interesting.

I thought Leon Redbone maybe or some unsung eccentric artist of the thirties discovered by these perceptive filmmakers. Then the music credits rolled. It was the Jerry Garcia Band. Unbelievable. To me that was the best thing he ever did. There was so much heart and mystery in it, so much intelligence, discretion and taste. I felt proud for Jerry. This was it. He finally made it."

BOB DYLAN: "There are a lot of spaces between The Carter Family, Buddy Holly and Ornette Coleman, but Jerry Garcia filled them all."

Remember me this way: Saying "Marijuana, exhibit A" in the Woodstock film but being unable to play when the time came.

DWAYNE GOETTEL

A member of the Canadian industrial innovators Skinny Puppy, Goettel died on August 23rd from a heroin overdose.

Remember me this way: Influencing a fledgling Trent Reznor to form Nine Inch Nails.

BIG DEE IRWIN

The lead singer in the doo-wop outfit The Pastels, Irwin is best known for his solo single version of 'Swinging On A Star' with Little Eva of 'Locomotion' fame.

Remember me this way: Not wanting to grow up to be a fish.

On the album cover:

STEREO

OOPS!
THE SWINGING SOUNDS OF
Bill Doggett
And His Combo

Honky Tonk—Part I & II
Canadian Sunset
'Deed I Do
Buster
Forest Green
Oops
Stop That Twistin' in Here
I Cover the Watertront
Lady's Choice
Mommy—Part I & II

SHANNON HOON

Died October 21st from an overdose of cocaine while on tour with his band Blind Melon. He was discovered by his childhood pal Axl Rose from Guns n' Roses. Hoon quit his sporting career at Columbus University and quickly fitted into the wild rock lifestyle and drug culture that eventually finished him off. Blind Melon's shares were, at the time, in the ascendancy.

Remember me this way: For inventing the 'Bee girl' image that stuck with the band through a million MTV plays of the single 'No Rain'.

BILL DOGGETT

Seasoned keyboard player with a blues, R&B and jazz background. Died November 13th.

Read it on record sleeves: *For the past nine years, Bill Doggett and Hammond organ have been transported about the country as the major cargo of a six-passenger bus. On at least 250 nights out of each year, the bus has parked outside of a dance hall somewhere between Vancouver and Orlando, Doggett and crew have unloaded and for the next four hours, hundreds of people have danced and smiled, laughed and sung.* From the sleeve of 'Oops! The Swinging Sounds Of Bill Doggett And His Combo'

Remember me this way: Steve Cropper: "I think 'Honky Tonk' by Bill Doggett changed my life and probably did the same for a lot of young guys who wanted to play guitar. If you wanted to play guitar in a dance band you had to know that song."

ALAN HULL

Lindisfarne singer and songwriter, died November 19th from a heart attack in Newcastle-upon-Tyne aged 50. Folkie veteran whose good time songs brought chart success.

Remember me this way: For penning the anthemic 'Fog On The Tyne'.

MATTHEW ASHMAN

A member of Bow Wow Wow, Adam And The Ants and The Chiefs Of Relief, Ashman died November 21st after falling into a diabetes-related coma.

Those Bow Wow Wow Classics: 'C30, C60, C90 Go' (1980), 'WORK (Ne No My Daddy Oh)' (1981), 'Prince Of Darkness' (81), 'Chihuahua' (81), 'Go Wild In The Country' (1982), 'See Jungle (Jungle Boy)' (82), 'I Want Candy' (82), "Louis Quatorze' (82) and 'Do You Want To Hold Me?' (1983).

Remember me this way: Playing 'C30, C60, C90 Go'.

CLARENCE C SATCHELL

The man behind The Ohio Players' sleazy horn sound also their penchant for scantily-clad, leather-bound ladies on their album sleeves died on December 30th.

Remember me this way: Getting full action from his 'Funky Worm'.

JUNIOR WALKER

Motown session stalwart turned successful soulful saxophonist, died December from cancer, aged 53. His biggest hit was 'What Does It Take (To Win Your Love)?'.

Read it in the press:
Junior Walker, the saxophonist and singer was a leading figure in the world-wide expansion of black American music during the 1960s. Records by Junior Walker And The Allstars were instantly recognisable for their leader's raw, crying tone and urgent, cryptic phrases. Aimed directly at the dancing and jukebox trade, pieces such as 'Shotgun' and 'Roadrunner' owed much of their charm to their lack of pretension.
Walker's obituary in The Telegraph

Remember me this way: He was the 'Roadrunner'.

Junior Walker

JUNIOR WALKER, the saxophonist and singer who has died aged 53, was a leading figure in the worldwide expansion of black American music during the 1960s.

Records by Junior Walker and the All-Stars were instantly recognisable for the leader's raw, crying tone and urgent, cryptic phrases. Unashamedly aimed at the dancing and jukebox trade, pieces such as *Shotgun* and *Road Runner* owed much of their charm to their lack of pretension; yet they proved to have greater staying power than many more elaborate products of the period.

Junior Walker was born Autry De Walt in 1942 at Blytheville, Arkansas, and began playing the tenor saxophone in his teens. His early musical influences included the saxophonists Illinois Jaquet, Sil Austin and Sam "The Man" Taylor, and the vocalists Louis Jordan, B B King and T-Bone Walker.

He formed his first band, the Jumping Jacks, in his late teens, and started by working in bars and clubs in the factory towns of the midwest.

He was spotted at Battle Creek, Michigan, in 1962 and signed to the Harvey label, owned by the singer and songwriter Harvey Fuqua.

Walker to Motown's boss, Berry Gordy. Their interview

"Go ahead and sign, we won't mess you around."

At first glance it was a strange alliance. Motown was the first black record company to aim at the general popular market, and its image was smooth and sophisticated. But Walker's rough vitality provided a valuable contrast to the surrounding refinement, and maintained Motown's connection with the traditional audience for rhythm and blues.

In the late 1960s and early 1970s Walker had great success with such numbers as *What Does It Take (To Win Your Love)* and *Walk In The Night*, performed in a somewhat toned-down version of his original style.

Later in the 1970s he adapted once more, this time to the disco fashion, scoring hits with party albums bearing such titles as *Whopper Bopper Show Stopper*. In the 1980s he recorded as guest artist with the pop group Foreigner.

Because his records contained little in the way of production effects or electronic trickery, he was able to reproduce his characteristic sound on stage with little difficulty, and he remained a tireless live performer until he was diagnosed with can-

Walker: Motown in the raw

"Give that boy a contract." Walker asked what he was

1996

THE LONDON BOYS

The successful Eurodisco duo (Edem Epharim and Dennis Fuller) died in a car crash in the Alps on January 21st.

Remember me this way: By their hits 'London Nights' and 'Requiem'.

HAMISH IMLACH

Folk singer and humorist, who worked with Christy Moore and Mary Black, died aged 55. A veteran of the UK folk circuit with an endearing guffaw and a piercing lyric.

Remember me this way: His live folk club rambles like 'Samson' or 'Oyster Girl'.

HAMISH IMLACH LIVE!

BROWNIE MCGHEE

Died February 16th from stomach cancer, aged 80. After touring the Deep South in the Thirties, he teamed up with Sonny Terry to form a 30-year legendary duo. From Knoxville, Tennessee, McGhee suffered from polio as a child. When he finally gave up his walking stick, he entered the world of Blind Boy Fuller, travelling to gigs and eventually meeting up with Sonny Terry. The duo set off to introduce the blues to as many people as possible and their journey never really ended.

Remember me this way: Playing a cameo in the movie Angel Heart.

JOSEPH POPE

Lead singer with '60s soul act The Tams who had hits in 1968 with 'Be Young, Be Foolish, Be Happy' and in '71 with 'Hey Girl Don't Bother Me'. Died from heart failure on March 16th.

Remember me this way: Young, foolish, etc.

JEFFREY LEE PIERCE

Gun Club singer, died March 31st from a brain haemorrhage while under doctor's care for drug and alcohol abuse. He was 37. Pierce had started the group back in LA and brought them to Europe, where their mix of swamp blues and basic rock 'n' roll had precipitated into a grinding drawl. Tipping a wink to Robert Johnson through their laboured cover of 'Preaching The Blues', they were the perfect band to accompany a Texas Chainsaw Massacre party.

Remember me this way: The Gun Club's brooding debut 'Fire Of Love'.

BERNARD EDWARDS

43-year old Chic bassist, founder member and producer died April 18th from pneumonia, after collapsing while on stage with the group in Japan. Edwards, along with Nile Rodgers, introduced the funk into soul with the disco-paced Chic.

NILE RODGERS: "Bernard had the whole sound for Chic in his head. He taught me how to play like that. He was the real driving force."

THOSE CHIC TOP TEN HITS IN FULL: 'Dance, Dance, Dance' (1977), 'Everybody Dance (1978), 'Le Freak' (78).

Remember me this way: Having 'Good Times'.

BRAD NOWELL

Remember me this way: Died May 25th from a heroin overdose after a protracted addiction. Nowell was a member of Sublime who moulded West Coast punk into DIY dub and ska.

His body was found by his dog, Lou, at around eight in the morning. Nowell left behind his wife of one week, Troy, and his 11-month old son, Jake.

Remember me this way: The band's posthumous single release 'What I Got'.

JIM ELLISON

The Material Issue singer committed suicide on June 20th, aged 32. The Big Star-influenced trio found a home on the circuit and had just released their major label debut.

Remember me this way: The 'International Pop Overthrow' album.

JONATHAN MELVOIN

Died July 11th from a drug overdose while on tour with The Smashing Pumpkins. He was discovered in a Manhattan hotel room by drummer Jimmy Chamberlin.

Read it in the press:

The Smashing Pumpkins' concert keyboard player, died of a heroin overdose after injecting the drug in his room at New York's Regency Hotel. Melvoin was the brother of Wendy Melvoin, former backing singer for Prince.

Melvoin's obituary in Q magazine

Remember me this way: Tinkling the ivories and simply over the moon.

CHAS CHANDLER

Animals' bassist and the latter day Hendrix and Slade manager, died July 17th from a heart attack. Chandler had seen Hendrix play live in the States and brought him over to the UK. London's rock aristocracy were suitably impressed, Hendrix knocked out three albums in a year but Chandler couldn't cope with the pace and dropped out of the proceedings. His second great management coup was snapping up Birmingham's Slade and turning them from would-be skinheads into pop Glamsters with a sense of humour.

Remember me this way: Making his first solid body guitar out of his old drawing board.

ROB COLLINS

Charlatans organist whose distinctive Hammond sound gave the group a modern retro feel, which resulted in their chart-topping debut 'Some Friendly'. Collins died on July 23rd in a car crash, aged 29.

Remember me this way: Baggier than the rest.

MARGIE GANSER

Member of the truly innovative all-girl trio The Shangri-Las who hit the charts with 'Remember (Walkin' In The Sand)' and 'Leader Of The Pack' in the '60s.

Remember me this way: Walkin' in the sand.

CHARLIE FEATHERS

The rockabilly pioneer, died in Memphis on August 29th. An early and reasonably unsuccessful signing to the Sun label, Feathers has become legendary over the years. There are confused anecdotes that claim he wrote the classic, 'Blue Moon Of Kentucky'. His overspill into country circles provided him with a wider audience for his ballads, but it's his rockabilly sides that have been elevated to the level of masterpiece over the years.

Remember me this way: With Elvis Presley's version of 'I Forget To Remember To Forget'.

BILL MONROE

The Bluegrass veteran died September 9th in Springfield, Tennessee, four days short of his 85th birthday. Monroe was part and parcel of the development of bluegrass music in the States. He constantly appeared on the Grand Ol' Opry and toured the country, developing a number of fine players who would inevitably complain about poor pay and be sacked for their troubles. Monroe constantly recorded and was a mean mandolin player in his own right.

Remember me this way: The man who introduced Elvis to 'Blue Moon Of Kentucky'.

TUPAC SHAKUR

Died September 13th following a drive-by shooting in Las Vegas, during which his manager 'Suge' Knight was also injured.

Read about it in books:

Hundreds of people walked the streets but didn't notice the late-model Cadillac with California plates pull up to the right of the rented BMW. One of its four passengers pulled a firearm. "I heard these sounds

THE SUNDAY TELEGRAPH SEPTEMBER 5, 1999

'Remember when I die, I'll be back'

So sang rap star Tupac Shakur in a song released a was shot three years ago. But was he really murd Plenty of his fans think not, as **William Langley** dis

Wall of death A memorial mural for Tupac Shakur in New York

"HE's dead," says Sgt Kevin Manning. "I saw the body with my own eyes. Cold on the slab. Three bullets through him. What more do you want?"

The body belonged to Lesane P. Crooks, better known as Tupac Shakur, a 25-year-old ghetto poet who, in a life filled with dissonance and thuggery, rose to become the biggest, and indisputably baddest, star in rap music. Three years ago, Shakur was killed in a drive-by shooting as he went to keep a date in a Las Vegas nightclub with former world heavyweight boxing champion Mike Tyson.

"Stone dead," says Sgt Manning, the homicide detective who headed the resoundingly unsuccessful hunt for Shakur's killer.

who hosts a nationally broadcast radio rap programme *Yo! Listen Up!* says, "What makes this a hot topic is that Tupac has become the black Elvis. There are too many question marks about this supposed death. There just isn't enough evidence for the public to let him go."

Three posthumous albums have been released since Shakur's death. All of them contain what have been construed as hidden messages or riddles to indicate that the artist's death was not what it seemed. One was titled *Don Killuminati: The Seven Day Theory*, and was recorded under the name Makaveli.

The first clue is that the letters, given a little imagination, can be rearranged to spell I'M

And then ther posedly signific ogy, all revolvin number seven, shot on Septemb at 4.03pm (4 plu He was 25 years equals 7.) He wa a BMW 7 Series was seven minu destination. Is th who dispute the death, some coo of the *Seven Day*

What happe body? Manning s but few others d funeral was he services in Ne Angeles and A abruptly cancell Shakur was crem family claim

"And, of co Cathy Scott, a

and I thought that it was someone shooting in the air," an eyewitness told Vibe (magazine).
Between ten and 15 shots rang out. Glass shattered.
Two men got out of the car.
"Then they just started spraying bullets. I could see Tupac jumping into the back seat, that's how his

138

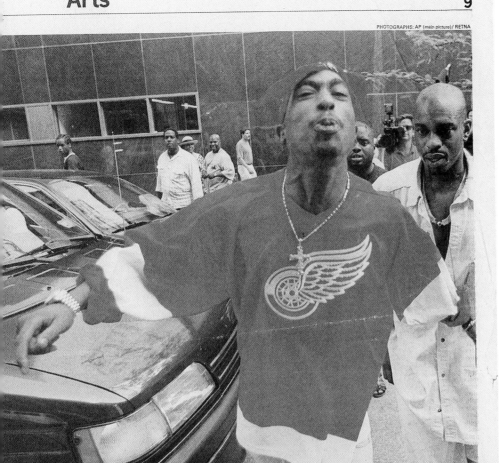

Spitting image Tupac Shakur, himself accused of violent crime, takes aim at reporters as he leaves a New York court two years before his death in 1996

San Diego-based psychologist who has studied the effects, from a basic human reluctance to attribute simple causes to shocking events. "Before we laugh and tell the people who believe this stuff to move on," he says, "we need to understand what Shakur meant to the fans who bought his records and saw his shows and shared the

on the streets."

The Shakur issue has, in a

spiring to plant bombs for the Black Panthers. She was later acquitted, but the violent, extreme and marginal pattern of Shakur's life was already established. His father vanished when he was four. His mother became a crack addict.

Born in New York, he drifted early into delinquency, soaking up the ghetto sogyny that underpins the "gangsta" variant of rap. He

ning Shakur climbed into a rented BMW driven by Marion "Suge" Knight, the owner of Death Row Record, the leading gangsta rap label.

As the BMW sped along East Flamingo Road, towards Club 662 where Shakur was to perform at a private party for Tyson, a pale coloured Cadillac drew alongside. Both cars slowed to a halt at a red light,

What happened

and as they did so the rear window of the Cadillac opened and one, or possibly two gunmen, opened fire. A volley of 13 bullets entered the BMW, hitting Shakur in the chest and legs. He died six days later in hospital.

The first hint of something strange came with the release of the video, accompanying Shakur's record *I Ain't Mad*

just before his death. It shows a beatific Shakur gazing down

get a huge, angry reaction from our readers. People are absolutely serious about this. There are Tupac fans who will be sitting at dinner parties in their fifties still talking about where they were when they heard he'd been murdered."

The most widely disseminated theory is that Shakur staged the Vegas shooting to escape the attentions of an

— directed, it is suggested by some, by Christopher Wallace

chest got exposed so much." Two bullets tore into his chest.

From Ronin Ro's excellent Have Gun Will Travel.

NICCOLO MACHIAVELLI: "I desire to go to Hell, not to Heaven. In Hell I shall enjoy the company of

popes, kings and princes, but in Heaven are only beggars, monks, hermits and apostles."

Remember me this way: As the gangsta who got "his" to the soundtrack of 'Me Against The World'. And allegedly, like Machiavelli, came back to life to tell the tale.

JO BAKER
Lead vocalist with The Elvin Bishop Group, who'd also sung with The Doobie Brothers and John Lee Hooker, died of liver disease on November 11th.

Remember me this way: With her distinctive Blues rock holler.

TINY TIM
Eccentric uke-carrying crooner, died November 30th from a heart attack. Not tip-toe-ing through the tulips no more.

Read it in the press:

Tiny Tim was born Herbert Khaury sometime between 1925 and 1930. While his show business career has lasted aeons, true fame was only his for the better part of two years. But one thing remains

OBITUARIES
Tiny Tim
American singer and ukulele player whose excruciating rendition of Tiptoe through the Tulips reached the To

Tiny Tim: weirder than the hippies

certain: Tiny Tim is the novelty act that won't go away! The success of 'Tiptoe through The Tulips With Me', Tiny's cover of a 1929 Nick Lucas hit, together with his marriage on the Tonight With Johnny Carson Show thrust him to national prominence in 1969. However, by 1971 he was more or less forgotten.

1993 Scram Interview

No one was ever quite sure how serious Tiny Tim was trying to be. "I am really a vampire of songs," he reflected, "and vampires suck blood. When I sing 'Great Balls Of Fire', I enter the body of Elvis Presley for a moment'."

Tiny Tim's obituary in The Telegraph

Remember me this way: Being eccentric.

PATTY DONAHUE

The Ohio-born singer with The Waitresses died December 6th from lung cancer.

Remember me this way: Doing the theme to TV show Square Peg, or the quirky 'I Know What Boys Like'

FARON YOUNG

The Louisiana-born country singer/songwriter who crossed over to the pop market shot himself on December 10th aged 64, while depressed about his deteriorating health. Young's progress on the Nashville scene was out-of-sync with the genre's traditions, but his rags-to-riches story, powered by his choice of brooding music and his distinctive tenor voice won him a huge following. After damaging his tongue in a car accident it was feared his career would be over but the Jerry Chestnut-penned 'Four In The Morning' was his biggest hit yet, establishing him as one of country music's greats.

Remember me this way: At 'Four In The Morning'.

1996

TOWNES VAN ZANDT

Texas-born singer/songwriter and western troubadour, died following a hip replacement operation on January 1st.

Read it in the press:

Trouble had a way of finding Townes Van Zandt, who was one of the greatest songwriters of our time. It came to him for the last time on New Year's Day when he died in his home in Mount Juliet, Tennessee. Van Zandt's obituary in Rolling Stone

TOWNES: "I don't think that I'm going to benefit from anything on this earth. If you have love on this earth, then that seems like number one. You know, there's food, water, air and love. And love is just basically heartbreak. Humans can't live in the past. So, it's a veil of tears man. I don't know anything that's going to benefit from me except more love."

TOWNES: "Actually, I do sell a lot of records, they just all go to Europe."

Remember me this way: Singing the tale of 'Pancho And Lefty'

RANDY CALIFORNIA

Drowned January 2nd, while saving his son, in an incident off Molokai in Hawaii. A keen environmentalist he jumped into the Thames in the '70s - for why we're not sure.

Read it in the press:

"California began his career with Jimi Hendrix in the mid-1960s, starting Spirit, in 1967, with his step father drummer Ed Cassidy. Spirit released four albums before disbanding in 1971. California recorded the solo album 'Kapt Kopter' before the group reformed in 1974.
California's obituary in Rolling Stone

Remember me this way: With Spirit's classic earth-friendly 45 'Nature's Way'.

BILLY MACKENZIE

Committed suicide in his garden shed, January 23rd. The former Associates' singer was aged just 39 and in the throes of a comeback.

TOM DOYLE (journalist): "His musical talent was undeniable. Inspired by the vocal gymnastics of Russell Mael and 'Station To Station' era David Bowie, his voice seemed otherworldly, his elastic range effortlessly scaling entire octaves, often within a single phrase. In the Associates more edgy moments his voice ached with paranoia."

Remember me this way: Intoning 'Party Fears Two'.

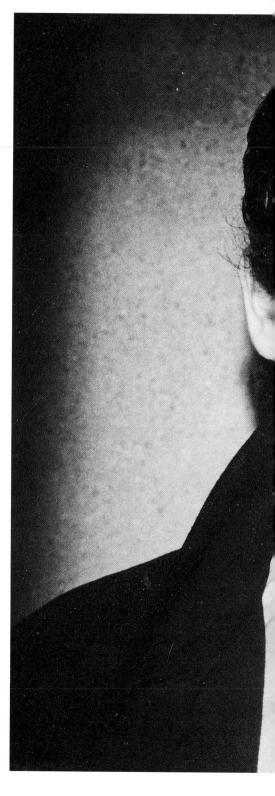

BRIAN CONNOLLY

The Sweet singer, died February 9th from liver failure, aged 52. Connolly had suffered from a muscle-wasting disease for years.

THOSE SWEET MOMENTS IN FULL: 'Funny Funny' (1971), 'Co-Co' (71), 'Alexander Graham Bell' (71), 'Poppa Joe' (1972), 'Little Willy' (72), 'Wig Wam Bam' (72), 'Blockbuster' (1973), 'Hell Raiser' (73), 'Ballroom Blitz' (73), 'Teenage Rampage' (1974), 'Turn It Down' (74), 'The Six Teens' (74), 'Fox On The Run' (1975), 'Action' (75), 'Lies In Your Eyes' (1976) and 'Love Is Like Oxygen' (1978).
Remember me this way: Delivering 'Ballroom Blitz' with a page boy haircut.

NOTORIOUS BIG

Murdered in a drive-by shooting, March 9th. The East Coast Bad Boy rapper had been linked with the murder of Tupac Shakur from West Coast label Death Row. In LA for a music biz event, Biggie was gunned down after leaving the shindig.

Read it on the internet:
BIGGY'S LAST DAY

8pm - The night began at the Peterson Automotive Museum on Wilshire Blvd at a party hosted by Vibe magazine, Qwest Records, and Tanqueray gin to celebrate the 11th annual Soul Train Music Awards.
9:30pm - The party really got going around 9:30 or 10:00pm, and Biggie appeared to be having a great time taking a table near the dance floor and chatting with friends.
12:35am - The party became overcrowded, and as is often the case in such situations in LA, the fire marshals were called in and the party was shut down.
12:45am - People poured out into the street and were waiting for their valet parked cars. According to a witness who spoke to USA Today, Biggie and Puff Daddy came out and talked to their friends about going on to another party. Puffy had his car brought around and drove off, and then Biggie and two friends (reportedly Lil Caesar from Jr MAFIA and Biggie's bodyguard, Damian) got into his GMC Suburban and drove up to the light with Biggie in the passenger side.
Biggie's car came to a stop at a red light at Wilshire and Fairfax when another car drove up on the right side. Six to ten shots were then fired from the other vehicle into the passenger side of Biggie's car. Panic obviously ensued and the Suburban drove straight to nearby Cedars Sinai Medical Center.
1:15am - Biggie Smalls was pronounced dead at Cedars Sinai.
From The Hip Hop Pages at **www.angelfire.com/wa/hiphopages/bigdeath.html)**

Read about it in books:
As Puffy drove away, Biggie settled into the GMC's front seat... One after one the vehicles stopped at the red light. They did not see the dark green vehicle driving erratically, stopping on the GMC's right side, discharging passengers. "All of a sudden I heard about five or six shots," said a security guard across the street. "Pow, pow, pow, pow, pow."
From Ronin Ro's excellent Have Gun Will Travel.

Read it in the press:
CAN'T THEY JUST GET ALONG?

And on it goes... Six months after Tupac Shakur died in a hail of bullets in Las Vegas, Suge Knight, owner of Death Row Records, was sentenced to nine years in prison for an act of violence. Then, on March 8th, the Notorious BIG, hugely successful rapper and sworn enemy of both Shakur and Knight, was shot in Los Angeles, finally dying in the famous Cedars Sinai hospital. All three incidents seem inextricably linked as rap writhes in an apparently unstoppable cycle of violence.
Danny Kelly in Q magazine.

RANDY NEWMAN: "There's some rap music I like, and some I don't, but 'Ready To Die' by Notorious BIG is one of the best records ever made. It starts talking about the "old days, when everybody was shootin' each other" and "Let's stop killing each other", then the rest of the album is all about people killing each other. It's the damndest thing. I don't know what he had in mind."
Remember me this way: Singing / rapping through "You're Nobody Till Somebody Kills You'.

HAROLD MELVIN

The pioneer of the Philly sound, Melvin died March 24th, aged 57. Coupled with Teddy Prendergrass the key period for his group Harold Melvin And The Bluenotes came in the '70s.

Read it in the press:

Some artists have golden voices made for hit singles; Harold Melvin's gift was to recognise those voices. By promoting his band's drummer, Teddy Prendergrass, to lead singer, Melvin transformed his journeymen vocal group, the Blue Notes, into one of the major R&B acts of the '70s. After suffering from a vascular disease and a series of strokes, Melvin passed away on March 24th.
Melvin's obituary in Rolling Stone.

Remember me this way: With the ballads 'If You Don't Know Me By Now' and 'Don't Leave Me This Way'.

LAURA NYRO

New York songwriter whose belated recognition coincided with her death, at 49, on April 8th from ovarian cancer. Her songs had already been hits for Barbara Streisand, The Fifth Dimension and Blood, Sweat And Tears, but finally she was beginning to gain respect for her own renditions of her songs.

PETER BUCK (REM): "Her album 'Eli And The Second Coming' is one of the most pop-jazz-psychedelic-demento records of all time. Beautiful songs, but I can't imagine how they learned to play all this stuff, there are so many time changes. I don't know much about her, except that she played at Monterey in '67 and everyone hated her."

Remember me this way: With 'Wedding Bell Blues' or 'Stony End', or a host of others. Seek out the retro flashback 'Stoned Soul Picnic', which was released just prior to her death and features her readings of those classics.

LAVERN BAKER

Died April 10th from complications linked to diabetes, which resulted in a heart attack. Heralded as the girl who put rhythm into the blues, her raucous vocal style is legendary.
Remember me this way: Hollering 'Jim Dandy'.

EL DUCE

Died in mysterious circumstances on April 19th, after being hit by a train while intoxicated.
Remember me this way: He was the singer for The Mentors but is probably best remembered as the man, allegedly, hired to kill Kurt Cobain.

JEFF BUCKLEY

Died May 29th when he drowned in The Mississippi River after going for a swim while on location to record his second album. The son of Tim and a huge international star thanks to sales of his awesome debut 'Grace'.

Buckley claimed he was born to be a singer, "first there was my mother's breasts, then music. All my life I sung to the radio. Singing onstage felt natural. It was like, "I'm going into the ocean, to the water.""

Read it in the press:

Jeff Buckley, who has died aged 30, was one of the most promising and musically adventurous singer/songwriters of his generation. He released only one album, 'Grace', in 1994; but its blend of rock and folk styles, fused by a voice likened to "a choirboy singing from the rafters of a whorehouse", drew critical acclaim and gave hope for great things to come.
Buckley's obituary in The Telegraph

KAZOO ELEGY FOR BUCKLEY

Elvis Costello and Marianne Faithfull were among mourners who performed at the official Jeff Buckley memorial in New York's Holy Trinity Church, held on July 31st. Faithfull played a traditional Irish ballad, while Costello sang a traditional classical piece accompanied by piano.

Patti Smith also attended and read out the lyrical poem 'The Wing' at the three-hour service. Buckley's girlfriend Joan Wasser, playing bass, joined Buckley's guitarist Michael Tighe and drummer Parker Kindred plus Shudder To Think's Nathan Larson and Katell Keinig in a tribute to Buckley.

A silver mirror ball hung in the church and kazoos were handed out, along with yellow guitar picks etched with Buckley's name. During the service mourners were asked to play the song 'You Are My Sunshine'. NME

Read it on the internet:

Deepest condolences and blessings. 'Grace' was one of those albums that changes your life. The sort of album that comes along every decade which enables you to pinpoint the exact place and time when you first heard it.

He did so much in so little time. He made the singer/songwriter cool again, and he

TRIBUTE

LAURA NYRO
1947-1997

SINGER/SONGWRITER LAURA Nyro, whose original, pioneering fusion of soul, gospel, jazz, R&B and pop created a catalog of million-selling hits for artists ranging from Three Dog Night to Barbra Streisand, died at her home in Danbury, Conn., on April 8. An intensely private woman, Nyro chose not to make public her two-year battle with ovarian cancer, which ended her life at age 49.

Debuting as a teen prodigy, Nyro was the youngest successful woman songwriter of her time. Her own records, while critically acclaimed, never drew a large audience, yet artists including Rickie Lee Jones, Alanis Morissette and Tori Amos bear the mark of her influence. Nyro's synthesis of American music genres had no precedent in popular music, and her literate, evocative lyrics also defied categorization, with themes ranging from sexual passion to spiritual redemption. Nyro's concerts were legendary for her riveting, transcendent performances. But her uncompromising style was not always appreciated; in fact, she was booed off the stage of the Monterey Pop Festival, in 1967.

Born Laura Nigro in the Bronx, N.Y., on Oct. 18, 1947, she began singing, playing piano and writing songs as a child. She was 19 when she recorded her 1966 debut, *More Than a New Discovery*, which included future Top 10 hits for Blood, Sweat and Tears ("And When I Die"), Barbra Streisand ("Stoney End") and the Fifth Dimension ("Wedding Bell Blues").

After becoming one of David Geffen's first clients when he was a manager, she signed with Columbia, where she recorded 1968's *Eli and the Thirteenth Confession*, featuring such songs as "Stoned Soul Picnic" and "Sweet Blindness." In 1971, she joined up with the R&B vocal group Labelle, featuring Patti LaBelle, Nona Hendryx and Sarah Dash, for *Gonna Take a Miracle*, a compelling collection of doo-wop and Motown classics.

Nyro retired to the New England countryside in the early '70s. Following a divorce, in 1976, she returned to recording with the subdued, jazz-tinged *Smile*. After the birth of her son, Gil Bianchini, in 1978, themes of motherhood, feminism, ecology and animal rights came to the forefront of her music, dominating 1978's *Nested*, 1984's *Mother's Spiritual* and 1993's *Walk the Dog and Light the Light*. In rare interviews, Nyro was guarded but philosophical. In 1988, after a 10-year hiatus from the concert stage, she told the *Los Angeles Times*, "Sometimes you trade one success to find another."

Singer Patti LaBelle, who named Nyro as the godmother of her son Zuri, said of Nyro, "Laura was a very spiritual person. She just wanted to live life; she didn't need the glitz and the glamour."

Earlier this year, Columbia released a retrospective, *The Best of Laura Nyro: Stoned Soul Picnic*. Set for release this month is the tribute album *Time and Love: The Music of Laura Nyro* (Astor Place Recordings), featuring Rosanne Cash, Lisa Germano, Suzanne Vega and Jill Sobule, among others. Vega, a Nyro admirer since age 12, said of her, "She had a lot of elements in her personality that I longed for. She seemed, in her music, to be very free and very passionate and very emotional – all those things I didn't think I could ever be." David Geffen remembers Nyro as "a consummate artist, and even though she is often referred to as a poet of her generation, in fact she is really a poet for past and future generations. . . . I am sad that she is gone."

None of the artists featured on the tribute album knew of Nyro's illness, but Peter Gallway, the album's executive producer, said Nyro had been listening to the finished tracks in recent weeks. According to her agent, Elizabeth Rush, earlier this year, Nyro "was in great voice . . . and was really hoping to tour behind these projects."

A private memorial service was held April 12, in Danbury. Nyro is survived by her son and her companion, Maria Desiderio. A memorial concert is being planned. — PATRICIA ROMANOWSKI

JEFF BUCKLEY
eternal life

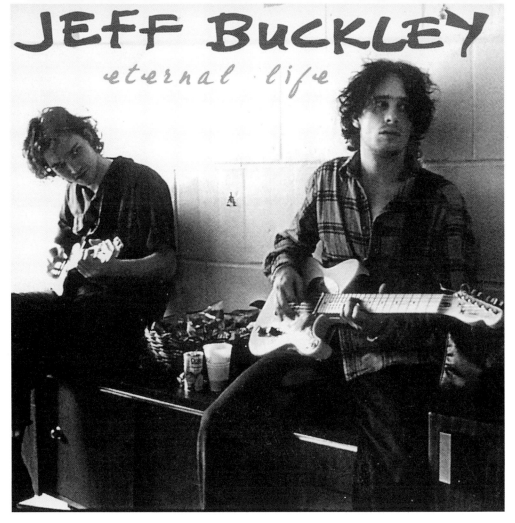

stood out in loud and direct opposition to grunge, which had a stranglehold on just about every other artist at the time. He was a genius because he changed and influenced just about every musician I know, which is the ultimate goal for a musician. And all this with one full-length album. It scares me to think what else he could have done.

'Corpus Christi' carol is the song that keeps going through my head ever since I found out about the news. He was the sort of guy that should have played at his own funeral, if you know what I mean.
kimwilkins@mailbox.uq.edu.au

ELVIS COSTELLO: "In 1995, I was director of a music festival on the South Bank and I invited Jeff to get involved. I was so impressed with his version of Benjamin Britten's 'Corpus Christi'. The thing that was so fascinating about him, apart from what he wrote, were the choices he made of songs to perform.

"He'd suddenly say he wanted to do something and just learn it. Like those Nusrat Fateh Ali Khan things. I'm sure he couldn't speak the language but his ear was so tuned to the sound, he could pick it up and create a really incredible version. At one point he was really ready to do this song by Mahler but I had to dissuade him. Not because I didn't think that h could do it, but because it would have been too frightening for the other musicians."
Remember me this way: Through all of 'Grace', but best tackling Leonard Cohen's 'Hallelujah'.

WEST ARKEEN
The songwriter and performer who worked closely with Guns n' Roses, died of a drug overdose on May 30th after taking too many opiates following an accident where his indoor barbecue blew up. And for that alone he has a place in this historic list.
Remember me this way: With Guns n' Roses' 'Patience'.

RONNIE LANE
Died June 4th from bodily deterioration caused by years of suffering from multiple sclerosis. Lane had tried all manner of cures and remedies, even resorting to snake venom at one point. As a member of The Small Faces and the Faces, he became a songwriter of great stature. He developed his unique folksy style on a handful of solo albums. Rod Stewart, when quizzed on the break-up of The Faces, once admitted that it all fell apart without Ronnie Lane, because he was "the true spirit of what it was all about".
Remember me this way: The Faces' mid tempo heartbreaker 'Debris'.

CERNUNNOS
The drummer with black metal band Enthroned, Cerununnos hung himself in Belgium after a two-month long depression.
Remember me this way: The posthumous Enthroned album 'Towards The Skullthrone Of Satan' which is dedicated to him.

LAWRENCE PAYTON
The Four Tops singer and arranger died June 20th from liver cancer. He'd been with the group since day one and worked at Motown with composers Holland/Dozier/Holland.
Remember me this way: Singing 'I Can't Help Myself'.

HOWARD PICKUP
Pickup was the guitarist†for 1977 punk rock faves The Adverts. In 1988, he was tracked down in his post-musical activity of running a taxi service and playing golf. Died on July 11th.
THE ADVERTS 45S: 'One Chord Wonders' (1977), 'Gary Gilmore's Eyes' (77), 'Safety In Numbers' (77), 'No Time To Be 21' (1978), 'Television's Over' (78), 'My Place' (1979).

FELA KUTI

The Nigerian singer and multi-instrumentalist, died August 2nd from AIDS.

Read it in the press:
Nigeria's Anikulapo Ransome-Kuti was rebel music for real, a man who walked it liked he talked it and, as a result found himself vilified, beaten, exiled and imprisoned.
Kuti's obituary in Mojo.

Remember me this way: For creating Afro Beat in the '60s when he mixed jazz, soul and African hi-life music with over 50 albums to his name.

LUTHER ALLISON

The 57-year-old blues guitarist died August 12th from lung cancer that resulted in brain tumours. A contemporary of Magic Sam and Buddy Guy.
Remember me this way: Acclaimed as a halfway house between Hendrix and Albert King.

NUSRAT FATEH ALI KHAN

Pakistani singer and performer of sufi poetry, died August 16th from a heart attack. Ironically, his public profile was beginning to increase through his work with Peter Gabriel.
What Nusrat said: "These are very pure messages. When I perform people should not be drinking or smoking."
Remember me this way: His music on the soundtrack to Natural Born Killers.

JIMMY WITHERSPOON

Died September 18th of natural causes at his home in Los Angeles aged 74. The R&B and jazz veteran developed throat cancer in the '80s but returned to the stage. He scored big back in 1946 with Jay McShann's band on 'Ain't Nobody's Business If I Do'.
Remember me this way: Mixing the sounds and style of Count Basie with Eric Burdon.

JOHN DENVER

The folkie that wanted to go to the moon (as an astronaut), died in a plane crash on October 12th.
Remember me this way: Being clean cut and whole-some on TV with the tune 'It's A Long Way From LA To Denver'.

GLEN BUXTON

Alice Cooper's guitarist, died October 19th from heart failure, while suffering from pneumonia.
Remember me this way: As the co-writer of Cooper's greatest 'School's Out'.

RAINER PTACEK

Virtuoso bottleneck guitarist, died November

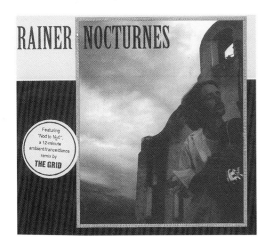

12th from a brain tumour. Ptacek had undergone chemotherapy in early 1996 but he suffered another seizure. He'd played extensively with Robert Plant, Giant Sand and ZZ Top and also released three solo albums. The world waits for the Robert Plant/Howe Gelb co-ordinated tribute album.
Remember me this way: His moody solo album 'Nocturnes'.

EPIC SOUNDTRACKS

The former Swell Maps, Crime And The City Solution and These Immortal Souls man committed suicide on November 22nd, aged 38. As part of the truly inventive Swell Maps he re-routed punk and established a global reputation, which was boosted by numerous album and single releases

and a whole host of collaborations.
Read it in the press:
His pseudonym was created by joining Epic, from the record company of the same name, with 'Soundtracks', the title of an album by Can who were at their height in the early '70s.
From Soundtracks' obituary in The Telegraph

Remember me this way: Banging out 'Gunboats In The Estuary'.

MICHAEL HUTCHENCE

The INXS singer hung himself in mysterious circumstances on November 22nd. At the height of his musical career, the world peeked through the keyhole and caught up with him. Debate

Epic Soundtracks

Drummer of the new wave band Swell Maps founded in the 1970s with Nikki Sudden

DIY aesthetic: the sleeve designed by Soundtracks for Swell Maps' album A Trip to Marineville (1979)

EPIC SOUNDTRACKS, who has died aged 38, was the inventive drummer of the new wave band Swell Maps.

Swell Maps (the name was a quote from an episode of the children's television puppet serial *Stingray*) was founded by Soundtracks and his elder brother Nikki Sudden. It first emerged in 1977 in the second wave of punk, after bands such as the Sex Pistols and the Damned had made themselves known through the tabloids.

The form of pop performed by Swell Maps was more idiosyncratic, and tended towards the avant garde. Album credits, listing who played what, might include, alongside bass, drums and guitar, "balloons", "microphone damage" and "vacuum cleaner". Their music was home-made and unpredictable, stretching from catchy pop melodies to experimental noise scratchings.

During their brief existence, Swell Maps released several singles and two albums, and built up a following through appearances on the John Peel show. Their improvisational, sometimes whimsical, sound was to endear

Soundtracks: gifted musician

Croydon, Surrey, on March 23 1959. When he was five, the family moved to

tain impromptu hand-made artworks, cartoons and doodlings. Perhaps the most striking sleeve design, featuring a burning house, was for their album *A Trip to Marineville*. Like most of the band's other sleeves, it was designed by Soundtracks himself. By early 1978, Swell Maps found themselves Number 1 in the English independent charts.

Other singles followed: *Dresden Style*, *Real Shocks* and *Let's Build A Car*. *A Trip to Marineville* was released in 1979, and contained such brittle, edgy classics as *Midget Submarines*. Their only other completed album was *Jane From Occupied Europe* (1980).

The band split up in 1980. Nikki Sudden went on to join The Jacobites; Soundtracks played with them, while also playing with The Red Krayola, the experimental band started by Mayo Thompson. He released two solo singles, *Jelly Babies* and *Rain Rain Rain*.

In 1984, Soundtracks joined Rowland S Howard, a guitarist who had played with The Birthday Party, and his brother Harry, who had restarted their

Michael Hutchence

The face of a new sound

MICHAEL Hutchence, who has died aged 37, lived the part of archetypal rock star. His good looks and stage presence as lead singer of the Australian group INXS led to comparisons with Jim Morrison of the Doors — with whom he had some vocal affinity — and Mick Jagger of the Rolling Stones. As for the band, they became the most successful rockers out of Australia.

The son of a wealthy champagne importer, Hutchence was born in Sydney but spent his early years in Hong Kong and Los Angeles, where he moved with his mother after his parents separated. At 13, Hutchence returned to Sydney, where he met his future songwriting partner, Andrew Farriss, at Davidson High School. There, according to one account, Farriss saved Hutchence from a playground beating.

Andrew and his brothers, Jon and Tim, were already proficient musicians when they formed the Farriss Brothers in 1977 with 17-year-old Hutchence as the principal vocalist — he had made his first recording some years earlier, singing Jingle Bells for a talking doll company. Isolated from the mid-1970s punk rock explosions of London and New York, the group put together a style which, as Andrew Farriss later recalled, was not delineated between rock, soul, pop funk or, indeed, anything. When the Farriss family moved to Perth for a year, the rest of the band went too, performing occasionally at local clubs.

By 1979 they were back in Sydney, renamed INXS — "in excess". Performances on Sydney's pub rock scene developed their audience — the

being responsible for most of the group's early compositions. Within a year their records were automatic Australian hits. Thus did Hutchence and Farriss travel to London and New York in search of contracts and concerts.

In 1983, INXS made their first US appearances on a tour with the Kinks, but it was the cable television music channel MTV which brought the Australian rockers to the attention of young Americans. With photogenic Hutchence to the fore, a string of arresting promotional videos — beginning with *The One Thing* — were central to the success of INXS.

After America came Europe and Japan. The international status of INXS was further boosted by the group's partic-

> With photogenic Hutchence to the fore, arresting promotional videos were central to the success of INXS

ipation in the 1985 Australian Live Aid concert. The music media accorded rock god status to Hutchence, and in 1986 he played a drug-crazed punk in the well-received Australian film *Dogs In Space*, directed by Richard Lowenstein, who had made several INXS videos. Hutchence's only other starring role was as the poet Shelley in Roger Corman's 1989 film *Frankenstein Unbound*.

INXS peaked artistically in the late 1980s with the albums *Listen Like Thieves* and *X*. *Kick* sold nine million and the Hutchence-Farriss rock ballad *Need You Tonight* was an American number one, while *Never Tear Us Apart* was an outstanding example of what one critic called Hutchence's "graphic lyrical style". Hutchence and INXS did not share the concern for

social issues of Australia's other major rock export, Midnight Oil, but *Original Sin*, his song about racial tolerance, was banned by radio stations in the American South. In 1989, Hutchence made the experimental album *Max Q*, his only recording away from INXS.

By 1993 the group appeared to be looking for a new direction with the *Full Moon, Dirty*

Hearts album, which was unfavourably compared with the work of the Irish group U2. Their last recording, *Elegantly Wasted*, received lukewarm praise.

Since 1990 Hutchence had based himself in London. His apparent adherence to a sex, drugs and rock'n'roll lifestyle made him a tabloid favourite, particularly through his high-profile relationships with

singer Kylie Minogue, model Helena Christensen and Paula Yates, with whom he had a daughter.

His death came as INXS were preparing for a 20th anniversary tour of Australia.

Dave Laing

Michael Hutchence, singer, born January 20, 1960; died November 22, 1997.

Hutchence ... accorded rock god status by the music media

and investigation followed his death. His girlfriend, Paula Yates, claims that his death was a result of a sex game gone wrong, while the family and the coroner's report state it was suicide.
Read it in the press:
Rocker Michael Hutchence died so he could date Princess Diana in Heaven, his grieving father joked yesterday. Kell Hutchence paid an affectionate tribute to his son, who romanced some of the most beautiful women in the world, including supermodel Helena Christensen.
The Daily Express, December 18th, 1997
Australian pop star Michael Hutchence, lead singer of the rock group INXS, has been found dead in a it

Sydney hotel, local media reported on Saturday. Australian Broadcasting Corporation radio quoted police as saying Hutchence had died of a drug overdose. Other radio reports said he had hanged himself. The media reports said Hutchence's body was found

at the Ritz-Carlton hotel in the exclusive harbour side suburb of Double Bay.

INXS, born in the Australian pub-circuit in 1977, has been one of the world's most durable music groups. Reuters

Remember me this way:
Giving it the funky chicken on 'Suicide Blonde'.

MICHAEL HEDGES

Died December 1st in a car crash attributed to worn tyres. The American guitarist, singer and composer developed a distinctive instrumental sound and signed to the new age Windham Hill label.

Remember me this way: Noodling in space.

NICOLETTE LARSON

Seasoned session singer (Neil Young, Beach Boys, etc), died December 16th of fluid to the brain following liver failure.

Remember me this way: With her very own solo hit 'Lotta Love' (written by Young).

FLOYD CRAMER

Much-praised Louisiana keyboard player died December 31st from cancer. Had hits in his own right and also tinkled the ivories on several Presley tracks.

Remember me this way: He wrote the theme tune to Dallas.

SONNY BONO

Died January 5th in a skiing accident, aged 62. The veteran peace and love protagonist eventually became a member of the US Congress and finally mayor of Palm Springs. But he's best remembered for his page boy crop and distinctive waistcoats 30 years previously.

Read it in the press:
Sonny Bono, a 1960s pop star-turned-politician, has died after crashing into a tree while skiing. He was 62. Bono, an avid skier, was skiing along an intermediate slope at Lake Tahoe's Heavenly Ski Resort on Monday when he struck a tree said resort organiser Stan Miller.
The congressman had been reported missing about two hours before his body was found, said spokesman Frank Cullen, adding Bono had been on holiday with his wife Mary Whitaker and their children Chianna, six, and Chesare, nine.
From Associated Press in Lake Tahoe, California

Remember me this way: Singing 'I Got U Babe' with Cher.

KEN FORSSI

The original Love bassist died January 5th from brain cancer.

Remember me this way: Trying to keep up on the breakneck 'Seven And Seven Is'

JUNIOR WELLS

Died January 15th from lymphoma, aged 63. The Memphis harmonica player was a regular blow with the Muddy Waters' group, renowned for trying on the shoes of the legendary Little Walter after he died.

Read it in the press:
Junior Wells, one of the greatest harmonica players in blues history, died of lymphatic cancer on January 15th in Chicago. Wells first emerged on the Chicago scene as a teenager, leading The Four Aces before joining Muddy Waters' band in 1952. Young enough to absorb rock 'n' roll, Wells fused traditional blues with the new sound, and he was instrumental in attracting a young, white audience to the blues.
Wells' obituary in Rolling Stone

Remember me this way: With 'Trouble In Mind'.

JUNIOR KIMBROUGH

Blues player from Mississippi who didn't make it big until the 1990s. Kimbrough released his first album at the age of 62. When Fat Possum Records released 'All Night Long' it was like nothing you'd ever heard before; The Washington Post called it "the best Delta Blues album in nearly 40 years." He died January 17th from a heart attack, leaving a staggering 36 children behind.

IGGY POP: "His music was the greatest. Nobody can hypnotise like this guy."

Remember me this way: In the style of John Lee Hooker.

CARL PERKINS

Suffering a stroke while ill with cancer, the 'Blue Suede Shoes' veteran died on January 19th. The Beatles covered several of his songs and he was idolised by Paul McCartney. In fact, his guitar playing style was an influence on many.

Read it in the press:
If Perkins had never made another record, then 'Blue Suede Shoes' would have placed him in the Rock 'n' Roll Hall Of Fame alone. At Sun between 1955 and 57, along with Johnny Cash, Elvis Presley and Jerry Lee Lewis, he was one of the principal architects of rock 'n' roll.
Perkins' obituary in Rolling Stone

Remember me this way: Wearing those blue suedes.

JOHNNY FUNCHES

Lead singer of original deep soul crooners The Dells. Their string of releases secured them endless chart positioning through the late '50s and '60s. Funches died of emphysema on January 25th.

Remember me this way: The bittersweet 'Dry Your Eyes'.

UNITED STATES

Sonny Bono dies after skiing into tree at resort

ASSOCIATED PRESS
in Lake Tahoe, California

Sonny Bono, a 1960s pop star-turned-politician, has died after crashing into a tree while skiing. He was 62.

Bono, an avid skier, was alone on an intermediate slope at Lake Tahoe's Heavenly Ski Resort on Monday when he struck a tree, said resort manager Stan Miller.

The congressman had been reported missing about two hours before his body was found, said spokesman Frank Cullen, adding Bono had been on holiday with his wife, Mary Whitaker, and their children, Chianna, six, and Chesare, nine.

An autopsy was to be carried out, but Lieutenant Ross Chichester, of the Sheriff's Department, said initial investigations indicated it was an accident.

His death follows that on New Year's Eve of another high-profile American, Michael Kennedy, the 39-year-old son of the late Robert F. Kennedy, when he, too, skied into a tree.

Bono and his second wife, Cher, gained fame in the 1960s with such hits as *I Got You, Babe* and *The Beat Goes On* before moving into television with their own show.

Last night, Cher was flying from London to Los Angeles to be with their daughter, lesbian activist Chastity, 29, after pulling out of the opening of the Harrods store's January sale.

Bono also leaves a child from his first marriage, about which little is known.

He was elected to Congress in 1994 as a Republican from Palm Springs, where he served as mayor from 1988-1992.

Sonny Bono

CARL WILSON

The Beach Boys crooner died February 6th from lung cancer complications, which spread to his brain, aged 51. He was the lead voice on 'Good Vibrations' and the often eulogised 'God Only Knows' and, in the light of brother Brian's mental instability, he took over as the driving force of the group feeding numerous songs into Brian's blueprint, most notably 'I Can Hear Music'. In fact, on later albums such as 'Holland' and 'Surf's Up' Carl took an ever-increasing role. However, with the group in disarray, he left to record a couple of solo albums, which featured some songs from his sad and lonely repertoire. But it wasn't until The Beach Boys reformed that Carl hit the limelight again.

Remember me this way: As the man who brought you 'Disney Girls' from the album 'Surf's Up'.

FALCO

The classically-trained Austrian musician died February 6th in a car crash in the Dominican Republic, aged 40. His Mozart-inspired pop hit was only the tip of his creativity, he'd also been banned for his punky lyrics when he played bass in Drahdiwaberl.

Wolfgang Amadeus Mozart: "As death, when we come to consider it closely, is the true goal of our existence, I have formed during the last few years such close relations with this best and truest friend of mankind, that his image is not only no longer terrifying to me, but is indeed very soothing and consoling! And I thank my God for graciously granting me the opportunity of learning that death is the key which unlocks the door to our true happiness."

Remember me this way: His bastardisation of the classics on 'Rock Me Amadeus'.

JUDGE DREAD

UK-based larger-than-life reggae rewriter and ska heavyweight, who died on March 12th from a heart attack on stage in Canterbury, aged 53.

Remember me this way: Bizarre versions of 'Je T'Aime' and the hoary 'Big Seven'.

COZY POWELL

Died April 5th in a high-speed car crash on the M4 near Bristol. The seasoned drummer played with Black Sabbath, Rainbow, Brian May and a host of others.

Remember me this way: His tub-thumping solo single 'Dance With The Devil'.

WENDY O WILLIAMS

Former Plasmatics front person, shot herself on April 6th in the woods by her home. The Plasmatics spiked their metallic sound by incorporating violent performances into their act. Amid the bedlam, former sex show star Wendy O was often seen upfront sporting a chainsaw.

Remember me this way: Topless, save for two pieces of insulating tape.

TAMMY WYNETTE

Died April 6th as the result of a blood clot at the age of 55. Five times married, Wynette upset the feminists with her big hits 'DIVORCE' and 'Stand By Your Man'. Her response was: "It's easier to sing about something you've done rather than something you've never experienced."

Her death led to controversy and intrigue when her family demanded she be exhumed to clarify how she died. The lawsuits go on.

MARLEE MACLEOD (New Country star): "After school, at some point I became much too cool for country. But my teenage disdain for those familiar songs gave way to respect for their peculiar artistry, and I particularly loved the premier women of country. Patsy crooned, Dolly soared,

TAMMY WYNETTE, 1942–1998

First lady of country music dies in Nashville at fifty-five

BY JAMES HUNTER

NO ONE HAS EVER HEARD A country singer more soulful than Tammy Wynette. Here was an internationally recognized woman always in bracing command of her own vocal style whose songs rendered emotions in ways both intricately subtle and boomingly direct. Here was a mother, a hairdresser, a striver, a wife, a fan, a lover, a *winner* who never shrank from declaring, often with heartbreaking tenderness, the tough stuff. Here was a country soprano of enormous heart and singular touch who recognized how effectively her music could accommodate the gravity of tangled domesticity and romance. Here was one of American popular music's iconic examples of transcendence. During the early evening of April 6th at her home in Nashville, a blood clot traveled to her lungs and she died in her sleep. She was fifty-five.

Wynette's health had been poor and complicated all her adult life. "She had so many stomach surgeries done in different cities and hospitals," explains Evelyn Shriver, Wynette's longtime publicist and now president of the Nashville-based Asylum Records. "She suffered the consequences of her lifestyle, of traveling and having people work on her who didn't always know the complexity of her conditions. There were times when I would see her go onstage when she could hardly talk. But she always sang great. She would say, 'I save everything for when I go onstage.' "

Born in 1942 near Tupelo, Mississippi, Virginia Wynette Pugh grew up on her grandparents' farm, picking cotton and dreaming of the Grand Ole Opry. A month before her high school graduation, she married Euple Byrd. Following the birth of their third daughter, in 1965, Wynette and Byrd divorced. She moved to be near her father's family in Birmingham, Alabama, where she worked in a beauty salon and sang every morning on local TV, rising at 4 a.m. to make a camera call before seeing her first hair client of the day. She and her children lived in a housing project.

A year later, Wynette piled her kids in a car and moved to Nashville, where she managed to slip past an absent secretary into the offices of producer Billy Sherrill. Sherrill – then overhauling the rhythms and tempos of country music to make a classier, more commercial machine – fell for Wynette's voice, the trademark "tear" down the middle of its lusciously imperfect tone already fully intact. He knew she was right for "Apartment #9," a minor single that Sherrill thought could be a hit. And he changed her name to Tammy.

The record was brilliant: Wynette summoned the courage to lace her self-styled vocal rhythms with sweetness and personal drama instead of trying to impersonate the big voice and dulcet phrasing with which Patsy Cline had triumphed. But the first of Wynette's many country-chart toppers was a year away. After "Your Good Girl's Gonna Go Bad" (Number Three), they tumbled out: the restrained bankings and ungodly swells of "I Don't Wanna Play House," the gorgeously wrought hope of "Take Me to Your World," the oddly circular sadness and dignity of "D-I-V-O-R-C-E" and, of course,

"Stand By Your Man," arguably the most stunning depiction of loyalty in recorded music.

"Her honesty, the way she chose her songs and the way she was never afraid to sing about anything – that's what I related to," says Trisha Yearwood.

In Nashville, Wynette married songwriter Don Chapel in 1967. Loretta Lynn met her then. "She had 'Your Good Girl's Gonna Go Bad,' " Lynn remembers. "We worked a show together, and Tammy was fixing her hair. I hadn't been singing but a couple three years myself, so we just bonded right then, and I guess we've been together ever since. Our lives were in our songs. We were just racing; we didn't feel like competition, but we raced. Tammy was the kind of person that, if she were your friend, it was forever. She died with things that she knew about me that will never be told, and I will die with things about her that will never be told. It's hard to lose your greatest friend in country music."

During Wynette's marriage to Chapel, which ended in 1968, a frequent guest at their house was George Jones, the legendary country singer, whom Wynette had long idolized. "He fell in love with Tammy," Billy Sherrill recalled in 1992. "They wanted to sing together so bad. Tammy was married to Don at the time they met. Then George took care of that." George and Tammy's stormy union produced one daughter, Georgette.

After three years, Wynette's third marriage also failed. But before then, she and Jones recorded their mythic early-Seventies duets, songs like "Near You," the wry "(We're Not) The Jet Set" and "Golden Ring," which appeared in 1976, a year after Wynette's divorce from Jones became final. They defined the Nashville duet deluxe, Wynette's crisp voice against Jones' plush sweeps. After their divorce, Wynette and Jones still recorded together sometimes; nowhere is Wynette more riveting than on the opening verse of "Southern California," a 1977 pairing with Jones, where she's lost in dreams of silver screens and limousines, explaining, "There's something I can't find in Tennessee."

In fact, from 1972's "Till I Get It Right" through 1976's "Till I Can Make It On My Own," Wynette's singing had only gained authority and refinement. And after yet another failed marriage, she finally found happiness with songwriter/producer/arranger George Richey, who became Wynette's manager in 1978. During the last decade of her life, her international renown produced a 1991 pop hit with England's the KLF, titled "Justified and Ancient," and Wynette, even awash in electrobeats and samples, was still all down-home cries and whispers.

"She was always just really curious about everything that was going on," Evelyn Shriver remembers, "always quick to jump up and bake you biscuits. She'd load you down with this great strawberry jam, this great peach jam, jars of chicken salad that she loved to make."

MCA Records Nashville president Tony Brown produced Wynette and Jones on their 1995 reunion album, *George and Tammy – One.* "Years from now, when I retire," he says, "one thing I'll be proud of is that I got to produce a duet album with George Jones and Tammy Wynette. Man, what a sweet woman."

PHOTOGRAPH BY MARK SELIGER

Loretta hollered, but Tammy... Tammy sobbed." (taken from a No Depression obit, August 1998) CLIFF RICHARD: "She was not afraid to be sentimental."

Remember me this way: Her career revival in 1992 with KLF or the original sobriety of her break-up reportage.

ROSE MADDOX

The country singer, rockabilly dabbler and smallest member of the Maddox Brothers And Sister

Rose died April 15th of kidney failure, aged 72.
Remember me this way: With 'When God Dips His Love In My Heart'.

LINDA MCCARTNEY

Canadian photographer (who produced classic shots of everyone from Hendrix to Morrison to The Grateful Dead) and humanist/activist who

married Paul McCartney and played keyboards in Wings. Linda was inseparable from Macca right up to her sad death on April 17th from breast cancer.
Remember me this way: With Paul singing 'Be With You'.

LESTER BUTLER

Red Devils' member, died May 10th from an overdose of heroin and cocaine. Two of his friends and co-sniffers were convicted with involuntary manslaughter following his demise. The Red Devils counted Mick Jagger as one of their fans and he used the band to back him on one of his solo projects.
Remember me this way: Rocking at the King King Club in uptown LA, as captured on the Rick Rubin-produced album.

LAL WATERSON

The legendary traditional English folk singer and sister of Norma, died September 4th of cancer.

Read it in the press:
A member of Britain's foremost family of traditional singers, Lal Waterson had a plaintive voice that was one of the great glories of English folk music. She formed the Watersons with her older siblings and cousin John Harrison and later her brother-in-law Martin Carthy. Their rich a cappella harmonies made them the most influential vocal group of the 1960s folk revival.
Waterson's obituary in The Times

Remember me this way: Her most recent recordings with son Oliver Knight, the album 'A Bed Of Roses'.

CHARLIE FOXX

Soul/R&B belter and half of Inez And Charlie Foxx (brother and sister partnership), Charlie Foxx died on September 18th, aged 58.
Remember me this way: The duo's often covered 1963 hit 'Mockingbird'.

ROLAND ALPHONSO

Mainstay and tenor saxophonist of The Skatalites and an all-round Jamaican musical motivator, died November 20th after collapsing on stage in Hollywood. His distinctive playing style powered 'Phoenix City', and 'El Pussycat' among many others. Alphonso began his career playing jazz and was heralded by none other than Louis Armstrong as "the next Charlie Parker".
Remember me this way: With The Skatalites' classic 'Guns Of Navarone'.

BRYAN MACLEAN

Arthur Lee's foil in Love, MacLean died on December 25th from a heart attack at his home in Los Angeles. He'd just released a comeback solo album called 'Ifyoubelievein', which featured a handful of recently discovered Love demos.
Remember me this way: With his 'Alone Again Or' from Love's greatest opus 'Forever Changes'.

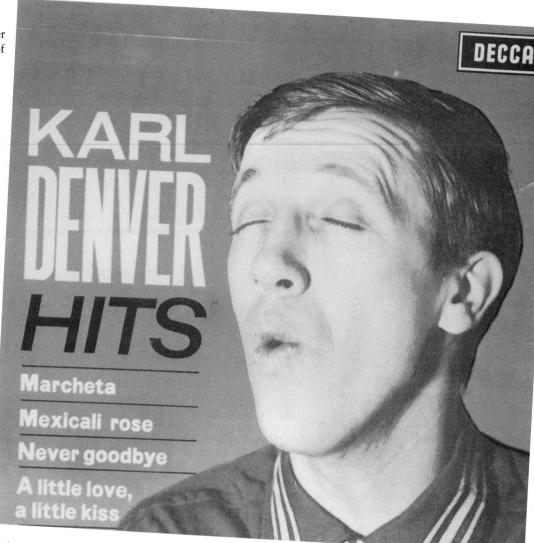

KARL DENVER

The hi-octane be-suited singer of 'Wimoweh', died December 25th. An early contemporary of Billy Fury Denver had fantastic pitch.

Read it in the press:
The annoyingly memorable falsetto sing (Wimoweh) - with its swooping yodel "Oh-Ooooooh, Wimoweh" and background vocal continuo "Wimoweh, Wimoweh, Wimoweh", was Denver said, an adaptation of a tribal chant he had heard as a merchant seaman in Johannesburg.
Denver's obituary in The Telegraph
Remember me this way: Screaming the house down.

BRYN JONES

Welsh rhythmic electronics expert obsessed with the Middle East who recorded as Muslimgauze. Died January 15th of a very rare blood fungus disorder, which led to pneumonia.
Remember me this way: Playing 'Milena Jenenska' on the 'Elephant Table Album'.

DAVID McCOMB

Gifted, but sadly unfulfilled, Triffids songwriter who died from a heart condition on February 2nd following a car crash.

MICK HOUGHTON (Triffids' press officer): "The songs still stand tall and true. 'Bury Me Deep In Love', 'Hometown Farewell Kiss' and the remarkable 'Jerdacuttup Man', to name but a few."

Remember me this way: The Triffids' 'Black Swan' or 'Born Sandy Devotional' albums.

JACKSON C FRANK

Once described as the most famous folk singer that no one ever heard of, Frank had schmoozed with Elvis, been Sandy Denny's boyfriend and had one of his tunes covered by Nick Drake. Cred? He had it all. His eponymous 1965 album was his legacy. The reason little else was recorded was due to the break up of his marriage and the death of his son, which threw him into an endless depression.

Remember me this way: The haunting ballad 'Blues Run The Game'.

GWEN GUTHRIE

A soul belter and seasoned session voice, Guthrie died on February 3rd from uterine cancer in Orange County, aged 48.

Remember me this way: Her social commentary on 'Ain't Nothing Goin' On But The Rent'.

DUSTY SPRINGFIELD

Legendary born-out-of-time belter who aspired to greatness and never quite got there. Ahead of her time and seemingly out of kilter with the world, she disappeared during the '70s and '80s and was only coaxed back into the public eye in recent years. Died March 2nd from breast cancer.

Ironically, Dusty died on the day she should have collected her OBE from the Queen at Buckingham Palace.

Read it in the press: *Dusty Springfield, who has died aged 59, was one of Britain's most successful female pop singers; she had nine top ten hits in the 1960s, and with her upswept hair and panda-shadowed eyes was among the emerging pop scene's most readily identifiable stars. She was distinguished from her contemporaries by her choice of material and her voice.*
Springfield's obituary in The Telegraph.

Evening Standard
WEST END FINAL

LONDON, WEDNESDAY, 3 MARCH 1999 — Incorporating THE EVENING NEWS — 35p

LONDON'S TWICE AS LUCKY WALLETS – SEE PAGE 56 FOR DETAILS

DUSTY DIES ON HER ROYAL DAY

Queen 'saddened' as cancer kills singer due to collect her OBE

by TIM COOPER

DUSTY SPRINGFIELD has died from breast cancer on the day she should have collected her OBE from the Queen at Buckingham Palace.

The 59-year-old singer died at 10.40 last night at her home in Henley-on-Thames, her agent Paul Fenn said today.

Dusty was awarded an OBE in the New Year Honours and her investiture had been due to be held yesterday. But, because she was too ill to go to the palace, she was allowed to have her medal collected for her ahead of the official date. A palace spokeswoman said today: "The Queen was saddened to hear of her death."

Dusty had also been due to receive a second major accolade — her induction into the Rock and Roll Hall of Fame in New York — in two weeks' time. Despite the reclusive life she led at her Henley mansion, she had been eager to meet the Queen, and also to join the traditional jam session at the Hall of Fame with fellow inductees, including Bruce Springsteen and Sir Paul McCartney. Her

The way she was: Dusty Springfield secured her place in pop history by becoming one of the biggest selling stars on both sides of the Atlantic

place in pop's hall of fame had already been assured, however.

Born Mary O'Brien in Hampstead in 1939, she became one of the top female singers of the Sixties. Her string of hits on both sides of the Atlantic included I Only Want To Be With You, I Just Don't Know What To Do With Myself, and You Don't Have To Say You Love Me.

Lulu, who knew Dusty for more than 30 years and was a close friend, said today: "I'm terribly, terribly sad at her loss but also at the same time relieved that she is no longer suffering."

Dusty was initially diagnosed with breast cancer in 1994. She thought she had beaten it but learned in the summer of 1996 that it had returned. She spent the next 18 months fighting the disease but a year ago she was too ill to attend the Brit Awards, where she had been due to be a guest of honour.

Just before Christmas she moved out of her converted granary in Oxfordshire to seek more seclusion in the larger house in Henley, with more picturesque views. Last May, shortly after the death of Linda McCartney from the same disease Dusty, whose mother Kay died of lung cancer, sold the rights to her 275 songs to Prudential Insurance for £6.25 million.

She never married and in the mid-Seventies consolidated her long-held status as a gay icon by finally admitting in the Evening Standard that she was bisexual.

With her sensuous, smoky voice, and an ability to sing anything from ballads to soul stompers, Dusty Springfield was one of the few white singers who could

Continued on Page 2 Col 3

President: I'll hunt Britons' murderers

UGANDA'S president today apologised for the massacre by Hutu rebels which claimed the lives of eight tourists. President Museveni vowed to hunt the gang which kidnapped a group of Westerners visisting Bwindi national park then hacked them to death with machetes. The victims included Britons Mark Lindgren, 33, and Stephen Roberts, 27. Britain's High Commissioner in Uganda, Michael Cook, said today that the attack was "an impressively organised operation."

Stephen Roberts: killed on his way to visit father

Uganda massacre: Pages 4 & 5

BANK'S EDDIE STAYS STEADY AND REFUSES TO LOWER LOAN RATE AGAIN: SEE PAGE TWO

Dusty Springfield, a singer whose voice simultaneously embodied Sixties pop elegance and seemed luminously timeless, died on March 2nd after a long struggle with breast cancer. On March 15th Springfield was posthumously inducted into the Rock 'n' Roll Hall Of Fame.
Springfield's obituary in Rolling Stone.

BLUE-EYED SOULSTRESS DIES

Bi-sexual white soul diva leaves life with promise tragically unfulfilled. But we'll always have Dusty In Memphis.

Considered the best British female voice of her generation, she should not only have been at the centre of what was 'swinging' but she should have

been ready for what was to come too. Instead, during the '60s she found herself increasingly out of sync both professionally and privately. The times had changed but never enough for Dusty Springfield. Though her peers were Lulu, Cilla Black and Sandie Shaw and she remained a sucker for ballads, stylistically she was more akin to Dionne Warwick. An early champion of Motown she was dubbed 'The White Negress' by Cliff Richard. Yet it took 'Son Of A Preacher Man', recorded in Memphis in 1968, to ratify her R&B credentials.
Peter Kane, Q Magazine

ANNIE LENNOX: "There was something about Dusty Springfield's voice that was very powerful, very expressive, a fantastic dynamic range. She's one of the few white singers where, if you shut your eyes, you'd think you were listening to a black singer, which was rare, particularly in those days."

Neil Tennant: "She was one of my favourites. My favourite album is 'Dusty In Memphis' and she told me herself that when she recorded this album she had laryngitis and they had to record it line by line, millions of takes. She's very husky and breathy. She's got a sort of intensity and desperation to her voice that's fantastically sensual. She sort of floats off onto another plane."

Dusty on 'Dusty In Memphis': "I hated it at first because I couldn't be Aretha Franklin. If only Jerry Wexler could realise what a deflating thing it is to say, 'Otis Redding stood there', or 'That's where Aretha sang'. Added to the natural critic in me, it was a paralysing experience. I was someone who'd come from thundering drums and Phil Spector, I didn't understand sparseness."

LUCY O'BRIEN (Journalist): Perhaps one of her greatest achievements was inventing that look, the impossible beehive, the smudged panda eyes, the glittering gowns.

DAVE STEWART: "She was one of Britain's most unbelievable voices."

Remember me this way: In Memphis.

DAVID ACKLES

Amazing but virtually-unsung American Gothic folklorist songwriter who inked great tomes of prose and shoehorned them into four minute songs. He died on March 2nd from cancer

Elvis Costello: "David Ackles made two really

terrific records for Elektra when I was about 15 or 16 and I used to listen to them avidly in my bedroom. It was kind of my teenage angst period. He sang all kinds of dark songs, but this particular one 'Down River' changed my life. I think that Elton John probably listened quite a lot to Ackles and stole quite a bit - in the nicest possible way."

ANDY GILL (journalist): "Of all the singer-songwriters signed to Elektra in the late '60s, David Ackles was by far the most original. It was his voice that first caught the ear, a warm, lugubrious baritone which reflected the, maturity of both the performer and his work."

Remember me this way: The 'American Gothic' album is the perfect place to begin.

LOWELL FULSON

Oklahoma-born blues institution, Lowell Fulson died on March 6th from complications due to kidney disease and diabetes, which resulted in congestive heart failure. He was 77. Remembered as the man who penned 'Reconsider Baby', he also had time to give away classics like 'Three O'Clock Blues' to BB King and 'Tramp' to Otis Redding.

Remember me this way: Introducing the world to Ray Charles.

ANANDA SHANKAR

Classical Indian fusionist and nephew of Ravi Shankar, suffered a cardiac arrest on March 26th.

During the Sixties he mixed Eastern mystique with rock 'n' roll timeframes.

Remember me this way: His insane version of 'Jumpin' Jack Flash'.

FREAKY TAH

The Lost Boyz rapper from New York was shot in the back of the head by a masked gunman on March 28th.

Remember me this way: The big-selling debut album 'Legal Drug Money'.

SKIP SPENCE

Highly influential psychedelic casualty who died in poverty from lung cancer and pneumonia on April 16th. He was on the verge of a benefit album release. The end came for Spence when he was pulled off an artificial respirator. "We tried our best to extend him," his son Omar told the San Francisco Chronicle, "But it got to the point where it would have been inhumane."

SPENCE SAID: (DURING AN INTERVIEW WITH JOHNNY ANGEL IN 1994): "YOU KNOW, I KEEP A DIARY TOO. IT'S IN MY OFFICE, IN HEAVEN."

Read it in the press:

Spence's genius cracked under the weight of Moby Grape's career troubles and his appetite for hallucinogens. A psychotic episode during the New York sessions for the group's 'Wow' LP landed Spence in Bellevue Hospital. On his release, Spence when to Nashville and cut 'Oar' in just four days, playing everything himself.
Spence's obituary in Rolling Stone.

Remember me this way: With the album 'Oar' and especially the song 'Lawrence Of Euphoria'.

THE TROUTMAN BROTHERS

Zapp members, brothers Roger and Larry, died April 25th, when Larry shot Roger then shot himself.

Remember me this way: Zapping like mad.

SHEL SILVERSTEIN

Seasoned songwriter who penned Johnny Cash's 'A Boy Named Sue' and Dr Hook's 'Sylvia's Mother'. Spent the rest of his time writing kids books and died May 10th.

Remember me this way: With the tune 'Your Credit Card Won't Get You Into Heaven'.

WILLIAM TUCKER

Chicago scenester and long term Ministry guitarist committed suicide May 14th just prior to the release of the band's long-awaited new album.

Remember me this way: Strumming out on 'Dark Side Of The Spoon'.

ROB GRETTON

Originally a DJ at Manchester's Rafters Club, Gretton went on to become the manager of both Joy Division and New Order and was a catalyst in the creation of the Hacienda club. He died May 15th from a heart attack.

Remember me this way: Screaming that he wasn't going to sink any more of New Order's money into the "poxy" Hacienda.

JEAN EAVIS

The Glastonbury Festival organiser who succumbed to cancer on May 16th during the build up to the June event.

Remember me this way: Sipping tea with Noel and Liam in her farmhouse kitchen.

AUGUSTUS PABLO

Dub reggae maestro, died May 18th from a nerve disorder, which he'd suffered from for many years. His melodica playing became well known in dub reggae circles and his 'Baby I Love You So' single was transformed into 'King Tubby Meets The Rockers Uptown' influencing The Clash, Pistols and their punk brethren.

Read it in the press:

After rising to prominence in the early 1970s, he influenced a range of artists from Joe Jackson to The Clash and Gang Of Four, and has since made his mark on artists as diverse as Stereolab, St Etienne, Andrew Weatherall and On-U Sound's Adrian Sherwood.
In 1973 he met King Tubby one of reggae's first dub producers along with Lee 'Scratch' Perry. They went on to produce 1977's 'King Tubby Meets The Rockers Uptown', an album widely acknowledged as a landmark of its genre.
Pablo's obituary in NME

Remember me this way: That King Tubby echo.

JUNIOR BRAITHWAITE

An original member of Bob Marley and The Wailers, Braithwaite was shot dead June 2nd.

Remember me this way: Creating some tension with 'Simmer Down'.

Skip Spence 1946-1999

SKIP SPENCE, THE DYNAMIC singer, guitarist and songwriter in the San Francisco band Moby Grape, died April 16th in a hospital in Santa Cruz, California. Spence had been hospitalized with pneumonia and was subsequently diagnosed with lung cancer. He died two days before his fifty-third birthday.

Born Alexander Lee Spence on April 18th, 1946, in Windsor, Ontario, Spence was a pivotal figure on the San Francisco scene even before the formation of Moby Grape, in 1966. Spence was in an embryonic lineup of Quicksilver Messenger Service; played drums on Jefferson Airplane's '66 debut, *Jefferson Airplane Takes Off*; and wrote or co-wrote some of the Airplane's finest early ballads, including "Blues From an Airplane" and "My Best Friend."

Spence's high-voltage charisma and inventive composing flowered in Moby Grape. "He was one of the most energetic people I'd ever met," says Grape guitarist Jerry Miller. "And when he grabbed that guitar and played rhythm, he was like a rock." Spence's songs "Omaha" and "Indifference," on 1967's *Moby Grape*, and "Seeing," on *Moby Grape '69*, capture his unique blend of pop savvy, eccentric melodicism and exuberant spirituality.

"You get this profound humanity, this manic lust for life," Grape singer and guitarist Peter Lewis says of Spence's songwriting. "The way he would change and play with chords, you couldn't tell where he was going. It was always a surprise."

But Spence's genius cracked under the weight of the Grape's career troubles and his appetite for hallucinogens. A psychotic episode during the New York sessions for the Grape's 1968 *Wow* LP landed Spence in Bellevue Hospital. Upon his release, Spence went to Nashville and – in four days, playing all of the instruments – cut the 1969 solo album *Oar*, a stark, ruminative record now considered a rock-noir classic.

Suffering from schizophrenia, Spence spent the next three decades in and out of treatment, often living on public assistance. He still wrote music, contributing songs to Grape reunion projects. Spence recorded a new original, "In the Land of the Sun," for the 1996 X-Files album, *Songs in the Key of X*; the track was rejected for being *too* spooky.

Sadly, Spence died on the eve of rediscovery. Sundazed Records is preparing a definitive reissue of *Oar*, and the Birdman label will soon release *More Oar: A Tribute to the Alexander "Skip" Spence Album*, featuring *Oar* covers performed by such all-star fans as Robert Plant, Beck, Tom Waits and Mudhoney. — DAVID FRICKE

EDDIE KURDZIEL

The Red Kross guitarist, died June 7th from a drug overdose.

Remember me this way: In a psychedelically-poppy haze.

SCREAMING LORD SUTCH

Eccentric quasi-politician and founder of the Monster Raving Loony Party. Sutch committed suicide after "losing the will to live" on June 24th. Recorded what's hailed as one of the worst albums ever in 'Lord Sutch And Heavy Friends'.

Read it on record sleeves:

Screaming Lord Sutch is about to wake up Southern California, if it's not too late. Lord Sutch, he's a hereditary Lord, originated the long hair trend back in 1960 and is a very popular performer in England. He ran for Parliament three times with a platform that included such planks as "Votes at 18", "Beatles Memorial College" and "Enforced Birth Control". Among his numerous awards is the Golden Hairnet, presented in 1965 by The Royal Society For The Prevention Of Accidents. Other recipients of the award have been Prince Charles and Mick Jagger.
Watching Lord Sutch perform is like watching Arthur Brown, Jerry Lee Lewis and James Brown all rolled into one. Make it your business to see him, he puts on quite a show.

Phil Flamm, Go Magazine, from the sleeve of 'Lord Sutch And Heavy Friends'

Remember me this way: With my heavy friends.

BRIAN O'HARA

Guitarist and singer with Beatles' contemporaries The Fourmost, O'Hara was found hanging at his home on June 27th.

Remember me this way: Singing the Lennon/McCartney song 'I'm In Love'.

DENNIS BROWN

The reggae star died July 1st from upper respiratory failure as a result of a collapsed lung. He had his first Jamaican hit when he was nine and died when he was 42, several chart toppers later.

Read it in the press:

The Jamaican reggae artist died of a collapsed lung on July 1st. Brown had hit records in his homeland from the age of 11 and enjoyed his biggest success in the '70s, under the guidance of producer Joe Gibbs.

Brown's obituary in Q magazine.

Remember me this way: Trying to get some 'Money in My Pocket'.

Guy Mitchell

Upbeat performer whose Singing the Blues sold 10 million

GUY MITCHELL, the American singer who has died in Las Vegas aged 72, helped to fill the gap between Bing Crosby and rock 'n' roll — with such success that during the 1950s he sold more than 40 million records.

Where so many popular singers have found success by wallowing in suffering and self-pity, Mitchell throve with a kind of up-beat joviality and sentimentality. It was pure deception that his most popular record, made in 1956, was entitled *Singing the Blues*, for Mitchell, backed by the Ray Conniff Orchestra, sounded very far from the depths of despair. Yet his recording sold 10 million copies and stands third in the list of the 1,000 top singles in the United States between 1955 and 1987, beaten only by Elvis Presley's *Don't Be Cruel* and *Hound Dog*.

Singing the Blues had been written by a polio victim called Melvin Endsley, and first recorded as a country number by Marty Robbins. Mitchell's version reached No 1 in Britain in January 1957, only to be displaced the next week by Tommy Steele's recording of the same song. Seven days later, however, Mitchell's record was back at No 1.

It did even better in America, holding the No 1 spot for 10 weeks. In general, though, Mitchell was more successful in Britain, where every record he made between November 1952 and July 1957 made the Top Twenty; six were in the Top Ten and four reached No 1. When he appeared for two weeks at the London Palladium in 1952 tickets sold out in 24 hours. Two years later he was chosen for the Royal Variety Show.

Many of the numbers which Mitchell sang in the 1950s were written by Bob Merrill and produced by Mitch Miller, the emphasis was on jaunty originality in the lyrics and on French horns in the accompaniment. One of their numbers was *She Wears Red Feathers* (1953), which peaked at 19 in America, but in Britain held the No 1 position for four weeks — not surprisingly, perhaps, given its theme of an English

banker's love for a girl from the tropics:

She wears red feathers and a hooly-hooly skirt,
She lives on just cokey-nuts and fish from the sea,
A rose in her hair, a gleam in her eyes
And love in her heart for me.

I went to her Ma and Pa and said I loved her only
And they both said we could be wed, oh, what a ceremony
An elephant brought her in, placed her by my side
While six baboons got out bassoons and played "Here Comes the Bride".

Mitchell's other No 1 hits in Britain were *Look At That Girl* (1953), and *Rock-a-Billy* (1957), the latter being as near as he and Mitch Miller ever came to acknowledging the existence of rock 'n' roll. True to form, neither of them played anything like so well in America.

Guy Mitchell was born Albert Cernick in Detroit on February 22 1927, the son of Yugoslav immigrants. They moved to California when he was 11. On arrival Albert signed for Warner Brothers as a potential child star, and soon had regular spots singing for KFWB Radio in Los Angeles.

The family moved again, to San Francisco, where Albert became an apprentice saddlemaker, and worked on ranches and rodeos in the San Joaquin Valley. But kept going with his music, singing country and western on Dude Martin's radio show.

After service in the navy, Cernick became a vocalist for the pianist Carmen Cavallaro's Orchestra, with whom he made his first recordings. He then tried his luck in New York, where, as Al Grant, he made a number of records for the King label. He was also a winner on the Arthur Godfrey Talent Show.

His breakthrough, however, did not come until 1950, when Mitch Miller, who was having trouble with Frank Sinatra, signed him for Columbia. The hope was that the public might appreciate some positive contrast to another singer, Johnnie Ray, who prospered by dint of copious sobbing. First,

though, Al Cernick had to go. "My name is Mitchell," Miller told him, "and you seem a nice guy, so we'll call you Guy Mitchell."

But it was not until his sixth record for Columbia, on which *My Heart Cries for You* (adapted from an 18th-century French song) was coupled with *The Roving Kind* (from the English sea shanty), that Mitchell made a breakthrough.

A string of catchy numbers followed, including *Sparrow in the Tree-Top* (1951), *My Truly, Truly Fair* (1951), *Pittsburgh, Pennsylvania* (1952), *Feet Up (Pat Him on the Po-Po)* (1952); *Pretty Little Black-Eyed Susie* (1953), *Cloud Lucky Seven* (1953), *Cuff of My Shirt* (1954), *Sippin' Soda* (1954) and *Knee Deep in the Blues* (1957).

Chicka Boom (1953) attempted to repeat the success of *She Wears Red Feathers*, by extolling the merits of an Eskimo woman. It reached No 4 in Britain and featured in Mitchell's first film, a 3-D musical entitled *Those Redheads from Seattle* (1953). He also starred with Rosemary Clooney in *Red Garters* (1954), which featured the song *A Dime and a Dollar*.

Mitchell's last hit single was *Heartaches* (by the Number (1959). Two divorces, and a great deal of drink, took their toll, and by the mid-1970s Mitchell was living on a ranch seemingly semi-retired from show business. "I've been so low," he reflected, "that even the bottom looks like up."

Yet he had showed himself to be an accomplished singer of ballads on his album *Guy in Love* (1959); and made two excellent country albums, *Travelling Shoes* (1967) and *Singing Up a Storm* (1968).

When he appeared on a television tribute to Mitch Miller at the start of the 1980s his contribution was ecstatically received. He began to record again, and 1984 made a tour of Britain, where his fans had never forgotten him. Indeed, a Guy Mitchell Appreciation Society had been formed in 1983.

Capitalising on this nostalgia, Mitchell made an album in 1985 entitled *Garden in the Rain*, an anthology of British songs, including Noël Coward's *I'll See You Again* and Paul McCartney's *Yesterday*. Two years later he returned triumphantly to the London Palladium. In 1990 he had a cameo role in the television series *Your Cheatin' Heart*, as Jim Bob O'May, with his band The Wild Bunch; seven of the songs he sang were released on BBC records.

During a tour of Australia in 1991, Mitchell had a bad riding accident, which left him with serious internal injuries. But he recovered to make further tours of Australia and Britain.

Latterly he lived in Las Vegas. His last record, *Dusty the Magic Elf* (1996) was for children. In Britain, though, nostalgia for his records of the 1950s remained undimmed, though the columnist Mary Kenny once identified a partiality for his records as a sure sign of midlife crisis.

Guy Mitchell married first, in 1952, Jackie Loughery, a former Miss USA; and secondly, in 1956, Elsa Soronson, a former Miss Denmark. His third wife, Betty, whom he married in 1974, survives him.

Mitchell: American even more popular in Britain

GUY MITCHELL

The UK's favourite clean-cut Yank, died July 1st from complications following surgery, aged 72. Never a huge star in his homeland of America, Mitchell had a string of UK hits, which assured him a lengthy British career.

Read it in the press:

Guy Mitchell, the American singer who has died in Las Vegas aged 72, helped to fill the gap between Bing Crosby and rock 'n' roll with such success that in the 1950s he sold more than 40 million records.

Mitchell's obituary in The Telegraph

Remember me this way: He never felt more like 'Singing the Blues'.

MARK SANDMAN

Died July 3rd from a heart attack while on stage in Rome with his jazz-punk fusion outfit Morphine. His group had forged new musical boundaries and developed an enviable global following.

Remember me this way: The 1993 album 'Cure For Pain'.

INA ANITA CARTER

A member of both The Carter Family and The Carter Sisters, as well as the offshoot Nita, Rita and Ruby and Mother Maybelle And The Carter Sisters, Ina Anita Carter was part of the Carter's development of traditional Appalachian country music. She died on July 29th, aged 65.

Remember me this way: With Bradley Kincaid's 'Bury Me Beneath The Willow'.

ROB FISHER

Half of Climie Fisher whose one huge 1980s hit was 'Love Changes Everything'. Fisher also played with Naked Eyes and Jules Shear among others. He died on August 25th aged 39.

Remember me this way: In ill-advised garb crooning that chart topper.

MOONDOG

Louis Hardin died Septmember 8th from heart failure. Renowned as dabbling in avant garde jazz, with a snatch of classical idealism, the blind composer produced a couple of excellent albums

in the early '70s. He also wrote 'All Is Loneliness' which was covered by Janis Joplin.
ROLLING STONE SAID: His melodic structures are classically inspired, while his use of percussion suggests a relationship with the more outside elements of rock and jazz rhythms.
MOONDOG SAID: "I began writing rounds in the late winter of 1951. I vaguely remember writing the first one 'All Is Loneliness', in a doorway on 51st street between 7th Avenue and Broadway."

DOUG SAHM

The legendary Tex-Mex, psyche-country, good time rock-a-boogie player died November 11th from a heart attack. A member of The Sir Douglas Quintet who charted with 'She's About A Mover' a spirited reply to the Beatles' US invasion in the early '60s. Later in his career Sahm dabbled in drugs and wigged out with the aid of numerous similarly hardy individuals as Doug Sahm And Band and eventually as The Texas Tornado's.
THE INDEPENDENT SAID: Despite his socialising and his excesses, Doug Sahm maintained an extraordinary output in his 44 years of recording. As he wrote in one of his songs, "I did a lot of cocaine but I did a lot of rhythm and blues".
DOUG SAID: "I'm a part of Willie Nelson's world and, at the same time, I'm a part of The Grateful Dead's. I don't ever stay in one bag."
REMEMBER ME THIS WAY: Singing 'Mendocino' at the peak of his hippie powers.

ALVIN CASH

Revered groovy soul popster who as Alvin Cash And The Crawlers and, later Alvin Cash And

The Registers recorded the soul shuffle 'It's Twine Time' and the memorable 'Funky Washing Machine' in the late '60s.0

Remember me this way: Sashaying his band across the floor.

RICK DANKO

An original member of Ronnie Hawkins And The Hawks, Levon And The

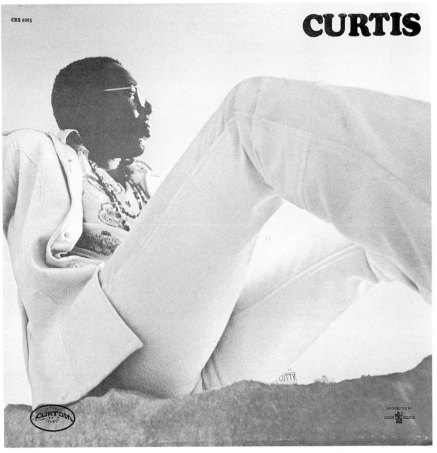
CURTIS
CRS 8005
CURTOM
CUTTY
DISTRIBUTED BY

Hawks, The Crackers and The Canadian Squires, Danko became bassist and a key player in The Band. His songwriting capabilities, however, weren't really recognised until his solo album in 1978 which Rolling Stone magazine acclaimed as a "moving and surprisingly fine record".
DID YOU KNOW: In his time in The Band, he also played with Dylan, contributed to the legendary 'Basement Tapes' and co-wrote the classic 'This Wheel's On Fire' with Bob.

Remember me this way: Carrying that weight.

HANK SNOW

Stylised whit Stetson-clad country singer who impressed Elvis a notched up a staggering 70 million record sales. Died on December 20th.
"(Snow's) toupee was a bad fit. Some claimed this was deliberate. But one violinist who chose to remove the offending item with his bow during a performance was instantly sacked."
Telegraph Obit outtake
Remember me this way: Singing 'I'm Movin' On'.

CURTIS MAYFIELD

Legendary soulman, songwriter and activist who produced influential harmonised classics with The Impressions, before cutting loose with socially aware items like 'Choice Of Colours'. Mayfield struck a chord with songs like 'Move On Up' before penning Blaxploitation movie music for the films Freddie's Dead and Superfly, which took him to a whole new audience. In a wheelchair since1990 when a lighting rig fell on him during a show, Mayfield continued to write provocative music right up to his death on Boxing Day.
THE OBITS SAID: "Curtis Mayfield turned soul music into a vehicle for politicised black consciousness while enjoying a series of hits."
Remember me this way: Singing "If you had a choice of colours, which one would you choose my brother?"

EPILOGUE

The dead have nothing except the memory they've left. **Ferenc Molnár**

TAMMY WYNETTE, 1942-1998

First lady of country music dies in Nashville at fifty-five

BY JAMES HUNTER

NO ONE HAS EVER HEARD A country singer more soulful than Tammy Wynette. Here was an internationally recognized woman always in bracing command of her own vocal style whose songs rendered emotions in ways both intricately subtle and boomingly direct. Here was a mother, a hairdresser, a striver, a wife, a fan, a lover, a *winner* who never shrank from declaring, often with heartbreaking tenderness, the tough stuff. Here was a country soprano of enormous heart and singular touch who recognized how effectively her music could accommodate the gravity of tangled domesticity and romance. Here was one of American popular music's iconic examples of transcendence. During the early evening of April 6th at her home in Nashville, a blood clot traveled to her lungs and she died in her sleep. She was fifty-five.

Wynette's health had been poor and complicated all her adult life. "She had so many stomach surgeries done in different cities and hospitals," explains Evelyn Shriver, Wynette's longtime publicist and now president of the Nashville-based Asylum Records. "She suffered the consequences of her lifestyle, of traveling and having people work on her who didn't always know the complexity of her conditions. There were times when I would see her go onstage when she could hardly talk. But she always sang great. She would say, 'I save everything for when I go onstage.'"

Born in 1942 near Tupelo, Mississippi, Virginia Wynette Pugh grew up on her grandparents' farm, picking cotton and dreaming of the Grand Ole Opry. A month before her high school graduation, she married Euple Byrd. Following the birth of their third daughter, in 1965, Wynette and Byrd divorced. She moved to be near her father's family in Birmingham, Alabama, where she worked in a beauty salon and sang every morning on local TV, rising at 4 a.m. to make a camera call before seeing her first hair client of the day. She and her children lived in a housing project.

A year later, Wynette piled her kids in a car and moved to Nashville, where she managed to slip past an absent secretary into the offices of producer Billy Sherrill. Sherrill – then overhauling the rhythms and tempos of country music to make a classier, more commercial machine – fell for Wynette's voice, the trademark "tear" down the middle of its lusciously imperfect tone already fully intact. He knew she was right for "Apartment #9," a minor single that Sherrill thought could be a hit. And he changed her name to Tammy.

The record was brilliant: Wynette summoned the courage to lace her self-styled vocal rhythms with sweetness and personal drama instead of trying to impersonate the big voice and dulcet phrasing with which Patsy Cline had triumphed. But the first of Wynette's many country-chart toppers was a year away. After "Your Good Girl's Gonna Go Bad" (Number Three), they tumbled out: the restrained bankings and ungodly swells of "I Don't Wanna Play House," the gorgeously wrought hope of "Take Me to Your World," the oddly circular sadness and dignity of "D-I-V-O-R-C-E" and, of course, "Stand By Your Man," arguably the most stunning depiction of loyalty in recorded music.

"Her honesty, the way she chose her songs and the way she was never afraid to sing about anything – that's what I related to," says Trisha Yearwood.

In Nashville, Wynette married songwriter Don Chapel in 1967. Loretta Lynn met her then. "She had 'Your Good Girl's Gonna Go Bad,'" Lynn remembers. "We worked a show together, and Tammy was fixing her hair. I hadn't been singing but a couple three years myself, so we just bonded right then, and I guess we've been together ever since. Our lives were in our songs. We were just racing; we didn't feel like competition, but we raced. Tammy was the kind of person that, if she were your friend, it was forever. She died with things that she knew about me that will never be told, and I will die with things about her that will never be told. It's hard to lose your greatest friend in country music."

During Wynette's marriage to Chapel, which ended in 1968, a frequent guest at their house was George Jones, the legendary country singer, whom Wynette had long idolized. "He fell in love with Tammy," Billy Sherrill recalled in 1992. "They wanted to sing together so bad. Tammy was married to Don at the time they met. Then George took care of that." George and Tammy's stormy union produced one daughter, Georgette.

After three years, Wynette's third marriage also failed. But before then, she and Jones recorded their mythic early-Seventies duets, songs like "Near You," the wry "(We're Not) The Jet Set" and "Golden Ring," which appeared in 1976, a year after Wynette's divorce from Jones became final. They defined the Nashville duet deluxe, Wynette's crisp voice against Jones' plush sweeps. After their divorce, Wynette and Jones still recorded together sometimes; nowhere is Wynette more riveting than on the opening verse of "Southern California," a 1977 pairing with Jones, where she's lost in dreams of silver screens and limousines, explaining, "There's something I can't find in Tennessee."

In fact, from 1972's "Till I Get It Right" through 1976's "Till I Can Make It On My Own," Wynette's singing had only gained authority and refinement. And after yet another failed marriage, she finally found happiness with songwriter/producer/arranger George Richey, who became Wynette's manager in 1978. During the last decade of her life, her international renown produced a 1991 pop hit with England's the KLF, titled "Justified and Ancient," and Wynette, even awash in electrobeats and samples, was still all down-home cries and whispers.

"She was always just really curious about everything that was going on," Evelyn Shriver remembers, "always quick to jump up and bake you biscuits. She'd load you down with this great strawberry jam, this great peach jam, jars of chicken salad that she loved to make."

MCA Records Nashville president Tony Brown produced Wynette and Jones on their 1995 reunion album, *George and Tammy – One.* "Years from now, when I retire," he says, "one thing I'll be proud of is that I got to produce a duet album with George Jones and Tammy Wynette. Man, what a sweet woman." ♫

PHOTOGRAPH BY MARK SELIGER

DEATH IS HERE TO STAY, whether we like it or not. In fact as I was editing this book death became a psychosomatic problem for me. I had constant chest pains and stomach rumbles metamorphosed into life-threatening ulcers. It clouded my thoughts, and the concept of bike riding and even gardening all became fraught with danger

The radio conspired against me too, segueing from Carpenters' singles to INXS via Frankie Lymon And The Teenagers, Dusty Springfield and Elvis. And there was always a Hendrix riff on the adverts.

Rock's dearly departed were following me everywhere. I was picking out Bessie Smith recordings in record stores and craving more information on Robert Johnson.

I'd try and blast death out of my system by playing something like the nonsensically excellent, 'Have You Seen Your Mother Baby Standing In The Shadow?' But the sleeve of 'Through The Past Darkly', the second volume of The Rolling Stones' hits, brought it all back to me, as it revealed "Brian Jones (1943 - 1969). When this you see, remember me, and bear me in your mind. Let all the world say, what they may, speak of me as you find."

The newspaper headlines were relentless. As the '90s closed Screaming Lord Sutch, that guy from Red Kross who we liked, and Moondog, the weird, blind composer of Americana symphonies all departed.

And, of course, the Michael Hutchence debate rattled on and on. The headlines moved on from 'Paula Yates Denies Sex Death Theory' to 'So He Was Having A Wank On A Door'. Just two years earlier the papers had resounded with 'Rage At 'Killer' Geldof' and 'Paula And Her Rock Stars At War', but now it was 'Police Retract Hutchence Suicide Claim' and 'Hutch Died To Go Out With Diana In Heaven'. Rum stuff. And none rummer than the TV documentary that attempted to shed more light on the story. Following which, the Evening Standard concluded:

Paula, unmade-up eyes wide, says she wants an enquiry for the sake of their little girl, Heavenly Hiraani Tiger Lilly. Better for the child to believe that he was a sexual deviant who took a deliberate and exciting risk with his own life, than to believe that he

would consciously and willingly leave her through the act of suicide.

Confused? You will be. The rock soap went into overdrive at the end of the '90s. Rock-related tragedy was also on the increase. The headline 'Boy's death is linked to rap music' drew me in. The Telegraph reported.

The head boy of a Church Of England school who was found hanged at his home may have been influenced by rap music with which he was obsessed, a coroner said yesterday.

Ohwevwo Omoma, 16, might have died while acting out sinister lyrics which he had written himself, Sir Montague Levine told an inquest.

Police investigating the death found a notebook of lyrics lying open on his desk. One verse referred to the act of hanging.

Ohwevwo, head boy at the Archbishop Tenison School in Kennington, South London, was described as a high achiever and was awaiting his GSCE results when he was found dead on June 23rd.

Police searching for a suicide note found lyrics he had written containing the words "Coming in is the Rellik/ So I'll hang your body by the neck".

Is that just fans taking things too seriously and too far? Or is it another remake of the old Ozzy story mentioned at the start of this book, where a 19-year-old student shot himself to death after hearing Ozzy's 'Suicide Solution' in 1984? Who knows? As the years roll on that song kept turning up like a bad penny for the double O as two, seemingly unrelated, deaths in 1986 and 1988 in Georgia, were blamed on Ozzy's music.

Michael Waller, 16, the son of a church deacon, shot himself in '86 while his friends watched. Waller was due in court for a minor offence and, so the story goes, he was so worried by the idea of appearing in court that he decided to look for other solutions. His father found a tape of Ozzy's 'Speak Of The Devil' on his tape deck and two and two were unceremoniously put together.

Two years on and Harold Hamilton, 17, was unlucky in love. Jilted, he borrowed a gun and his friend's car and drove to a secluded spot. There he slipped a copy of Ozzy's 'Tribute' album on the death deck and put a bullet in his head.

Both sets of parents sued Osbourne, claiming

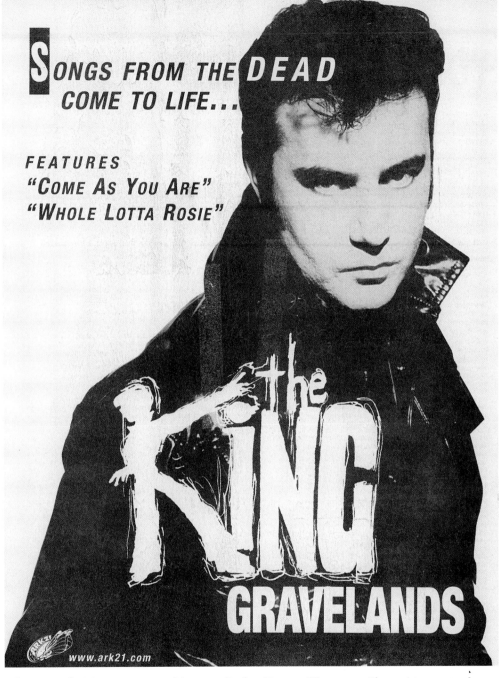

SONGS FROM THE DEAD
COME TO LIFE...

FEATURES
"COME AS YOU ARE"
"WHOLE LOTTA ROSIE"

the KING
GRAVELANDS
www.ark21.com

there were hidden messages in his songs. Both cases were dismissed.

The behavioural patterns of fans have been endlessly dissected but it's the behaviour of the family when death comes around that brings in the column inches.

The litigation concerning the demise of Tammy Wynette and her subsequent exhumation and autopsy will run and run. The resultant reports revealed a different cause of death than had been originally suggested; it was not so much a blood clot but heart failure. However the verdict remained the same, death by natural causes. This left the will-contesting daughters Jackie Daly, Tina Jones and Georgette Smith, further out of pocket as Tammy's will declared anyone contesting the will would lose their inheritance.

If Wynette's exhumation was carried out for financial reasons, then the recently reported concept of exhuming Elvis is surely borne from madness. It seems Lisa Marie Presley wants to exhume the King's body to finally put an end to those 'Elvis Not Dead' rumours. Lisa Marie, inherited the King's estimated 125 million dollar fortune on turning 30 and wants to quell the sordid stories once and for all.

So, will we finally be able to put the King to rest? Well, perhaps not, because The King is the chosen nom de plume of a new music sensation (sort of), whose act is based around exploiting the dead. The King produced a whole album of cover versions of songs made famous by people who are now dead. His album Gravelands (geddit?) boasts his interpretations of Nirvana's 'Come As You Are' and AC/DC's 'Whole Lotta Rosie'. Who could ask for more?

Music fans are indeed strange people. I know, because I count myself as one of them. I can vividly remember the death of Jimi Hendrix and the enclave of Hendrix fans at school who queued to buy his commemorative single 'Voodoo Chile (Slight Return)', which came for 6/3d in a picture sleeve. It was our natural bond and a link with Jimi that would remain with me forever.

And, having been weaned on the Grateful Dead after seeing them live in 1972 when I was an impressionable 14-year-old, the death of Jerry Garcia left me feeling similarly empty.

As soon as I read the news, I slipped on 'American Beauty' and played 'Ripple' again and again. I don't think I cried. I don't think I pontificated about the cause of death or his recurring drug problems. It just struck me, as I read the newspaper reports that a part of me had gone forever.

Jerry Garcia, lead singer of the Grateful Dead, was found dead yesterday in his room at a drug treatment centre in Marin County, California. He was 53. He was found at 4am by a counsellor at Serenity Knowles, a residential facility, said Dan Murphy of the Marin County Sheriff's Office. The leader of the perennial touring band was rumoured to have been struggling with a heroin addiction for the past few years, but the sheriff's department said that he died of natural causes.

Edward Helmore, Los Angeles, in the The Times, August 1st, 1995

Jerry Garcia, leader of the Grateful Dead rock band and a seminal figure in the hippy movement, has died in a California drug rehabilitation centre. He was 53. A singer, guitarist and charismatic amateur philosopher, Garcia managed to express the yearnings and frustrations of an entire generation in music that drew on rock, jazz, folk and mind-bending drugs to become the signature sound of San Francisco in the 1960s

He had suffered health problems for the past decade, and was found unconscious in his room at Serenity Knowles Centre north of San Francisco early yesterday morning. He was pronounced dead in spite of attempts to resuscitate him and is believed to have suffered a heart attack.

Garcia was almost as famous for his relentless touring as for his music. For more than 30 years The Grateful Dead pursued a global odyssey, stopping almost nightly to perform and followed everywhere by dishevelled but amiable armies of fans who were better known as 'Deadheads'.

Giles Whittel in The Times

Dolly Collins

Dolly Collins (seated at the organ) with her sister, Shirley, in 1961

DOLLY COLLINS, who has died of a heart attack at the age of 62, played an influential role in collaboration with her sister, Shirley, in the early years of the English folk revival.

Drawing on her knowledge of early music instrumentation, Dolly Collins provided unusual yet compelling accompaniments to her sister's distinctive rendering of the songs they learned when they were growing up in Sussex.

Their achievements were at least as important as those of Steeleye Span, Fairport Convention and other folk groups which courted youthful audiences with heavy amplification of the material.

A delightful example of the Collins sisters' work was their 1967 album *The Sweet Primeroses*.

This essentially English collection of ballads was sung by Shirley with what *The Sunday Telegraph* described as "skilful roughness", while Dolly gave unusual yet effective backing on a portative organ, copied from a wooden-piped instrument made in the 17th century. The album has recently been reissued as a CD to renewed acclaim.

Dorothy Ann Collins was born at Hastings on March 6 1933. She combined her musical career with such mundane jobs as telex operator and bus conductress; and at one stage she lived in a converted bus in a field.

She played the piano and harmonium, and studied composition with Alan Bush, producing a number of original works, including a secular Mass to a libretto by the novelist Maureen Duffy.

With Shirley, she appeared on the same concert bills as more fashionable musicians such as the Incredible String Band. John Peel's enthusiastic championing of the sisters' music on his Radio 1 programme also brought it to the notice of a broader audience than might be found in the back rooms of public houses. Shirley's first solo album, *The Power of the True Love Knot*, was a sumptuous evocation of medieval England, featuring Dolly's organ accompaniments.

When the sisters recorded *Anthems in Eden* in 1969, Dolly made arrangements for members of David Munrow's Early Music Consort. The instruments included crumhorns, sackbuts, rebecs and shawms and produced a sound described as a "cross between Court music and a Salvation Army band".

The Collins sisters made two other albums together: *Love, Death and the Lady* (1970), and *For As Many As Will* (1974).

A gifted but self-effacing musician, Dolly Collins contributed as a session musician to the albums of other artists. In later years she spent more time composing than playing, as her keyboard dexterity was increasingly impaired by a form of arthritis.

She was married and had a son.

KAREN DALTON

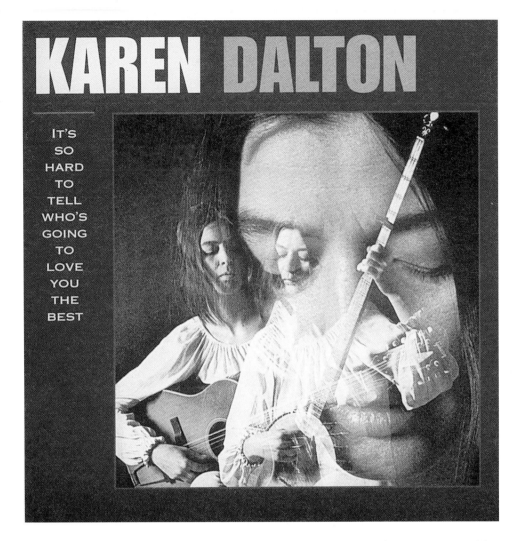

IT'S
SO
HARD
TO
TELL
WHO'S
GOING
TO
LOVE
YOU
THE
BEST

If the death of Jerry Garcia marks the end of The Grateful Dead it will end a phenomenon which has involved a massive cult following for nearly 30 years.

Garcia, 53, was lead guitarist, singer and songwriter with the group and had fought against heroin addiction for 20 years. Yesterday he lost the battle when he was found dead in his room at a drug treatment centre in California. A nurse had attempted to revive him.

The Grateful Dead have been a perennial touring band, and to attend a concert was to watch not just a strikingly good band playing improvised rock and roll, country and jazz music. It was also to absorb an audience like no other. The Deadheads, as they became known, followed the band across America and across the world, often leaving home

as teenagers to do so, and getting temporary jobs wherever the band might be playing.
David Lister in The Independent

"We are a group that is earnestly trying to accomplish something and we don't quite know quite what it is," Jerry Garcia said once.

More than any other musician produced by the Sixties he could suggest in his playing the presence of something indescribable, possibly unattainable, but still hugely worth striving for. He could be idle, uninspired, cliched or simply too stoned to function on stage, but for hundreds of thousands of people none of this mattered beside the moments when he set off in search of some eldritch tranquillity and then brought it home for us all to share.
Andrew Brown in The Telegraph

Beyond Jerry and Jimi, I'd always felt pangs of loss, tears of rage and the inevitable need to buy back catalogue when my heroes had disappeared. When Dennis Wilson drowned I even watched Two Lane Blacktop again. And similar rituals took place for Gene Clark, Mary Wells, Kurt, Major Lance, Dino Valente, Townes Van Zandt, Laura Nyro, Jeff Buckley, Rainer Ptaceck, Bryan McLean, Dusty and Skip Spence. They'd all been part of my life and when they died I was left feeling that I didn't know enough about them. They'd gone all too soon and I wanted a badge to show my allegiance.

Most of the people in this book I'd been aware of and, in many cases had music by, but there were some who were brought into sharp focus by their death. Stripped of their mortal image, their songs were a revelation. In death you can even find time for Tiny Tim.

And then there were the true revelations. For example Dolly Collins, who died of a heart attack, aged 62 at the tail end of the '90s. She'd played an influential role in the early years of the English folk revival, collaborated with her sister Shirley and had an eerie voice and phrasing that chilled any room. I dare say, had she still been alive, her importance and the great beauty of her recordings would have been another thing that I might have put off hearing until later. But, in death, it seemed like the perfect time.

During the preparation of this book I've wallowed in the blues music of Mance Lipscomb and revisited Cap Rock courtesy of Gram Parsons. I headed down to the Dustbowl with Woody and Hank, and shared a few late sessions with Roy Orbison, Sandy, Janis, Nick Drake and even Faron Young.

And I also heard new things by people who I never knew existed. Some of them were breathtaking, none moreso than Karen Dalton.

Dalton died in 1994 but, unfortunately I haven't been able to find out anything about how she died. But I've heard her sing and she sums up everything about the myth and mystery of music celebrity and how, in death it achieves far greater magnitude. I love her album.

So the story goes, Karen Dalton arrived in New York's Greenwich Village in the early '60s with her little girl Abby, a big red Gibson 12-string, a long-neck banjo and an incredible voice. She moved into the heart of the Village, an apartment in Bleecker Street, where she'd play the coffee house circuit alongside Fred Neil, Dylan, Tim Hardin and Dino Valente.

According to those who were around at the time: "Her guitar style was as unique as her singing and musicians could have a pretty hard time playing with her because of her very laid-back sense of beat." And when you hear her recordings you'll certainly agree with that description.

But it all went pear-shaped for Karen's music career and, as the years rolled on, everyone lost touch with her. The eventual reports of her death were hazy at best. Her second short-term husband, Dick Weisman met up with former Greenwich Villager Happy Traum in 1995 and was told that she had died in Woodstock a year earlier.

Weisman: "I am certain that neither of Karen's albums sold very well. She performed rarely in clubs and I can just see some fat cat record executive chomping on a cigar and asking, 'what's the image we're selling here?'."

So Karen Dalton went nowhere very slowly. And she is now remembered only by the sleevenotes of the excellent album 'It's So Hard To Tell Who's Going To Love You The Best', which features her interpretations of songs by Fred Neil, Eddie Floyd, Leroy Carr, Leadbelly and Jelly Roll Morton.

The album is a treasure and her beautiful Billie Holliday-styled vocals give it a haunting quality. It took her death and the creative archiving of Holy Modal Rounders' mainstay Peter Stampfel to dig out the story, search out the tracks and get the thing released. It's the perfect epitaph.

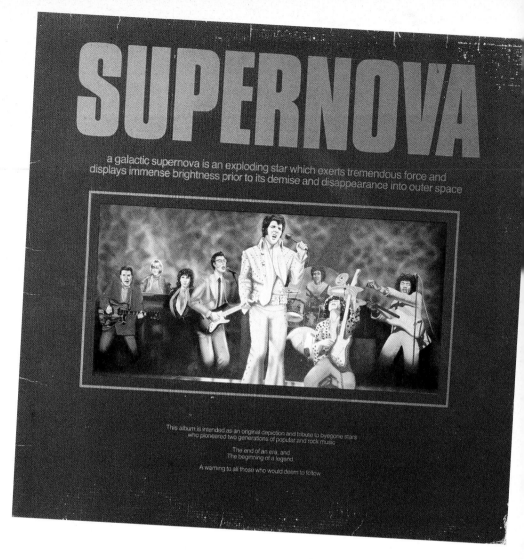

By some contrast, I've also unearthed some very strange items that wear the shroud of rock obituary. None more strange than 'Supernova' and album put together by producer Dave Montague. Montague was also fascinated by the death of the rock hierarchy and he attempted to create a rock opera about it.

Recorded by a bunch of people who have gone on to remain anonymous, it features songs about dead rock stars, topped and tailed by some scene setting reportage.

Included are tributes to Buddy Holly, Eddie Cochran, Brian Jones, Jimi Hendrix, Jim Morrison, Marc Bolan, Elvis, Keith Moon; all done loosely in the style of the dead icon. So there's drums aplenty for Moon and wah-wah guitar for Jimi. As an entity the album sounds like a cross between Mott The Hoople and a bad cabaret act. And, if the sleeve paintings weren't bad enough, the lyrics take some beating:

"He was living on the edge, but he pushed his luck too far
Burned himself out, like an exploding star
He was playing Russian roulette
Pulled the trigger, but lost the bet."
(from 'Supernova')

Well, it's hardly Shakespeare. Or even James Barron Hope, who summed up the whole reason for 'Supernova,' and indeed this book, when he said "Tis after death that we measure men."

As you traverse the music of the people in this book, you can hook up with Blind Willie Jefferson's 'In My Time Of Dying', or fast forward through to Jeff Buckley's 'Grace' album, which is just sodden with tears. Skip to track three 'Last Goodbye'. It's a story about a broken relationship, but it's every bit as meaningful when you relate it to Buckley's lost soul and, indeed, the hundreds of others in this book.

"I'll only make you cry,
This is our last goodbye."

CREDIT IS DUE...

CREDIT IS DUE TO THE FOLLOWING...

NEWSPAPERS AND NEWSPAPER ARCHIVES:

The Daily Telegraph, The Sunday Sport, The People, The News Of The World, The Times, The Independent, The Guardian, The Daily Mail, The Observer, The Los Angeles Herald, The San Francisco Chronicle, The Evening Standard, Variety and Metro.

MUSIC MAGAZINES AND PERIODICALS:

Q, Mojo, NME, Sounds, Uncut, Record Collector, Billboard, Vibe and Rolling Stone.

MUSIC FANZINES:

Answer Me, Motorbooty, Scram and Brutarian.

BOOKS

An Ideal For Living by Mark Johnston (Proteus)

Angry Women In Rock (Juno Press) Blues Legends by Tony Russell *The Blues From Robert Johnson To Robert Cray by* Tony Russell (Aurum

Carlton)

Born To Win by Woody Guthrie

Kurt Cobain And Courtney Love In Their Own Words by Nick Wise (Omnibus)

Karen Dalton: *'It's So Hard To Tell Who's Going To Love You The Best'* (Unveiled)

Bob Dylan by Anthony Scaduto (Rogan House/Helter Skelter)

The Encyclopaedia Of Rock Obituaries by Nick Talevski (Omnibus)

Fandemonium by Judy and

Fred Vermorel (Omnibus)

Follow The Music – The Life And High Times Of Elektra Records In The Great Years Of American Pop Culture by Jac Holzman and

Gavan Dawes (Firstmedia)

The Great Rock Discography by MC Strong (Canongate)

The Guinness Book Of British Hit Singles by Jo and Tim Rice (Guinness)

The Guinness Who's Who Of Folk Music by Colin Larkin (Guinness)

The Guinness Who's Who Of Country Music by Colin Larkin (Guinness)

The Guinness Who's Who Of Sixties Music by Colin Larkin (Guinness)

The Guinness Who's Who Of Seventies Music by Colin Larkin (Guinness)

Have Gun Will Travel – The Spectacular Rise And Violent Fall Of Death Row Records by Ronin Ro (Quartet)

Illustrated Encyclopedia Of Jazz by Brian Case and Stan Britt (Salamander)

In The Country Of Country by Nicholas Dawidoff (Faber and Faber)

Janis Joplin, Her Life And Times by Deborah Landau

The Kerrang! Direktory Of Heavy Metal by Neil Jeffries (Virgin)

Gram Parsons by Sid Griffin (Sierra)

The Penguin Guide To Jazz by Richard Cook and Brian Morton (Penguin)

Road Mangler Deluxe by Phil Kaufman and Colin White

Rock 'n' Roll Babylon by Gary Herman (Plexus)

The Rolling Stone Record Guide (Virgin)

Searching for Robert Johnson by Peter Guralnick (Penguin)

Story Of Pop (Octopus)

The Best Of Sunday Sport (Sphere)

The Daily Telegraph Book Of Obituaries (Ted Smart)

The Daily Telegraph Book Of Obituaries – Entertainers (Ted Smart)

The Virgin Encyclopedia Of R&B And Soul by Colin Larkin (Virgin)

Without You, The Tragic Story Of Badfinger by Dan Matovina (Francis Glover Books)

Your Record Stars, 1957 (Eldon Press)

QUOTES

William Shakespeare, *Hamlet*
The Bible

FROM THE INTERNET

'A Letter To Janis' by Sam Andrew
www.bbhc.com/samwritings.htm

Dead Rock Star Club
http://users.efortress.com/doc-rock/links.html

Music Central
www.angelfire.com/biz/music_central

The Official Unofficial Joy Division/Ian Curtis Home Page
http://member.xoom.com/joy_division/

Bobby Shred's Lizzy Tribute Site
www.angelfire.com/nj/thinlizzy

All-Music Guide
www.aent.com/amg/all_music.html

Fuller Up. The Dead Musician Directory
http://elvispelvis.com/aids.htm

The Hip Hop Pages
http://eigg.com/rap.htm

The Holy Death Site
www.av1611.org/rockdead.html

The Death Of Kurt D Cobain
www.angelfire.com/me/ComeAsYouAre

The Murder Of Kurt Cobain by Toby Amirault
www.tiac.net/users/tobya/

Kurt Cobain webring
www.angelfire.com/pe/clique/webrings.html

We Will Always Remember
www.hotshotdigital.com/WellAlways Remember.html

The Rock 'n' Roll Hall Of Fame Website
www.rockhall.com/K

A Fan's Tribute To Patsy Cline
www.geocities.com/Nashville/5710/index1.html

POEMS
Billy Fury © *bongobeat.com/poems/bfury.html*
Nick Drake © Dana Perry 1999
Sid Viscous © Virgil Hervey
Jeff Buckley © Leslie (Cloud Tiger)

A FAN'S TRIBUTE TO PATSY CLINE by GUY CESARIO
http://www.geocities.com/Nashville/5710/index1.html

SPECIFIC WRITERS
Andy Gill, Charles Shaar Murray and Adrian Deevoy.

PRESS AGENCY ARCHIVES
API
UPI

ALBUM SLEEVE NOTES
The Association: *'And Then… Along Comes The Association'* (Valiant)
Chet Baker: *'Chet Baker Sextet And Quartet'* (Vogue)
The Bonzo Dog Doodah Band: *'The Doughnut In Granny's Greenhouse'* (Liberty)
Paul Butterfield Blues Band: *The Paul Butterfield Blues Band'* (Elektra)
Alex Campbell: *'Way Out West'* (ARC)
Gene Clark: *'Flying High'* (A&M)
Eddie Cochran: *'Legends Of The 20th Century'* (EMI Records)
John Coltrane: *'The Complete 1961 Village Vanguard Recordings'* (Verve)
Xavier Cugat: *'Viva Cugat!'* (Mercury)
Bill Doggett: *'Oops! The Swinging Sounds Of Bill Doggett And His Combo'* (Columbia)
Sleepy John Estes: *'Stone Blind Blues'* (Catfish)
Sleepy John Estes: *'Brownsville Blues'* (Delmark)
Tim Hardin: *'Hang On To A Dream - The Verve Recordings'* (Mercury)
Tim Hardin: *'Simple Songs Of Freedom - the CBS Recordings'* (Sony)

Billie Holliday: *'Lady Day'* (Saga)
Mahalia Jackson: *'Great Songs Of Love And Faith'* (Columbia)
Mahalia Jackson: *'Newport 1958'* (Philips)
Joe And Eddie: *'Walkin' Down The Line'* (Vogue)
Leadbelly: *'Pretty Flower In My Backyard'* (Saga)
The Louvin Brothers: *'Tragic Songs Of Life'* (Stetson)
The Mamas And The Papas: *'If You Can Believe Your Eyes And Ears… The Mamas And Papas'* (RCA)
Joe Meek: *'I Hear A New World'* (RPM Records)
Nico: *'Chelsea Girl'* (MGM)
Nilsson: *'Aerial Ballet'* (RCA)
Phil Ochs: *'I Ain't Marching Anymore'* (Elektra)
Roy Orbison: *'Crying'* (London)
Charlie Parker: *'Ornithology'* (Society)
Gram Parsons: *'Warm Evenings, Pale Mornings, Bottled Blues'* (Raven)
Jimmy Reed: *'Boss Man Of The Blues'* (Stateside)
Jimmy Reed: *'Blues Is My Business'* (Stateside)
The Rolling Stones: *'Through The Past Darkly'* (Decca)
Jimmie Rodgers: *'Jimmie The Kid'* (RCA)
Bessie Smith: *Bessie Smith. The World's Greatest Blues Singer'* (CBS)
Lord Sutch: *'Lord Sutch And Heavy Friends'* (Atlantic)
Sister Rosetta Tharpe: *'Gospel Train'* (Mercury)
Dino Valente: *'Dino Valente'*
Josh White: *'Good Morning Blues'* (MFP)
Hank Williams: *'Let Me Sing A Blue Song'* (MGM)

SONGS
'Runnin' Blue' by The Doors (Elektra Records) © Doors Music Co/ASCAP
'Supernova' by Dave Montague (Circular Sounds) © Circular Sounds Ltd
'Last Goodbye' by Jeff Buckley (Columbia Records) © Sony Songs Inc/El Viejito Music/Gary Lucas Music/BMI

AND THE BLACK BOOK TEAM
Dave Henderson, Howard Johnson, Keith Drummond, Gail Robir•on, David Black, Gary Perry and Nick Clode.

WHILE WE WERE WRITING WE MADE A TAPE
SIDE ONE
1 TERRY by Twinkle, Decca 45
2 OLD SHEP by Hank Snow from 'When Tragedy Struck'
3 VIVA LAS VEGAS by Elvis Presley, RCA 45
4 STACKOLEE by Paul Clayton from 'Bloody Ballads'
5 ENDLESS SLEEP by Nick Lowe, Stiff 45
6 THE GOOD TIMES by Nat King Cole, Capitol 45
7 THERE'LL BE NO TEARDROPS TONIGHT by George Jones from 'Blue And Lonesome'
8 POOR ELLEN SMITH by The Kossoy Sisters with Erik Darling from 'Bowling Green'
9 SEASONS IN THE SUN by Terry Jacks, Bell 45
10 WHERE THE WILD ROSES GROW by Nick Cave from 'Murder Ballads'

SIDE TWO
1 SLAUGHTER ON TENTH AVENUE by Mick Ronson, RCA 45
2 THE SNIPER by Harry Chapin from 'The Sniper'
3 LOVE WILL TEAR US APART by Joy Division, Factory 45
4 WHERE DID OUR LOVE GO by Donnie Elbert, London 45
5 UP JUMPED THE DEVIL by Robert Johnson, Columbia Legacy track
6 DAY AFTER DAT by Badfinger, Apple 45
7 LOST HIGHWAY by Jeff Buckley, Columbia single
8 BURY ME BENEATH THE WILLOW by The Carter Family from 'The Carter Family Album'
9 THE GALLIS POLE by Leadbelly from 'Pretty Flower In My Backyard'
10 ARE YOU LONESOME TONIGHT by Elvis Presley, RCA 45

THE BLACK BOOK COMPANY

PO BOX 2030
PEWSEY
SN9 5QZ
ENGLAND

TELEPHONE
44 (0) 1672 564929
FAX
44 (0) 1672 564433
EMAIL
dhende7730@aol.com
INTERNET
www.blackbookco.com

The regular guys:
Dave Henderson
Howard Johnson
Keith Drummond
David Black
Gary Perry
Nick Clode
Karyn Hansell

DISTRIBUTION UK
Turnaround 44 (0) 181
329 3009

DISTRUBUTION
AUSTRALIA
Tower Books (02) 9975
5566

"Death becomes them."

"Book 'em Danno!"

So, the Black Book Company manifesto...
We're interested in music. Hearing new things. And our books look at the effect that music has on the fans and the famous.

In Touched By The Hand Of Bob and Get Your Jumbo Jet Out Of My Airport, we examined the power of, respectively, Bob Dylan and AC/DC. We investigated the obsessions of fandom and the effect that these heroes have on the world.

Leaving The 20th Century examines the effects of the rock legend in death and the effect that those people and their passing has on us all.

OUR BACK PAGES...

Touched By The Hand Of Bob

EPIPHANAL BOB DYLAN EXPERIENCES FROM A BUICK SIX
by Dave Henderson. PUBLISHED: June 1, 1999
Paperback, heavyweight matt finish, fully illustrated. ISBN: 1-902799-00-3

Like remembering how you heard about the assassination of John Lennon, the world and their Walkman all have a story about their experience with Bob Dylan. The fans and the famous all tell the tale of being touched by the hand of Bob.

Dave Henderson delves deep into Dylanland, discovering Fatwa-invoking fanatics, rune-juggling astrologers, hi-brow intellectuals and a bizarre circus of followers. Touched By The Hand Of Bob follows Dylan's miracle-strewn journey, meeting the people who covered his songs, copied his haircut and grabbed at the hem of his frock coat. They walk among us...

THE AUTHOR
After spending a year trying to entice Bob Dylan to attend the Q Awards, Dave Henderson saw the blind devotion which surrounded Dylan's appearance at the Glastonbury Festival, he became enthralled by the mercurial music, then by the global effect of Dylan's very presence. While planning the 1999 Q Awards, he dived head first into the mysterious power of Bob.

Get Your Jumbo Jet Out Of My Airport

RANDOM NOTES FOR AC/DC OBSESSIVES
by Howard Johnson. PUBLISHED: June 1, 1999
Pbk, hweight matt finish, fully illustrated. ISBN: 1-902799-01-1

When AC/DC vocalist Bon Scott died in 1980 few could have envisaged that 19 years later the group would still be one of the world's biggest rockacts. Why are they still so popular on the back of a few boogie chords and a schoolboy uniform? Read on...

Get Your Jumbo Jet Out Of My Airport is the first book ever to fully document the group's massive appeal. From the obsessive owners of 500 bootlegs to the record company execs and producers who have brought AC/DC to the world, Howard Johnson has interviewed them all. The result is a collection of the finest anecdotes and most revealing tales, revealing why AC/DC remain so special, so important and so influential. Delivering one of the most revealing pictures of the band ever, with a wealth of previously unseen pictures, this is a work of frankly lunatic devotion.

THE AUTHOR
Howard Johnson saw his first AC/DC gig in 1979 aged 15, wearing shorts and school blazer. His dress sense, however, has improved in the last 20 years and he's managed to persuade such publications as Mojo, Q, FHM, The Daily Telegraph, FourFourTwo, New Woman and Total Sport among others that he can write a bit too. Last book he authored? British Lions rugby captain Martin Johnson's diary of the incredible 1997 Tour To South Africa. This has very little to do with AC/DC, of course, but we thought you might find it interesting anyway.

You can order books published by the Black Book Company direct from us, or through our website at www.blackbookco.com

DIRECT BY MAIL

You can order copies of our titles for £13.50 each (including post and packing in the UK and within the EC).

For overseas orders, please add £1 (outside of EC but within Europe) or £3 (USA, Canada and Australia).

If you'd like to order more than one copy, please add £1 per additional copy.

If you'd like to order in bulk (over five copies), then please fax your request to us at
+44 (0) 1672 564433

Or email us on dhende7730@aol.com

IF YOU'D LIKE TO GET ON OUR MAILING LIST...

For special offers, limited edition items and news on upcoming projects, then send your address to us by fax or email, or write to us at

THE BLACK BOOK COMPANY
BOX 2030
PEWSEY
SN9 5QZ
ENGLAND

WHAT THE PAPER'S SAID ABOUT...

TOUCHED BY THE HAND OF BOB

TIME OUT " A rule of thumb. You can never have too many Dylan books. Best of the most recent bunch is Dave Henderson's Touched By The Hand Of Bob. Henderson entertainingly delves into the 'psyche of Bob';s faithful'. All aspects of Bob's mixed up legend are rifled, explored, documented and exposed in what is a genuinely compelling, funny and fantastic book."

Q MAGAZINE "Dave Henderson has opted for a fan's eye view of what it means to have been metaphorically nuzzled by the great man. It's a brisk volume filled with bite-sized anecdotes, remembrances and the odd critical opinion; ideal for dipping into."

UNCUT MAGAZINE "What we get here is a trot through Dylan's career as seen through the eyes of numerous witnesses, both contemporary and modern. There are quotes from stars and the unknown and several endearing tales of people meeting Dylan and instantly making complete prats of themselves. Enormously enjoyable: Dylan book of the year!"

MOJO MAGAZINE "This is a real ragbag of a book- fans recalling epiphanic Bob moments, as well as discographies, cuttings and other fascinating odds and ends - which makes it one of the more enjoyable Dylan books of late."

BEAT SCENE MAGAZINE "There are elements of Nick Hornby's Fever Pitch here even, and more relevantly, High Fidelity. Henderson concedes his record collector passions but strives for meaning to it all and tries to elicit some sane answers from everyone he meets who shares this predeliction for Bob Dylan. A massive treasure chest of Dylan stuff to absorb and written with a lot of spark."

RECORD COLLECTOR "Touched By The Hand of Bob captures the bizarre intoxication of being a Dylan fan, in an era which has chosen to ignore everything for which he stands. Whether you lost your virginity to Nashville Skyline or sacrificed friendships, marriages or faithful dogs in your devotion to Dylan's art, anyone who has been touched by Bob's apparently sweaty hands will recognise themselves or their close friends in Henderson's anthology of neurosis and nostalgia."

WHAT THE PAPER'S SAID ABOUT...

GET YOUR JUMBO JET OUT OF MY AIRPORT

Q MAGAZINE "Johnson's teenage confessions offer a stark but welcome contrast to those of most thirtysomething journalists fixated with The Clash. "I had records by The Scorpions, UFO and Journey." he crows, while stapling together 1,000 copies of Phoenix, the north's premier heavy metal fanzine. The result is an irresistible read but, perhaps for like-minded souls only."

RECORD COLLECTOR MAGAZINE "Howard Johnson provides an informative, entertaining text, while allowing it to be a framework for more juicy material, care of fanzine writers, video extras, journalists, ex-AC/DC members and, most importantly, the fan obsessives. On the whole, this is a witty, well-researched package."

COMING SOON

GLASTONBURY 2000
30 Years In The Field Of Dreams
by Dave Henderson

Published June 1, 2000
ISBN: 1-902799.03.8
230mmx230mm paperback
Price: £12.99
The story of the world's most enduring festival. Told by the fans, the bands, the oragnisers and the instigators. From its inception in 1970 through the sun-baked nirvanas and rain-saoked quagmires.

THE BEATLES UNCOVERED
The Fab Four's Legacy:
Butchered and Bedraggled
by Dave Henderson
Published: September 1, 2000
ISBN: 1-902799.04.6
230mmx230mm paperback
Price: £12.99

A dangerous voyage into the underbelly of the cover versions, featuring The Beatles' catalogue interpreted by The Royal Philharmonic Orchestra, Joe Cocker, Dr John, Marmalade, MP Derek Enright, The Army Of Halfwits and a thousand others.

THE OFFBEAT 500
Mad men, women, icons and psycopaths - all making music
by Dave Henderson

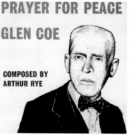

Published: November 1, 2000
ISBN: 1-902799.05.4
230mmx230mm paperback
Price: £12.99
Enter the world of crazed record collecting. Witness albums by trains, school choirs and dogs. Religious tracts, self-help experiments, psycho-analysis, strange cover versions, songs about Satan and simple musical homages to the paintings of Paul Klee.

ALSO IN PRODUCTION
NEIL YOUNG: MY PART IN HIS DOWNFALL

BOB DYLAN UNCOVERED

I FOUGHT THE LAW: PURGERY, POOR BEHAVIOUR AND PAYBACK IN THE MUSIC INDUSTRY

AND ANOTHER THING (OR TWO)…

WE HAVE MODERN TECHNOLOGY
A WEBSITE
WITH STUFF OTHER THAN OUR BOOKS

www.blackbookco.com

HOME OF LOTS OF STUFF ABOUT MUSIC WE LIKE
So, if you're intrigued by…

APOCRHYPHAL TALES, THE WORLD OF BECK, STRANGE BEATLES' COVERS, OBSCURE STARS LIKE NICODEMUS AND MICHAEL PENN, THE SOUNDTRACKED LIFE OF DANNY ELFMAN, JOHNNY CASH'S RELIGIOUS OPERATTA, ALBUMS BY DOGS, THE CONCEPT OF MYSTIC VINYL, MICKEY NEWBURY, PEOPLE WHO SAMPLE INSECTS, THE CHURCH OF SNEAKY PETE, THE SOULFUL DRONE OF TYRONE DAVIS, THE NEW WAVE OF ORCHESTRAL BRIAN WILSONISM, LADIES WHO PLAY WATERING CANS, MUSIC CRIMINALS, JOE HENRY, TINY TIM, MARK WIRTZ, MYRACLE BRAH, GINAT SAND, NEAL CASAL, THE IDIO‑SYNCRACIES OF PROG ROCK, HAPPENSTANCE MAGAZINE, THE KULT OF KURT COBAIN, ELVIS SIGHTINGS, SCREAMING LORD SUTCH, SHIRELY COLLINS, FRANCOIS BREUT, KAREN DALTON AND WHY SOME SONGS MAKE PEOPLE CRY… THEN DROP BY